Leon Day

ALSO BY BOB LUKE
AND FROM MCFARLAND

Pete Hill: Black Baseball's First Superstar (2023)

*Bromo-Seltzer King: The Opulent Life of
Captain Isaac "Ike" Emerson, 1859–1931* (2020)

*Integrating the Orioles: Baseball and Race
in Baltimore* (2016)

*Dean of Umpires: A Biography of
Bill McGowan, 1896–1954* (2005)

Leon Day
A Baseball Life from the Negro Leagues to the Hall of Fame

Bob Luke

McFarland & Company, Inc., Publishers
Jefferson, North Carolina

ISBN (print) 978-1-4766-9627-0
ISBN (ebook) 978-1-4766-5649-6

LIBRARY OF CONGRESS CATALOGING DATA ARE AVAILABLE

Library of Congress Control Number 2025042970

© 2025 Bob Luke. All rights reserved

No part of this book may be reproduced or transmitted in any form or by any means, electronic or mechanical, including photocopying or recording, or by any information storage and retrieval system, without permission in writing from the publisher.

Front cover image: Brooklyn/Newark Eagles pitcher Leon Day
(National Baseball Hall of Fame and Museum, Cooperstown, New York)

Printed in the United States of America

*McFarland & Company, Inc., Publishers
Box 611, Jefferson, North Carolina 28640
www.mcfarlandpub.com*

For my daughters
Jennifer Morgan and Allyson Frusciano

Table of Contents

Acknowledgments   ix
Introduction   1

1. "I'm in"   9
2. The Player and the Person   13
3. Growing Up   17
4. A Career Takes Off   23
5. Newark   32
6. Cuba and a Career Pause   38
7. Mexico Beckons   46
8. Strides Toward Integration   50
9. Day Vacates the Mound   56
10. Pathways to the National and American Leagues   65
11. From Ruppert Stadium to Utah Beach   74
12. Baseball and the War   82
13. Racial Tensions at Home   86
14. He's Back and Rarin' to Go   90
15. Uneven Progress in Race Relations   98
16. Two Seasons in Mexico   102
17. A Mixed Blessing   104
18. More Baseball for Day   113

Table of Contents

19.	On to Organized Baseball	120
20.	The East-West Games	130
21.	Post Career	135
22.	Cooperstown Beckons	142

Epilogue   157
Appendix A: Geraldine Day's Acceptance Speech for Leon Day   159
Appendix B: Questionnaire Completed by Leon Day in 1951   161
Chapter Notes   163
Bibliography   183
Index   185

Acknowledgments

MANY PEOPLE CONTRIBUTED to this book.
 Society for American Baseball Research editor and writer Thomas Kern and prolific baseball writer Paul Dickson read drafts of the manuscript, corrected errors, and suggested revisions that measurably improved its accuracy and readability. Dr. Bob Hieronimus, Baltimore artist and entrepreneur, and his executive producer, Laura Cortner, supplied a number of documents, helped arrange informative interviews with Leon Day's widow Geraldine Day, and carefully reviewed the manuscript with Geraldine.
 Those who provided information from libraries and archives are Cassidy Lent, library director at the Baseball Hall of Fame and Museum, who sent a copy of Day's file and answered innumerable questions fully and promptly, and Claudette Scrafford who provided invaluable assistance in obtaining photographs of Day from the Hall of Fame. Others include Dr. William Walker, associate professor of education at the State University of New York's Cooperstown graduate program; Mary Anne Moran at the Savakinus Lackawanna Historical Society; Amanda Faelnel at Kent State University's library; Mike Klingaman, sportswriter for the *Baltimore Sun*; James Kominewski, archivist at the University of Manitoba, Winnipeg, Canada; Lisa Keith-Lucas, archivist at the Camp Gordon Johnston World War II Museum; Dr. David Siegel, emeritus professor of political science at Brock University in St. Catharines, Ontario, Canada; Everette F. Coppock, command sergeant major, U.S. Army, retired; and Jorge Colón Delgado, official historian of the Puerto Rico Professional Baseball League.
 Others who provided advice and encouragement include Larry Lester, widely recognized authority on the Negro Leagues and for 30 years chairman of the Society for American Baseball Research's Negro Leagues Committee; prolific author Tim Wendel; Oliver Lee at Robert Edward Auctions; and Matt Flores at Huggins and Scott Auctions.

Acknowledgments

As always, my wife Judy Wentworth has been a constant source of encouragement and understanding of my hours at the computer.

All errors are mine alone.

Introduction

"LITTLE BITTY GUY. He looked too small to be the batboy, but oh could he throw." That's how George Giles, a skilled and flashy first baseman for 18 seasons and Leon Day's manager, as the Brooklyn Eagles opened their 1935 season, described Day, one of the least known of baseball's Hall of Fame members.[1] Eric Brady in a 1987 *USA Today* article asked, "Never heard of Leon Day? Old-timers say Day was a dominating pitcher. He holds the Negro Leagues' record of 18 strikeouts in a game; Roy Campanella was his victim three times. And yet Day is largely unknown. He's 70 now and lives in Baltimore."[2]

This book is Day's biography: the times in which he played, those he played with and against, and his lengthy trek to Cooperstown. An African American, Leon Day had the ability but not the right skin color to play in the National or American League. So he and hundreds of other Black ballplayers plied their trade in America in the Negro Leagues and in Latin America and Canada, places where ability trumped complexion.[3]

We follow Day's Negro Leagues career from Baltimore's semipro teams, to the Baltimore Black Sox, to the Brooklyn Eagles, and then to the Newark Eagles, with winter stops in Puerto Rico, Mexico, Cuba, and Venezuela mixed in. We see several National and American League executives flirt with the prospect of Black players in the National and American League in 1942 as World War II was getting underway. Day's baseball career is interrupted by two and a half years in the army as a private first class[4] during World War II with service on Utah Beach during the D-Day invasion and then back to Newark for a spectacular 1946 season with the Eagles and on to Mexico for two summer seasons and finally to Baltimore with the Baltimore Elite Giants where his Negro Leagues career ends in June 1950. We then see him go to Canada for his post–Negro Leagues career, two half seasons (the end of 1950 and the first half of 1951) in Winnipeg, Canada. From Winnipeg he goes

Introduction

to Toronto to play the last half of the 1951 season with the minor league Toronto Maple Leafs. The year 1952 finds him with the minor league Scranton (Pennsylvania) Miners. By 1953 he's back in Canada with the Eskimos in the Western International League. He makes his last stop with the ManDak League's Brandon Greys before retiring at the end of the 1954 season.

We follow his appearances in seven East-West games, the equivalent of the National and American Leagues' All-Star games, where he set the record for strikeouts and games played.

Not much is known about his personal life. Ship manifests that document Day's travels to Puerto Rico, Cuba, and Venezuela from 1936 to 1943 record his marital status as married to Helen Elizabeth Day, née Johnson. The couple resided at 66 Washington Avenue in Belleville, New Jersey, about five miles from Newark, since at least 1939. His 1943 service record also listed him as married. They had no children. Little else is known about Helen Day.[5]

We also follow his life after baseball. He remarries after his relationship with his first wife ends, works as a bartender and security guard, signs autographs at memorabilia shows, sends autographs through the mail for a $10 fee, and is the beneficiary of many people's successful efforts to get him elected to the Cooperstown Baseball Hall of Fame just six days before he dies on March 13, 1995.

We discuss the racial dynamics, particularly in Newark and Baltimore, during the times he played in both cities to highlight Black baseball's contributions to African American communities and the stresses for Blacks brought on by segregation and discrimination.

Much of the information in Day's biography comes from the Black press of the day. Published weekly, unlike the white dailies that gave but scant coverage to the Negro Leagues, Black newspapers kept fans well informed. We rely heavily on them, a number of books, and interviews with Leon Day's widow Geraldine Day and Dr. Bob Hieronimus (a Baltimore radio personality and community activist, known as "Dr. Bob" to many) and his executive assistant Laura Cortner.

America was a mirror society during Day's career, 1934–1954. Blacks and whites each, with some exceptions, had their own organizations: schools, cemeteries, insurance companies, hotels and motels, restaurants, churches, barbershops, beauty parlors, army units, newspapers, beaches, and the like. And so it was with baseball until 1947 when

Introduction

Jackie Robinson finally cracked the National and American Leagues' color barriers with the Brooklyn Dodgers. While Robinson's debut was a momentous breakthrough, it would take 12 more years before a player of color appeared on the roster of every National and American League team. Tom Yawkey, Boston Red Sox owner, had the honor of being last. He signed infielder Elijah "Pumpsie" Green in 1959 after Green had spent several years in the Red Sox farm system.

Newark, New Jersey, where Day spent the bulk of his Negro Leagues career as a member of the Newark Eagles, saw similarly slow movement toward integration in its public school system, government, and industries. Significant progress toward equality wouldn't happen in Newark until the civil rights movements of the 1950s and '60s.

Leon Day and the Negro Leagues

At first glance, life in the Negro Leagues was no bed of roses. Players experienced long rides in dilapidated buses where sweaty uniforms were hung out of windows to dry. Showers could be infrequent in Southern towns where Negro Leaguers were often refused use of locker rooms. Day, a rookie playing winter baseball in Puerto Rico, recalled in a 1974 interview with Doug Davis an instance where the team stunk so badly that the bus driver pulled up alongside a pond, ordered the players off the bus and into the pond to wash their uniforms and themselves. Some teams, Day continued, hired a white boy to ride with them to order food from white-owned restaurants. Some eateries, seeing a busload of Blacks, wouldn't sell food to the white boy. Threats of mob violence to Black players who beat a white team caused many a Black team to throw a game. Davis was told, "Doug, we could have beaten them with our eyes closed, but the consequences just weren't worth it, and we wouldn't have gotten paid." Segregated hotels, precarious team finances, racial taunts from white spectators, and sparse salaries added to the challenge. Few made their living from their baseball salaries alone. By 1938 the average salary was $175 a month for a four-month season. Most found whatever employment they could during the off season.[6]

Many worked as laborers, teachers, industrial workers, or waiters to supplement their baseball income. The better players, including Leon Day, made extra money during the winter months playing on teams in

Introduction

Puerto Rico, Cuba, Mexico, the Dominican Republic, and Venezuela. During the season some had access to greener pastures by "jumping" from one team to another, despite loud objections from team owners and league officials, where the pay was better.

The most money Day made in the States was $1,800 (about $29,000 in 2024 dollars) for one season. His peak earning seasons, by contrast, were in Mexico where he pulled down $5,000 (about $61,000 in 2024 dollars) for a four-month season in 1947 and again in 1948. In addition to his salary, Leon, as did many players in Latin America, had his apartment paid for by the team, which allowed him to bring his wife Helen Johnson with him in 1947.[7] The two had married on July 17 of that year.[8]

Puerto Rico was his most frequent winter season stop—1935–36, 1936–37, 1939–40, 1940–41, 1941–42, and 1949–50—where not only was the money better, but also, Day recalled, "they treated you like a man. You could stay in any hotel unlike in the States."[9]

Day summed up his days in the Negro Leagues, telling *Baltimore Sun* reporter Kent Baker, "we didn't have no money and we'd be riding all night, then get off the bus and play a game. We weren't eating right and my corns would be killin' my feet. The only time I got rubbed down was by myself. Unless there was a colored restaurant in town," Day continued, "we'd mostly go to the grocery store and get bologna sandwiches. $2 a day was the most meal money we ever got; most of the time it was $1. You couldn't eat but two meals, but fortunately they didn't cost much in those days. You had to love it to go through it."[10] He loved it. "The Negro League," he said, "was a great experience. It was fun to play. It always felt good being able to play against some of the best talent that baseball has ever known."[11]

Day loved life in the Negro Leagues in spite of experiencing none of the luxuries afforded National and American Leaguers. *Brooklyn Eagle* columnist Lew Zeidler offers an example of typical hardships faced by Negro Leagues players. After listing luxuries enjoyed by National and American League players—"the best food in the finest hotels, luxurious sleeping quarters in the feathered berths of the railroads which whisk the players from one city to another"—Zeidler describes how Day and the Brooklyn Eagles made it from a late August 1935 night game in Buffalo, New York, to an evening encounter the next night in New York City, a distance of about 400 miles in the days before the interstate turnpike system. Once the Buffalo game ended, players boarded

Introduction

their bus without showering. Fifty miles later one of the pistons in the bus's motor shot its way out of the cylinder head. The bus rolled to a stop. Several players edged the bus to the shoulder while the team's traveling secretary, Eric Illidge, went in search of a mechanic. About 7:00 a.m. the mechanic arrived. He delivered the verdict that it would take two days to repair the bus. Unable to wait that long, Illidge rounded up three cars for hire. The drowsy players arrived at their New York hotel at 4:00 p.m., just three hours before their game against the Negro National League's league-leading New York Cubans. The cost of hiring the cars was almost as much as the guarantees the team received for the upcoming game. Eighteen-year-old Leon Day, who couldn't stop yawning, rose to the occasion, pitching the Eagles to a win.[12]

Such unexpected hardships, and there were many, didn't diminish Leon's love of the game. Nor did the passage of time change his feelings. Years later he gave Bill Glauber, a writer for the *Baltimore Sun*, an upbeat account: "We were a good bunch of guys traveling down the highway. One guy would start telling lies, then another and another. Then we'd start singing [led by Day's rich tenor voice] 'Sweet Adeline,' play cards, get to the ballpark, play the game, and get right back on the bus."[13] A writer for the *Baltimore Afro-American* concluded after interviewing Day in 1992, three years before he died, "The only thing that mattered was that he was playing baseball, the sport he loved, with people he loved. All else was water under the dam."[14] Day's older sister Ida Mae Bolton said at the time of his death, "I think he was born to be a ball player, because Leon never did anything else. He loved it and talked about it all the time. When we were little we used to make fun of him, but he stuck to it."[15]

Max Manning, nicknamed "Dr. Cyclops" for the thick glasses he wore as a fellow hurler with Day on the Newark Eagles, and, like Day, a veteran of World War II, also loved it. "I was able to support my family and live comfortably during those times. We had fun. We traveled by bus from town to town. There was singing and good natured bantering among teammates. We sometimes played a double header with each game in a different city in order to make the payroll. Whatever was necessary to play the game of baseball the players did." "If it wasn't raining we was playing," Day told *Sun* reporter Wayne Coffey. Four games in a day was not unheard of. Day recalled playing four games on July 4, 1935, starting with a morning doubleheader at Ebbets Field.[16]

Introduction

Other players echoed Day's and Manning's sentiments. Monte Irvin, a teammate of Day's with the Newark Eagles before a Hall of Fame eight-year career with the New York Giants and Chicago Cubs, noted conditions were better in the National and American Leagues. "You didn't have a uniform to bother with. You got a good place to sleep. You ain't got to worry about traveling and all that. I made more money and the caliber of baseball and playing conditions were better." Still, he lamented, "I had more fun in the Negro Leagues."[17]

At a 1994 meeting of the Negro Leagues Baseball Players Association in Baltimore, 13 former players, all of whom had a hard time understanding the huge salaries commanded by National and American Leaguers, shared their attitudes toward their playing days. Russell Awkard, an outfielder from Rockville, Maryland, who played only two seasons (1940–41) split between the Newark Eagles and New York Cubans, remembered, "Playing baseball was a great way to see the country. We played the game we loved, got to travel, and got a paycheck for it." Larry Kimbrough, a 10-year veteran mostly with the Philadelphia Stars, recalled, "Back when I played, you took what they gave you." In his case it was $350 a month, nowhere near the million-dollar annual contracts enjoyed by some in later years. "We were happy to be playing baseball," Kimbrough said. "I probably would have played for nothing."[18] This is not to say they would have turned down the hefty salaries paid to American and National Leaguers of the 1990s but that they had few, if any, regrets about their time in a Negro Leagues team uniform.

Although regrets may have been few, the stark difference in salaries was a hot topic of discussion. "I can't even relate to the type of money they're getting now," proclaimed Wilmer Harris, who starred for the Philadelphia Stars as a pitcher. "We all played because we loved the game," he continued, "and it was an honest way to make a living. Today it seems like everyone's in it just for the money."[19]

Playing in American and National League ballparks such as Griffith Stadium, Yankee Stadium, the Polo Grounds, and Comiskey Park where spectators usually numbered in the thousands was a highlight for Day. Well-groomed fields and covered grandstands were a welcome improvement over the amenities found in many small-town parks that hosted Negro Leagues games. Smaller audiences, wooden benches for seats (sometimes covered and sometimes not), and playing fields with stones and bumpy terrain were not uncommon.

Introduction

"The best thing about playing in the big league parks," Day remembered, "was the showers. Really great showers, lot of water pressure. And they always had plenty of soap and towels. Sometimes we would see no water for a long time after a game. If we were staying in a private home, three of us would sometimes have to take a bath using the same water. But the big league parks, now they were special. There'd be soap all over. We'd load up, stuff it everywhere. I remember the Dodgers used Lifebuoy. And the managers would give us socks, those real nice white kind to play in. A lot of the major leaguers wouldn't wear them if they'd been worn before, so they'd just give them to us."[20]

Some were not as sanguine. First baseman Clinton "Butch" McCord, who played three seasons in the Negro Leagues and 11 in the minors, said in 1996, "We were in the slave market back then.... If we wanted to play baseball, we had to play when and where the owners told us to play. It took me 15 years to get over the hurt of not making it to the majors."[21] A notable criticism of Negro Leagues life was uttered by Jackie Robinson who played one year in the Negro Leagues, 1945, as a shortstop with the Kansas City Monarchs. He cited low pay, long rides in uncomfortable buses, unprofessional umpiring, lack of coaching, and conflicts of interest in cases where league presidents owned a team. Robinson could have added the lack of a disabled list. If a player didn't play, he didn't get paid no matter the severity of the injury or illness. Russell Awkard once took a pitch in his right eye and was given a piece of raw meat to cover it. "I was back the next day," he said. "Couldn't afford not to be."[22]

Richard Powell, longtime executive with the Baltimore Elite Giants, acknowledged that conditions were not the best but that the attention given to the "poor" conditions confronting players was overblown. "Hell," he said, "we played on major league fields.... And for the issue of not getting served in restaurants, that applied to all coloreds, not just ball players.... They were riding buses but going to cities they'd never seen before and the buses were taking them to play ball. Baseball was all that mattered."[23]

At the start of Day's career there were no minor leagues where Black players could hone their skills. Full-time scouts were unheard of. Scouting was most often done as part of one's job as owner, manager, or player. Word of mouth was a popular recruiting strategy. In Day's case, a catcher with the Baltimore Black Sox of the Eastern Colored League,

Introduction

Maeajah "Mac" Eggelston, an "always on the move" catcher and infielder during his 1919–34 career, mentioned Day's name to the Sox's manager, Rap Dixon, who signed Day after seeing him play on Baltimore's sandlots.[24]

In spite of it all, many players acknowledged the situation for what it was and played the game they loved with pride to the best of their considerable abilities. Otherwise, as Day put it, "you'd have to get a real job."[25]

A real job eluded Day until his retirement from baseball in 1954. Over his 22-year career he was a fixture on leading Negro Leagues teams, notably the Newark Eagles and the Baltimore Elite Giants, and played winter ball in Latin America. While serving his country in World War II, he propelled an integrated U.S. Army team to a European Theater of Operations championship in 1945 and, toward the end of his career, played in Canada and on two previously all-white minor league teams. Bill Veeck, flamboyant owner of several major and minor league teams, expressed an interest in the aging star in the early 1950s. Veeck signed him to a brief contract with the Toronto Maple Leafs, a St. Louis Browns farm club, but didn't promote him to the parent club.[26]

Leon Day

Leon was a natural athlete, and his love of the game started at an early age. He dropped out of high school in the tenth grade to play ball. He excelled as a pitcher, the position for which he is best known, as well as an infielder and outfielder. He let his exploits on the diamond do the talking for him. He avoided the bravado and showmanship displayed by other equally talented players such as Satchel Paige whom Day beat three of the four times they faced each other. Some claimed Leon's modesty delayed his eventual journey to Cooperstown.

A WORD ABOUT TERMINOLOGY. In place of "the majors" or "major leagues" I have used National and American League to avoid the implication that the Negro Leagues players were of lesser ability.

Chapter 1

"I'm in"

EARLY ON TUESDAY MORNING, March 7, 1995, 79-year-old Leon Day called his wife Geraldine at home from his bed at Baltimore's St. Agnes Hospital where he was being treated for a heart condition, diabetes, and gout. "Baby, I'm in!" he shouted into the phone.

"You're in where?" she asked.

"I'm in the Hall of Fame. Didn't you hear it?" he said.

Geraldine replied, "Leon, don't you know they haven't even voted yet. It's only 8 o'clock in the morning." Undeterred, he admonished her. "Girl, don't you play around like you do. I'm in. I'm in," he said. But he soon realized Geraldine was right. Day had dreamed the night before that Ed Stack, Hall of Fame board chairman, appeared in his room, told Day he had been elected, and slipped a Hall of Fame ring on his finger.

"They" referred to members of the Hall of Fame's 1995 Veterans Committee who were to vote that day on new members. The committee consisted of 15 members—five Hall of Fame former National and American League players, five former executives, and five members of the media. Leon had missed a call to the hall two years earlier by a single vote. "Leon was so down," Geraldine remembered. He said at the time, "You know what, baby, they're trying to wait until I die. But I'm going to make them a liar."[1] He did.

Elected with Day by the Veterans Committee were turn-of-the-century pitcher Vic Willis, National League founder William Hulbert, and Philadelphia Phillies outfielder Richie Ashburn, perhaps the best leadoff hitter in the National and American Leagues from 1948 to 1962. The Baseball Writers' Association of America (BBWAA), authorized to hold an election every year, selected Phillies third baseman Mike Schmidt with 548 home runs to his credit. Longtime Washington Senators broadcaster Bob Wolff, who also called games in other sports, was selected as the 1995 Ford C. Frick Award winner.[2] Presented annually to a broadcaster for "major contributions to baseball," the award is named after the late broadcaster, National League president, commissioner, and Hall of Famer. Frick was a driving force behind the creation of the Hall of Fame and helped foster the relationship between radio and baseball. Mel Allen and Red Barber were the first two recipients in 1978. A single winner has been selected in each subsequent year.[3]

A Wealth of Praise

Former teammates and writers showered the right-handed hurler with high praise following his death. Pioneering Negro Leagues baseball historian John Holway called him "Baltimore's mighty mite." Baseball historian Donn Rogosin, author of *Invisible Men: Life in Baseball's Negro Leagues*, said of Day, "He became the league's number two pitcher, just a step behind Satchel Paige." Monte Irvin, fellow Hall of Famer and Newark Eagle teammate, and one of the first Negro Leaguers to make the National and American Leagues when he signed with the New York Giants in 1949, said of Day, "I would say he's the most complete ballplayer. I've never seen a better athlete, never seen a better baseball player all around. He had a great fastball and a good curve. He wasn't that big, maybe 5'10"." Irvin added, "One day we were playing against Satchel Paige and locked in a scoreless game. 'Get me just one run,' Leon pleaded, and then Leon hit a home run that won the game. That's the kind of player he was."

Larry Doby, a teammate of Day's as the star second baseman for the Newark Eagles from 1941 to 1943 and 1946 to 1947 and the first Black to sign an American League contract when Bill Veeck, owner of the Cleveland Indians, signed him in 1947, agreed with Irvin's assessment. Both Irvin and Doby compared Day favorably with National League Hall of Fame pitcher Bob Gibson. A right-handed hurler for the St. Louis Cardinals, Gibson, an eight-time All-Star, delivered a wicked fastball. Batters feared his high inside bullet that set them up for a missile on the outside corner of the plate. A 20-game winner for five seasons, Gibson won both the National League's Most Valuable Player and the Cy Young Award, signifying the league's best pitcher, in 1968. That year he posted an earned run average of 1.12, the lowest since the lively ball was introduced in 1920 and the fourth lowest in major league history at the time of his death in 2020. Two years later in 1970, Gibson again won the

National League's Cy Young Award. Unlike Day, he was voted into the Hall of Fame in 1981, his first year of eligibility.

Doby, a future Hall of Famer himself, also noted that Day always called him "Bring Me Back." Growing up in Paterson, New Jersey, Doby didn't like going to the back door of restaurants in the South. So when the team stopped for food at such an eatery, Doby stayed on the bus and called out to Day, "Bring me back something to eat." Leon always did.[4]

Celebrations

Friends and family gathered the evening of March 7 at the Pikesville, Maryland, Hilton, just a few miles from the hospital. Day was too ill to attend, but his 80-year-old sister Ida Mae Bolton, then living with Leon and Geraldine, did. "I got chills. My body just shook," she exclaimed. "We thought it wouldn't happen unless he passed away. I hope," she continued, "Mom and Pop know about this." Day's mother died in 1935 and his father in 1941. Ida added she thought her brother "waited for that [the election] because Leon had been sick for quite a while. But he did make it, and I thank the Lord for that."[5]

Others joined in the celebration of Day's life at his funeral. Three hundred people—including 30 former Negro Leagues players, Baltimore's mayor Kurt L. Schmoke, Maryland's governor Parris Glendening, Maryland U.S. senator Paul S. Sarbanes, Congressman Kweisi Mfume, and Baltimore city councilwoman for Day's district, Agnes Welch—attended his funeral on March 17. Schmoke caught Day's essence, saying, "In an age when baseball seems to be only about money and replacement players [in early 1995, MLB threatened to break the players' strike by fielding teams of replacement players], Leon Day's life was about dignity, class, and talent and so much more." Mfume offered similar accolades, saying, "It is rare that you find an individual with talent, ambition, and humility. But those are just some of the defining and wonderful qualities of Leon Day, one of Baltimore's true heroes."[6]

Pallbearers who carried Day's coffin from Central Church of Christ to the waiting hearse included former players Max Manning, Mahlon Duckett, Gene Benson, and Leroy Ferrell (who was a good enough pitcher with the Baltimore Elite Giants from 1948 to 1950 to be invited to the Brooklyn Dodgers' 1950 spring training where "he ate his way out of camp"); Bob Hieronimus, who led the Baltimore campaign to see Day elected to the hall; and Todd Bolton, a National Park Service ranger born in Alexandria, Virginia (as was Day), inveterate baseball fan, and confidant of Leon in his later years. After the funeral, Day was laid to rest in Baltimore's Arbutus Memorial Park. A detail of National Guardsmen honored Day's army service with a three-gun salute and "Taps." His final resting place is just steps from that of Ben Taylor, Day's manager for a time with the Newark Eagles. Taylor died in 1954.[7]

Geraldine Grieves

Day's death was an emotional as well as a financial blow to his widow. "For a year," she said, "I went to the cemetery every day. I sat by Leon's grave on a bench under a big tree and read my Bible, unless the Orioles were playing. Then I'd turn on the car radio and leave the door open so I could sit there and hear the ball game. That's how I grieved. Leon loved baseball."[8]

Day's love of the game had rubbed off on her. When they met, she did not know Leon was a nationally known ballplayer, let alone anything about baseball. That changed over the course of their 35-year relationship. "The love she has for the [Baltimore] Orioles is unbelievable," said Ray Banks, curator of the Hubert V. Simmons Museum of Negro Leagues Baseball in Owings Mills, Maryland. "If she's at Camden Yards and those around her aren't talking baseball, she'll get up and move to a seat where she can concentrate on the game. Baseball is mental therapy for her."[9]

Chapter 2

The Player and the Person

SMALL IN STATURE, standing 5'7", Day tipped the scales at a trim 170 pounds. The Hall of Famer was best known as a right-handed pitcher with a devastating fastball and sharp-breaking curve, both delivered in an unorthodox manner. In place of a windup or stretch, Day started his pitches from beside his ear much as a third baseman or catcher would, giving the batter less time to swing than when facing a more orthodox delivery. Gene Benson, a friend of Day's who faced him many times as a member of the Philadelphia Stars, said, "He threw the ball more or less from his hip. He didn't rear back and come right over his shoulder. He came right from his thigh, but he would whistle the ball and make it move. He could bring it."[1]

Day explained his delivery. "When I threw overhand, it would hurt my shoulder," Day said. "But from here [motioning to his ear], I'd feel nothing. I threw my fastball straight up. I couldn't throw overhand, so I jerked it at them. It fooled a lot of hitters." That it did. Although Negro Leagues statistics are notoriously incomplete, baseball historian John Holway credits Day with a 76–29 won-loss record in official Negro Leagues games, good for a winning percentage of .698, the highest of any Hall of Fame pitcher, Black or white, at the time of his election. The *Pittsburgh Courier*, one of the country's most respected Black weeklies, rated him as the best pitcher in the Negro Leagues in 1942 and 1943, better even than the much venerated Satchel Paige.[2]

Day did more than pitch. An all-round athlete, he excelled as a second baseman and as an outfielder. Often used as a pinch hitter or runner, Day amassed a lifetime batting average over .300 and was always a threat to steal a base. Always fast afoot, he once covered 100 yards in 11.1 seconds dressed in full uniform and spikes. As a 16-year-old in 1932, he took first place in the boys' 80-yard dash and the boys' sack race in a track and field meet sponsored by the Consolidated Gas and Electric Company of Baltimore.[3]

A player with Day's multiple talents—pitching, running, batting, and fielding—was a big deal. Negro Leagues teams, largely for financial reasons, were limited to 16–18 players and could not afford the luxury of a player who specialized in only one position. As a result many Negro Leaguers played multiple positions, but few did so with the range of skills Leon Day possessed. Managers could confidently slot him into any position except catcher and know he'd also be a threat on the base paths and in the batter's box.

On the field his competitive flame burned brightly. Asked about his best pitch he would often say, "My dust off pitch. I knew I had great control so I could take that ball right up by their face. Then they got up and dusted themselves off. Then I'd strike 'em out. They don't know which way it's coming." Newark Eagle Monte Irvin dusted himself off following one of Day's "dust off" pitches in a Puerto Rican league game. Irvin yelled at his Eagles teammate as he got up, "Whadya do that for? I'm your teammate, and I'm hitting .250." "I want to make sure you don't hit .251," Day yelled back.[4]

He rarely hit a batter he didn't intend to hit, but he did throw at them occasionally. In 1934 Rap Dixon, manager of the Baltimore Black Sox, who had recently signed Day to his first professional contract, ordered the young right-hander to hit Jud "Boojum" Wilson, a hard-hitting superstar with the Philadelphia Stars and possessor of a violent temper. Day did. Boojum stared at him and yelled, "You son-of-a-bitch, if you hit me again, goddamn it, I'm gonna kill you. You hear me?" "Yes sir, Mr. Boojum," the teenage rookie called back. "I didn't hit him no more either," Day told baseball writer James Riley.[5]

This was not the young rookie's first encounter with Ernest Judson "Boojum" Wilson, one of the toughest players in the Negro National League. His nickname was inspired by the sound of his batted ball careening off outfield fences. Day had seen the slugger's outbursts as a child when he sneaked into the Black Sox's stadium. Police were often called to take control of Boojum when he went on one of his rampages. "He," Day told Riley, "used to fight them in Baltimore. It would take the whole department to lock him up. He'd knock them down just as fast as they'd get up, and they'd hit him in the head with that 'billy' and he wasn't feeling nothing. Boojum was crazy. He was *crazy*. I ain't kidding."[6] Crazy, no doubt, but he eventually made the Hall of Fame in 2006.

Chapter 2. The Player and the Person

Day enjoyed a challenge. After a game in Puerto Rico, Josh Gibson, often called the Black Babe Ruth (or was Ruth the white Josh Gibson?) for his prodigious homers and a legend with the Pittsburgh Grays and Crawfords, taunted Day that he couldn't hit him. "Old Josh," Day recalled, "told me, 'You can't hit me,'" to which Leon replied, "Oh, yes I can." The next time Day, pitching in Puerto Rico for the Aguadilla Sharks, faced Gibson, playing for Santurce, and took up Gibson's challenge. Knowing that Gibson tended to back away from pitches he didn't like, Day told Riley, "I threw one about a foot behind him and he backed right into it. It hit him ... boom! Just like a base drum! I hit him dead in the ribs.... I knew I could hit him," Leon gloated. "You didn't hit the ball hard," remembered Stanley Glenn, "because if you did he was going to hit you the next time around."[7]

The fastballer, as many pitchers did, observed the code "if one of my guys gets hit, I'll hit one of yours." A knockdown duel erupted between Leon and Chet Brewer, a well-regarded and well-traveled right-handed pitcher with a 24-year career in the Negro Leagues, during a game in Puerto Rico. Brewer was "knocking my men down ... boom, boom, boom," he told Riley. "I said 'that's alright' and I went out there and started knocking them suckers down ... boom, boom, boom!"[8]

Off the Field

Little is known about his personal life during his career, but thanks to a questionnaire he completed in 1951, we know he was married at the time, enjoyed fishing and photography, and had as his ambition "to reach the Majors"[9] (see Appendix B).

When discussions about his career came up, he adopted a soft-spoken and modest, some said to a fault, demeanor. He preferred to talk about others' feats. When asked in later years by reporters and admirers to talk about his career, he deflected their questions with responses like "Oh, I could hold my own" before launching into a discussion of other players. His favorites were Baltimore Elite Giants pitcher Bill Byrd, called "El Maestro" in Puerto Rico, where he and Day frequently squared off against each other; outfielder Turkey Stearnes, a Nashville, Tennessee, native and outfielder who starred for the Detroit Stars; and the versatile Sam Bankhead, a good friend of Josh Gibson, who could play any

Leon Day

position except catcher and hit with power. If somebody pressed Leon about his feats, he'd tell them, "Go to the library."[10]

When talking with visitors in his Baltimore home after he'd retired, he often shot a look at Geraldine, who, standing nearby, urged him to talk more about himself. The look meant "you go back to the kitchen."[11] "You didn't get too many stories out of him," Geraldine told an interviewer, except the one about games they had to throw in the South to stay out of jail. The big sheriff would appear on the field and tell Day's team, "If y'all Ns beat my Ns, y'all going to jail. Y'all won't leave from here." When the couple were alone, Geraldine found a little Johnny Walker Red did wonders for Leon's storytelling.[12]

"Leon was as good as Satchel Paige," Irvin said just days after Day's death, "as good as any pitcher who ever lived and that would include Bob Gibson. But he never made any noise. Leon was never the promoter Satch was."[13]

Chapter 3

Growing Up

Born with the assistance of a midwife on October 30, 1916, at home, 504 Oronoco Street in Alexandria, Virginia, Leon had three older siblings. The oldest, named after his father, was Ellis Day, Jr., followed by William H. Day, nicknamed "Piggy," and sister Ida Mae. Their parents were Ellis Day, 42, a laborer in a glass factory, and Hattie Lee Day, 35, a domestic and an active member of the Eva Jenifer Neighborhood Club, an association to help working girls and women. Both were born in Virginia.

The family left Alexandria in May 1917, crossed the Potomac River, and took up residence on Eutaw Street in Baltimore, Maryland, where Ellis Sr. found work in a glass factory. A younger brother, Robert, died as an infant. Leon recalled as a five-year-old walking with his family behind a horse-drawn wagon on which was placed a small white coffin making its way to the cemetery.

By 1930 the family moved again, this time to 2506 Puget Street in Baltimore's Mount Winans neighborhood, three and a half miles south of Baltimore's Inner Harbor. The area was originally known as "Hull's Village" and "Hullsville" after Charles J. Hull, who purchased the 50-acre tract in 1872. Hull built modest homes for laborers who worked at nearby businesses including the B&O Railroad, stockyards, and glassworks. The community was developed for African Americans and had both a post office and a "colored" school by the end of the 19th century.[1] Neither of the Day residences in Baltimore had electricity or indoor plumbing.[2]

No record could be found of his father attending any of his son's games, but it's not hard to imagine that he did when Day's Newark Eagles came to town to play the Baltimore Elite Giants during the Giants' seasons in the Queen City.

Leon Day's birth certificate documenting his birth at 6:00 a.m. on October 30, 1916, in Alexandria, Virginia. The family soon left Alexandria for Baltimore where Day grew up and started and ended his Negro Leagues baseball career (Ancestry.com).

An Early Love of the Game

Day, like millions of youngsters, fell in love with baseball at an early age. Up until age 12 he played ball with neighborhood kids using a broomstick and old tennis balls. While his playmates would grow up still being baseball fans but pursuing other interests, baseball would be Day's ticket out of his poverty-stricken neighborhood.

By age eight, he was finding his way into the Baltimore Black Sox's Maryland Stadium where he spent his Sundays. He got in any way he could. "It was within walking distance," he told Riley, "but it was a good walk, about two miles. I'd go over the fence, under the fence, sometimes I'd get a foul ball and they'd let me in, but I got in there some kind

Chapter 3. Growing Up

of way." One way was help from his favorite Black Sox player, pitcher Lamon Yokely, who hailed from Winston-Salem, North Carolina, and was so popular with fans that he was called a "matinee idol."[3]

Wanting desperately to see a packed exhibition doubleheader between the Black Sox and a barnstorming team of National and American League players including Hall of Famers Jimmie Foxx and Lefty Grove, Leon tried to get in "any which way," but added security foiled his attempts. Somehow Yokely spotted the youngster and escorted him into the park. Other times he'd wait just beyond the right field wall "where an old guy had made a little gate in the wall and would let people in for 25 or 50 cents. When he let someone in, we flew in there behind him. The guy," he told Riley, "couldn't say anything 'cause he was cheating himself."[4]

By age 12 he had hooked up with his first team, the Mt. Winan Athletic Club, where he displayed his God-given abilities. Halfway through the tenth grade, the 17-year-old dropped out of Frederick Douglass High School where he was a standout on the baseball, basketball, and track teams.[5] His disappointed mother tried, to no avail, to change his mind. He quickly joined a semipro team, the Silver Moons. It wasn't long before his pitching and play at second base came to the attention of Rap Dixon, manager of the Baltimore Black Sox. The well-traveled Dixon was a superb outfielder and heavy hitter as well as a man with a hot temper. Also a good judge of baseball talent, he had seen Day's play with the Silver Moons. While published accounts of the Silver Moons are scarce, the *Afro-American* shows Day pinch hitting in a September 1932 game against a local team, the Twelfth Ward Democratic Club, and playing shortstop in a May 1934 game against the semipro Bethlehem Gray Sox in which he scored two runs and banged out two hits.

Going Pro

One day during the first half of the 1934 season, Dixon asked the youngster, "Young man, how would you like to play professional baseball?" "You'll have to ask my papa," Day replied. Papa gave his blessing after extracting a promise from Dixon to take care of 17-year-old Leon and asking his son to "promise me that whatever you do you'll always give it your best." Day promised and left the Silver Moons for the

Black Sox who had reentered the Negro National League for the last half of the 1934 season. Other notables on the team included Rap's brother Paul, a somewhat less accomplished ballplayer than his older brother, and pitcher and infielder Jimmy Johnson. Day left home with more than his father's good wishes. He carried a small penknife that his daddy had given him along with some advice. "Keep it in your pocket," Papa told him. "You meet a lot of different people when you travel."[6]

Soon afterward the Sox left for a ten-game road trip and never returned to Baltimore. Dissension between J.B. Hairstone, a former Black Sox player and manager who umpired occasional games and dabbled in baseball poetry, and Black Sox owner Joe Cambria led to a confusing turn of events. Hairstone charged that Cambria, by failing to pay taxes in 1930, had lost the rights to use the team's name. Cambria prevailed in court in 1933 and fielded a team that year called the Baltimore Sox. Meanwhile Hairstone put together his own team, using the name the Baltimore Black Sox, giving the city two teams with almost identical names. Neither team distinguished itself in 1933.

Halfway through the 1934 season, as tensions continued to grow between Hairstone and Cambria, Cambria sold his team, which had gained admittance to the Negro National League, to Jack Farrell who relocated the team to his hometown, Chester, Pennsylvania. For a short time he called the team the Chester Baltimore Black Sox. Farrell, a Black entrepreneur, also purchased the beleaguered Washington Pilots and folded some of their better players into the Baltimore Black Sox, the team name he settled on for the remainder of the 1934 season. Farrell was the first Black owner of the Baltimore Black Sox since 1917. The team did well against regional semipro teams but played only 13 league games, winning three, losing eight, and tying two.[7]

In addition to his baseball interests, Farrell was the first Black to be licensed as a boxing promoter in Pennsylvania. He staged bouts for years including one in 1924 featuring the 46-year-old former World Heavyweight champion Jack Johnson, the first Black man to hold the title. Farrell also promoted dances throughout Delaware's and Maryland's Eastern Shore. The press referred to him as "the sultan of Mary and Market Streets."[8]

Dixon promised the 17-year-old Day, now playing out of Chester, Pennsylvania, $60 a month plus room and board for the remainder of the 1934 season. Leon saw some money occasionally but claimed he

Chapter 3. Growing Up

didn't care about the money because "I loved the game." Day explained how the payment he did receive worked. "They were playing percentage ball, but I didn't know it," he told Ed Hines, a reporter for the *Sports Collector Digest*, in 1934. "At the end of the game they'd split up the pot and give me 3 or 4 dollars, or something like that." Papa was happy with the three meals a day Leon did get. It was one less mouth to feed at home.[9]

Almost a Gray

Best known for his play with the Newark Eagles, the young pitcher almost became a Homestead Gray near the end of his tenure with the Black Sox. "Buck tried to steal me after a game in Johnstown, Pennsylvania, in 1934. I struck out about 15," Day told Riley. Buck was Buck Leonard, star first baseman and outfielder for 17 seasons with the Homestead Grays and often called the "Black Lou Gehrig," who, along with Josh Gibson, was inducted into the Hall of Fame in 1972. Buck offered the youngster $125 a month, an offer Day, promised $60 but actually receiving much less, found enticing. Carrying his cardboard suitcase down the stairs of the hotel in Johnstown, he ran into Rap Dixon coming up the stairs. "Where do you think you're going?" Rap growled. "I'm going over there," Day said pointing to the Grays' bus. "You ain't going nowhere. Take that bag back upstairs," Dixon ordered. Leon did as he was told.

Had Day not run into Dixon on the stairs and joined the Grays, Cum Posey's entourage, already regarded as the best Negro Leagues team ever to don uniforms, would have been unbeatable. Without Day, the Grays would win six undisputed consecutive Negro National League pennants, 1940–45. The Baltimore Elite Giants were awarded the 1939 pennant after winning a playoff series, but the Grays won more games that year than the Elites and hotly contested the decision. The Grays won another National Negro League pennant in 1948 and appeared in five of the seven World Series between the Negro National League and the Negro American League, winning three.[10] One can only imagine what the Grays could have done with Day in the lineup.

Leon's time with the Black Sox was less than impressive. He appeared in only three league games. He started one in July but found the going rough. By the second inning he had given up six hits and seven runs to the Nashville Elite Giants who won the game 10–9.

Burnalle (Bun) Hayes, a journeyman pitcher whose Negro Leagues career spanned eight seasons and four teams, relieved him. In total Day faced 25 bona fide Negro Leagues batters in his rookie year, gave up 11 hits and 11 runs, and struck out two and walked two,[11] but he was on his way. He had played, however briefly, with a professional Negro Leagues team. The Black Sox folded due to financial reasons after the 1934 season. The Depression was in full swing, and Negro Leagues baseball suffered along with the rest of the country.

Chapter 4

A Career Takes Off

Although Rap Dixon put the kibosh on Leon joining the Grays, he didn't impede the teenager's career. In 1935 Rap took Leon with him to the Brooklyn Eagles, occasionally referred to in the press as the Brooklyn Black Eagles, founded by a newcomer to the Negro Leagues, Abraham Lincoln Manley, Abe for short.[1]

The Moguls

Team owners in the Negro Leagues were called "moguls," shorthand for important and prominent people, by the Black press. The term was an apt description of the men at the helms of the teams. The Eagles' owner Abe Manley was one. He made his money in real estate and the numbers game in Camden, New Jersey, during the 1920s. He liked to hang with the players, often playing poker with them and traveling with them on their bus. He was active in league affairs, serving terms as vice president and treasurer.

Gus Greenlee, owner of the Pittsburgh Crawfords, which dominated the Negro National League in the 1930s, was a respected bookie, community leader, moneylender, and entrepreneur. Born in a log cabin in North Carolina, he moved to Pittsburgh after his freshman year in college and worked as a shoeshine boy, taxi driver, and steel mill worker. Prohibition-era nightclubs served as a front for his numbers activity. He managed several boxers. Everyone who was anybody in Pittsburgh's Black neighborhoods patronized his Crawford Grill.

Thomas T. (Smiling Tom) Wilson, owner of the Elite Giants, lived in Nashville, Tennessee, where he ran numbers and entertained clients at his Paradise Ballroom, a legitimate business that helped finance his baseball interests. He served a term as chairman of the board of the Pride of Tennessee Elks Lodge No. 1102. A sharp dresser favoring tailor-made suits whose pockets held wads of cash, he loved the good life and was a favorite of the ladies.

James "Soldier Boy" Semler, owner of the New York Black Yankees, made his fortune in real estate, running numbers, and the restaurant business. With a reputation as a "charming, smooth-talking, con artist," he was disliked by some business associates and players, several of whom left the team when he became owner.

Cumberland "Cum" Posey, the Homestead Grays' owner, represented a variation on the theme. As a player and manager with the Grays from 1911 to 1929, he also excelled in basketball and golf. When the Depression hit, he took Rufus "Sonnyman" Jackson on as a co-owner of the Grays. Jackson's job was to raise money for Posey. Jackson ran numbers games, rented jukeboxes by the hundreds to bars and cafés, and owned the Sky Rocket Café, a nightclub. Posey called the shots but stayed above the fray serving on the Homestead school board, writing a column, "Posey's Points," for the *Pittsburgh Courier*, and holding memberships in several elite Pittsburgh clubs.

Alex Pompez owned the New York Cubans. One of the wealthiest men in Harlem, he was indicted in 1936 by a grand jury for racketeering. He fled to Mexico where officials refused New York governor Thomas Dewey's extradition request. He later voluntarily returned to testify against members of Dutch Schultz's mob, the only man to testify against fellow Mafia members and live. He resumed ownership of the Cubans in 1938. Ten years later the team became a farm club to the New York Giants who hired Pompez as a scout. Later he served as a member of the Hall of Fame's special committee for the Negro Leagues.[2] The committee elected the first Negro Leaguers during 1970–77.

The Eagles Get Underway

Abe convinced the moguls to award him a franchise in Brooklyn, New York. Abe rented Ebbets Field directly from the National League Brooklyn Dodgers, thereby avoiding fees charged by middlemen—Nat Strong, among others—to arrange games. Strong retaliated by charging half price for games at nearby fields. Abe hired Ben Taylor as his manager. Formerly a slick fielding infielder who wielded a fearsome bat and pitched as well, Taylor was enshrined in Cooperstown in 2006. Each

Chapter 4. A Career Takes Off

owner of the existing teams made several of their players available to Abe who ordered them to report to Jacksonville, Florida, for spring training. Among those who reported was Leon Day, a free agent after the Black Sox folded.[3]

Youngsters such as Day, with innate skills and a passion for the game, looked to established players for guidance. Credit is often given to pitcher Layman Yokely, Day's childhood idol, for developing Day into the Hall of Fame pitcher he would shortly become. Yokely had been the Black Sox's "ace" in the late '20s and early '30s. A sore arm contributed to his decline by the time Day joined the Sox, but he could still play.[4]

In 1934 postseason play, Yokely took the mound for the Black Sox in two games of a 12-game series against a barnstorming team of white players simply called the All-Stars. Yokely lost both games played in Baltimore. By the spring of 1935, a newspaper article had both Yokeley and Day in spring training with the Brooklyn Eagles in Jacksonville, Florida. No mention of Yokely with the Eagles after that could be found.[5] It may have been during that spring when Yokely provided Day with many a lesson. "I'd tell him what to do, what not to do. He was my boy," Yokely told baseball historian John Holway.[6] Another mentor was Ted "Double Duty" Radcliffe, so purportedly nicknamed by short story writer Damon Runyon, for Radcliffe's ability to pitch one game of a doubleheader and catch the next one or vice versa. "Duty" taught Day a pickoff move known as a half balk which is illegal today, but it fooled many a base runner during Leon's career.[7]

The mentoring resulted in a vastly improved Leon Day. He was a standout during spring training. Noting his small stature, five feet seven inches tall and weighing just 155 pounds,[8] a far cry from the 180 pounds carried by the six-foot four-inch frame of Satchel Paige. A writer for the *New York Age* noted, "The right-handed pitching prospect from Baltimore continues to show a good delivery and is almost certain to be taken north."[9] Not only did he go north for the 1935 season, but manager Ben Taylor used him exclusively as a starting pitcher for the 1935 campaign.

A week before the campaign got underway, Day led the Brooklyn Eagles to a 10–1 shellacking of the Newark Dodgers in the second game of an exhibition doubleheader at Olemar Field in Irvington, New Jersey.

A *New York Age* writer covering the games that season reported that spectators seeing Day for the first time were "agreeably surprised" with Day's appearing "cool as the proverbial cucumber" as he delivered his "snappy drop and biting fast one."[10]

Leon took the mound for Taylor in the opening game of another Sunday doubleheader against the defending Negro National League champion Philadelphia Stars. The "youthful Baltimorean" went the distance, yielding but "five scattered bingles and poled out two hits, both doubles." The Stars managed but three runs to the Eagles' eight. "It was," the *New York Amsterdam News* reported, "the hitting and twirling of Day that made the difference." A writer for the *Times Union*, a Brooklyn paper, reported Day "had the league champions eating out of his hand." Leon had won his second straight Negro Leagues game. The youngest player on the team at age 18, Yokely's and Radcliffe's protégé would go on a 7–4 won-lost record in 103 innings.[11] His performance earned him his first of seven appearances in an East-West game, the Negro Leagues' equivalent of the National and American Leagues' All-Star game.[12]

The Eagles returned to Ebbets Field for their home opener against the Homestead Grays. In a rare event in those segregated days, a white man, New York City mayor Fiorello H. La Guardia, threw out the ceremonial first ball. Day didn't pitch, but had he, the Eagles may have fared better than their 20–7 slaughter at the hands of the Grays.[13]

Day's pitching soon became one of the few Brooklyn Black Eagles highlights. But by late June the team languished in last place in the eight-team Negro National League with a 3–16 won-loss record.[14] Manley had made a flurry of trades and acquisitions trying desperately to field a winning roster. He'd fired Ben Taylor a month into the season over a dispute about acquiring new players. Taylor sued Manley but lost in court. One move of Abe's that did pay big dividends was the acquisition of George Giles from the Kansas City Monarchs. At six feet two inches and weighing 190 pounds, Giles was considered one of the fastest players for his size. Abe appointed Giles team captain and filled the managerial void himself created by his firing of Taylor.[15]

By late June Abe's frustration was showing. "I've searched every little highway and byway for new material…. No one seems to be the man we want," he complained to a *Chicago Defender* reporter. "The only reliable pitchers," he continued, "seem to be Jackman, Day, and Radcliffe and they are going none too well."[16] Bill "Cannonball" Jackman, who played only briefly for Manley, was 38, Radcliffe 30, and Day 19.

New York Black Yankees owner Semler could have made Abe's

Chapter 4. A Career Takes Off

frustration worse if the rumor that he was contemplating raiding the Eagles for the services of Day and "Rap" Dixon was true. Raiding another's team was commonplace. Semler had lost two players to raids, but he said, "I accepted the situation for what it was" and added, "If I took Day and Dixon anybody with the least spark of fairness would say I was right in so doing." Semler, no doubt aware that some looked upon him unfavorably, took neither player, explaining, "I will not do anything at this time to create any further ill feeling." Whether his decision and explanation enhanced his reputation among the other moguls is not known.[17]

Abe's frustration eased a bit after the Eagles took three of four games from the strong Chicago American Giants as the first half of the 1935 season ended. "A rousing finale can make us forget early disappointments," a reporter for the *New York Amsterdam News* said in early July. "They've settled themselves," he continued, "and they're sure there'll be a pot of gold at the end of the rainbow in the second half."[18] The reach for gold was premature. The Eagles did move up from last place but only to sixth in the second half.

Day won another of the Eagles' games against the Chicago American Giants by pitching what a *Chicago Defender* writer described as "a stingy game"[19] in the second game of a Sunday doubleheader. Leon put in another notable performance in July as the second half began by defeating the Pittsburgh Crawfords, who featured sluggers Josh Gibson, Buck Leonard, and Oscar Charleston, considered by many to be the best Negro Leagues player of all time, 4–3. A month later, Leon took one of his only four losses. The Philadelphia Stars shut out Day and the Eagles 6–0.[20]

That the Eagles failed to break into the league's first division disappointed Abe, but Day fared well. His earned run average ranked third among all pitchers in the Negro National League. His won-loss record ranked fourth. A writer for the *Delaware County Daily Times* said Day's performance "stamped him as a peer of the first water." A writer for the *New Journal and Guide* called Day the "ace" of the staff and noted just prior to the East-West game, "the chunky right-handed pitcher of the Brooklyn Black Eagles is en route to Chicago for the big East-West Game."

Day's 1935 season qualified him as one of three Eagles players to join New York Cubans catcher Frank Duncan's postseason San Juan, Puerto Rico–bound all-star team. The two other Eagles were outfielder

New York Cubans catcher Frank Duncan's nattily-dressed All-Star team just before their departure from New York City for Puerto Rico where, using the team name Brooklyn Dodgers, they captured the island's 1935–36 winter season championship. Top row, from left: Ed Stone, Slim Jones, Ray Brown, Rufus Lewis, Terris McDuffie, Buck Leonard, Johnny Hayes. Bottom row, from left: Ray Dandridge, Dickey Sway, Bill Sadler, Leon Day, Frank Duncan, Vic Harris (courtesy Noir-Tech).

Ed Stone, a solid hitting outfielder with a strong arm, and pitcher Terris McDuffie.[21]

McDuffie was known not only for his large array of pitches but his ego as well. The lettering on the back of his warm-up jacket read, "The Great McDuffie." "To hear him boast of his prowess and invincibility you would think there has never been a Satchel Paige, Jose Mendez, Rube Foster or Phil Cockrell," wrote sports scribe Randy Dixon of the *Philadelphia Tribune*. Dixon went on to say McDuffie would have to be forgiven "because he is delivering the goods."[22]

Getting off to a strong start in the warm climes of Puerto Rico, the team, carrying the name Brooklyn Eagles, won their first five games. By mid–January 1936, their won-loss record stood at 14–1–2. Of particular note was an exhibition doubleheader against the National League Cincinnati Reds' starting nine. The Eagles won the morning game 5–4 and

Chapter 4. A Career Takes Off

dropped the afternoon encounter 3–2. The 1935 Reds had finished below .500 with a 68–85–1 record. Two eventual Hall of Famers, catcher Ernie Lombardi and first baseman Jim Bottomley, were on the roster. The Eagles' win was a testament to the fact that Negro Leaguers could hold their own against National League competition. By mid–March 1936 the Eagles had won the island's championship and a trophy symbolic of the title.[23]

Abe stayed behind in Brooklyn to continue his pursuit of players who could win the pennant for him. At the same time, he made plans to leave Brooklyn for Newark, New Jersey, in search of a better financial return. He had lost $30,000 (about $680,000 in 2024 dollars) in the New York market. Three National and American League teams (Brooklyn Dodgers, New York Yankees, and New York Giants), another Negro Leagues team (New York Cubans), plus several semipro teams, such as the Brooklyn Bushwicks, the Bay Parkways of Brooklyn, and the Farmers of Glendale, competed with him for the increasingly scarce New York ticket dollar as the Depression wore on.

Particularly notable among the semipro teams were the Bushwicks, an all-white team, led by owner Max Rosen, a Jewish immigrant from Hungary who quickly developed a passion for baseball. He owned the team from 1913 to 1951. Baseball writer Thomas Barthel claims, "No other semi-pro team ever challenged so many good teams and beat them so regularly."[24] One reason being that Rosen stocked the Bushwicks with many National and American Leaguers either on their way up or after their retirement. Teams in the National Negro Leagues were frequent victims. The newly named Newark Eagles suffered a doubleheader loss, including one game with Day on the mound in 1938. The Bushwicks outmanned the Eagles again 10–2 on July 12, 1942.[25] The Crawfords, Stars, Black Yankees, and Grays regularly supplied the opposition to the Bushwicks at games usually played on the Bushwicks' home turf, New York City's Dexter Park. The Negro Leagues opposition could also be strong at times as testified to by the Grays' five straight wins over the white boys from Brooklyn in 1943.[26]

Abe would not be free of all Negro Leagues competition in the Garden State as the New York Black Yankees held forth in home games at Hinchliffe Stadium, 15 miles north of Newark in Paterson, New Jersey, in 1936–37 and again from 1939 to 1945 far from the hustle and bustle of the Big Apple, but Newark was a welcome respite from the city's congested playing fields.

In Newark he struck a deal with George Weiss, vice president of the New York Yankees' affiliate minor league team, the Newark Bears, to rent Ruppert Field, which unlike Ebbets Field had lights. By renting from Weiss, Manley again avoided paying a middleman to arrange games. Abe avoided any Newark competition by buying the city's only Negro Leagues team, the Newark Dodgers. He also arranged for Eagle players to stay at Newark's Grand Hotel, which would become the players' and their admirers' watering hole of choice for years to come.[27]

People gathered at the Grand after a game to socialize around the bar and sample the food which Monte Irvin described as "outstanding." "Effa" (Abe's wife), Irvin said, "never had to pay for a drink when she put in an appearance." "Women," he said, "sought out their favorite player. If they didn't know the player's name, they would ask for them by their uniform number." Then the two could dance to the music of bandleaders like Fletcher Henderson, Charles Johnson, and Count Basie and performers like Cab Calloway, Earl "Fatha" Hines, Lionel Hampton, and Fats Waller. Poet Amiri Baraka frequented the Grand as a young child with his father. He remembered "everybody highliftin' glasses jingling with ice, black peoples' eyes sparkling and showing their teeth in the hippest way possible ... seeing Larry Doby and Lennie Pearson and Pat Patterson ... and wearin' my ears and eyes out drinking a Coca Cola, checking everything out." Baraka's biggest thrill was the time his father pushed him forward for an introduction to Monte Irvin who "would bend down and take my little hand in his."[28]

Effa Manley

Abe appointed his wife Effa Manley to oversee the team's administration and logistics while he focused on recruiting players. Effa, as attractive as she was smart, was well-suited for her assignment. She, like Abe, loved baseball. Before tying the knot with Abe on June 15, 1933, she would walk from her Harlem apartment to Yankee Stadium to root for the "Bambino." "I was crazy about Babe Ruth," she said. "I used to see all the Yankees games hoping he'd hit the ball out of the park."[29]

A high school graduate with ten years of experience in New York City's millinery industry, her leadership, organizational, and persuasive skills were on display in the summer of 1934. Partnering with the

Chapter 4. A Career Takes Off

Reverend John H. Johnson, rector of St. Martin's Episcopal Church in Harlem, she led a boycott of white stores that refused to hire Blacks. Protesters she organized carried signs reading "We won't shop where we can't work" up and down Harlem's 125th Street in the summer heat. She and Johnson confronted the owners of Blumstein Department Store with two weeks of receipts showing that the vast majority of their customers were Black. The owners and their lawyer refused to budge after two meetings with Effa and Johnson. Effa then switched from confrontation to a more humane appeal. "You know," she told the Blumsteins, "we think just as much of our young colored girls as you do your young white girls. The only thing they can find to do is work in someone's home as a maid or become prostitutes." Her statement shocked the Blumsteins. On July 26, 1934, after asserting they never practiced discrimination, William Blumstein issued a statement promising to hire as many "colored" sales clerks as the business would allow. They hired 35 by September.[30]

Effa put her skills to use for the Eagles by scheduling and promoting games, negotiating players' salaries, dealing with the U.S. State Department in a failed bid to stem the flow of players to the Caribbean, and as the only woman to attend meetings of Negro National League moguls, constantly urged them to take a businesslike approach that would bring credit to "the race." Pleas by the other moguls to Abe "to keep your wife home where she belongs" fell on deaf ears.

Effa put so much energy, compassion, and creativity into her work that in 2006 she was elected the first, and so far only, female member of the Baseball Hall of Fame.

CHAPTER 5

Newark

THE NEWARK THAT GREETED the newly formed Eagles in 1936 was 90 percent white and 8 percent Black. Discrimination relegated most Blacks to the Hill District, so named for its terrain, in Newark's Third Ward. The Hargrave Commission's survey of New Jersey, a summary of which was published in the January 22, 1940, issue of the *Afro-American*, described the Third Ward as "Newark's largest slums where social diseases are rampant."[1] The enabling legislation for the survey was introduced into the New Jersey Assembly by delegate Frank Hargrave and passed by both chambers. The findings cited hundreds of instances of workplace segregation and concluded with recommendations for additional legislation and studies.[2]

The survey's findings did not come as news to Newark's Black population. While tempers occasionally flared over the employment rights of Blacks, despite laws prohibiting segregation in public schools, industries, restaurants, and hotels being on the books since 1888, many Blacks shied away from confrontation. They put more energy into building their own institutions. Black businessmen founded the People's Finance Corporation. Professional societies such as the Negro Funeral Directors of New Jersey, the Newark Barbers' Protective Association, and the Modern Beauticians served as support groups for many Blacks in the city.

Entertainment was everywhere. Taverns and saloons (one for every 429 residents, the highest ratio of any American city) got their beer from one or more of Newark's five breweries, Ballentine, Hensler, Krueger, Feigenspan, and Wiedenmayer. Black jazz artists such as Ella Fitzgerald, Billy Eckstine, Sarah Vaughan, and Duke Ellington performed regularly in both white and Black theaters. Black artists could perform in white theaters, but Black patrons were seated in the balconies. White comedians, such as Jackie Gleason, were also popular.[3]

Chapter 5. Newark

The New Team

While Newarkers partied, a pitching staff, led by the two aces of the Brooklyn Eagles' pennant-winning Puerto Rico team the previous winter, Leon Day, now only 19, and Terris McDuffie gave Newark fans two reasons to look forward to a winning season. The success of McDuffie and Day, both names often mentioned in the same sentence, prompted Calvin Service, sports editor of the *Chicago Defender*, to call Abe's team the league's most improved team and the probable pennant winner. Wanting to develop players once he found them, Abe soon formed a farm club, the Winston Salem Eagles, who played in Winston-Salem, North Carolina, as a barnstorming team during the 1936–38 seasons but without developing any player of note.[4]

Service's prophesy notwithstanding, the Eagles stumbled out of the gate losing their first two league games of 1936, 5–1 and 9–5, to the Washington Elite Giants before 2,500 spectators in Washington, D.C.'s Griffith Stadium. Day started the second game but was tagged for four runs in the first inning. Player-manager Bill Bell, a top-flight pitcher for 15 seasons with the Kansas City Monarchs and Homestead Grays before receiving the managerial reins from Abe and known as a good teacher and role model for young pitchers, relieved Day in the third inning.[5]

The team's struggles continued. The Eagles lost three of four games to the New York Cubans in early June. Day went the distance in game one but lost 1–0. Martín Dihigo, an eventual Hall of Famer and the most versatile of all Negro Leaguers who played every position well, clubbed a solo homer in the ninth inning. A less-than-stellar outing by Day in late June reflected the Eagles' ongoing pain. He started, went the distance, but gave up four runs in the first inning, leading to a 5–3 loss against the Brooklyn Bushwicks. The second half of the 1936 season saw Abe's charges improve to 15 wins and 11 losses, good for second place for the season behind the Pittsburgh Crawfords in the Negro National League—a distinct improvement over 1935 but one place short of Abe's aspirations.[6]

Day continued pitching through 1936. He gave one of his best performances in a game he lost: a pitchers' duel with Chet Brewer of the New York Cubans. Brewer, ten years into his 24 Negro Leagues career, and Day both pitched into the ninth inning of a June 7 game at Hinchliffe Stadium in Paterson, New Jersey, when Martín Dihigo, of Cuban birth, singled in the winning run. Two months later, as Day's won-lost ratio turned positive, the *Pittsburgh Courier* ran a stand-alone photo titled, "Great Day." The caption read, "Leon Day, the brilliant 19-year old pitcher ranks as one of the greatest young pitchers in the Negro National League."[7]

As winter approached, Effa Manley summoned her administrative skills, contacted Puerto Rican officials, and arranged for players from the Eagles, Crawfords, Black Yankees, and Homestead Grays to form a team in the Puerto Rican League. "I was very unhappy about the boys not having any work," she said. "So I proceeded to make us contacts in Puerto Rico."

While she was making contacts, Abe was choosing the players: Day; McDuffie; Bob Evans, a pitcher who had lost the sight in one eye due to a knife fight as a teenager and came to the Newark Eagles from the Brooklyn Eagles; plus third sacker Ray Dandridge, master of the hot corner by being "relaxed, smooth as silk, and possessing a great pair of hands with a velvet touch"[8]; and right fielder Ed Stone represented the Newark Eagles. Others included luminaries Satchel Paige, whose wife Janet accompanied him, and Josh Gibson. Using Newark Eagles uniforms and equipment, they called themselves the Newark Eagles. A *Philadelphia Tribune* writer applauded the project saying, "We hope this team will live up to our expectations and be the worthy successors to the one and only Brooklyn Eagles of last year." The *Pittsburgh Courier* went beyond hope, asserting, "The team is expected to sweep all opposition." The players set sail from New York on November 19, 1936, on the American steamship the SS *Coama*. They arrived in San Juan four days later. Day, 20, was the youngest. The player closest in age to him was Ray Dandridge, 23. The oldest player was George Scales, 35.

The 1936–37 outfit easily captured the championship in part by beating the Newark Bears, who were also enjoying the warmer climes, six games in a row. Day's appendectomy prevented him from playing a major role in these games.[9]

Abe Continues the Hunt

Abe continued trading players while the games in Puerto Rico went on. One trade in particular paid big dividends. Abe swapped moderately

Chapter 5. Newark

talented outfielder Thadist Christopher, whose strength was at the plate as attested to by once powering a ball completely out of the Polo Grounds, and Harry Williams, a journeyman second baseman, for outfielder Jimmy Crutchfield and second baseman Dick Seay from Gus Greenlee's Pittsburgh Crawfords. Seay's addition to an infield already composed of Mule Suttles, a power hitter who swung a 50-ounce bat, at first; Willie Wells, the best shortstop in Black baseball in the '30s and early '40s; and Ray Dandridge at the hot corner, cemented what became known as "the million-dollar infield." All but Seay, as of this writing, eventually reached the Hall of Fame. Crutchfield added speed to the outfield. Day, and the rest of the pitching staff, now had a much improved defense behind them.[10]

As the team headed north after 1937's spring training in High Point, North Carolina, Effa arranged for three games with Abe's minor league aggregation, the Winston-Salem Eagles. The series proved a useful and prescient tune-up to the regular season. The Newark nine took all three games. Day won a 6–0 shutout in the third game while striking out ten batters in the seven innings he pitched.[11]

As opening day, 1937, approached, columnists offered their usual preseason predictions. E.B. Rea, sportswriter for the *New Journal and Guide*, chose the Homestead Grays and the Eagles as the prime contenders for the upcoming pennant race. "I am convinced now," he added, "that the Eagles will be a hard bunch to stop."[12]

In the spirit of Rea's prediction, the Eagles reeled off nine-straight wins, good for first place in the Negro National League. The streak came to an end in late May in the second game of a Sunday doubleheader against the New York Black Yankees. McDuffie took the loss 5–4. In the opening game, however, Day, cited "as one of the prime reasons the Eagles occupy first place," threw a shutout to the tune of 12–0. He helped his cause with two singles and two runs scored while striking out seven. It was one of two shutouts the Yankees suffered that season at Day's hands.[13]

Leon continued baffling hitters. Two other outings of note occurred in early August. Three thousand fans turned out to witness McDuffie and Day team up to sweep a doubleheader from the New York Black Yankees. McDuffie won the first game 9–4. Day held the opposition scoreless through the first three innings of the second game but surrendered four runs in the fourth. He pitched shutout balls the rest of the way and won the game 10–4 thanks to his heavy-hitting teammates. A week later against a barnstorming white team, the All Phils, in a game that the *Philadelphia Tribune* called "the greatest game seen here this season and one of the most absorbing played anywhere," Leon dueled 38-year-old George Earnshaw for 11 innings. Earnshaw was one year retired from a 127-games-won-and-93-lost career with the Philadelphia Athletics, Chicago White Sox, Brooklyn Dodgers, and St. Louis Cardinals. His performance had declined noticeably in his last two seasons. The curfew law ended the game tied 3–3, but Leon had a memorable outing by notching 16 strikeouts.

As the season went on, the *New York Age* touted the Eagles as "having the best infield in Negro baseball history and a pitcher in Leon Day worth going miles to see."[14] Such praise notwithstanding, the Eagles placed second in the Negro National League standings due to losing six games late in the season to the perpetual pennant-winning Homestead Grays. Day, on the other hand, had what would be the best season of his illustrious career. He won 13 games and lost none.[15]

He actually lost one, but as he told Riley, "the game was only an exhibition." His 13 wins were accomplished over the course of 61 league games during which he batted .320.[16]

Abe as Chief Scout

Now more determined than ever to field a pennant-winning team, Manley kept up his talent hunt. On a tour of semipro games in his chauffeur-driven black Lincoln Continental, he spotted an 18-year-old high school senior playing for the semipro Orange Triangles in Orange, New Jersey: Monford "Monte" Irvin. After a brief negotiation, Irvin signed for $125 a month (about $2,700 in 2023 dollars). It was big money for his family, which included 11 children. "My Dad," Irvin said later, "never made more than $15.00 a week. Many guys started at a dollar a day, then you might get a little raise up to $10.00 a week. At $15.00 you're doing pretty good."[17]

Abe also had his eyes fixed on veteran Satchel Paige. Salivating over the prospect of a pitching staff featuring Paige, Leon Day, and Terris McDuffie, Abe offered Paige's employer of record, Pittsburgh Crawfords owner Gus Greenlee, $5,000 ($110,000 in 2024 dollars). Paige, never a

Chapter 5. Newark

stickler for contracts, had let it be known he was for sale to anyone for $2,000 (about $44,000 in 2024 dollars), presumably to be paid to him, not to a team owner. Thumbing his nose at a $200 fine levied by Negro National League owners on Paige and three other players who had "jumped" their teams for Santo Domingo the previous spring, the lanky hurler quietly set sail for Argentina as the Eagles' spring training was starting in Jacksonville, Florida. New York Supreme Court justice Ferdinand Pecora belatedly issued a restraining order barring Paige from leaving the country. Greenlee, a Pittsburgh sheriff, and Abe teamed up to search for the wandering pitcher whom the sheriff wanted in connection with a suit filed earlier against him by Greenlee. The press loved the spectacle, calling for Scotland Yard and Sherlock Holmes to join in. Paige ended up in Mexico and Abe in Jacksonville, Florida, with a wallet lighter by $5,000.[18]

Chapter 6

Cuba and a Career Pause

Day chose the Cuban Baseball League for his 1937–38 winter exploits. He got off to a good start. Pitching for the Almendares, which represented the Almendares district on the outskirts of the old city of Havana, he tossed a shutout at the Santa Clara roster. The *New York Age* described the encounter "as a beautifully hurled game." A writer for the New *York Amsterdam News* credited Day in November with "hurling regular big league ball." More shutouts were to come. By late January 1938, the *New York Amsterdam News* trumpeted, "Leon Day ... continues to baffle the sluggers of the league with his blinding speed and is piling up a shutout list which is terrific."[1]

Even though doing well, he was pitching with a sore right arm sprained in a shower accident. "I'm in the shower," he told Rick Hines, "after a game and I slipped and caught myself with my right arm. I felt something pull right then." Even with a diminished wing, Leon posted a 7–4 record with the Almendares.[2]

He enjoyed his time in Cuba. Day reported, "My stay had been most pleasant and there were too many lovely Cuban lasses to look at." The soreness in his arm, however, was no secret. Effa got wind of it and ordered Day, described by the *Philadelphia Tribune* as "the master of the cannonball," back to Newark. Day disembarked by himself from the SS *Florida* in Miami, Florida, on January 14, 1938, and continued on to Newark. There, he submitted to a doctor's care and rested his arm, which appeared to be improving by late February.[3]

His enforced rest perhaps gave him time to think about his future. He joined Eagles third baseman Ray Dandridge, right fielder Ed Stone, and pitcher Bob Evans in holding out for more money, though Day reportedly did so reluctantly. Day's holdout was of particular concern to the Manleys given his stellar performance in 1937 and Abe's expectation that he would do even better this year. News of Day's holdout, according to Bill Mills, a writer for the *Crusader News Agency*, a national Black

Chapter 6. Cuba and a Career Pause

news service based in New York City from 1935 to 1940, was of particular interest to fans. An article in the *New Pittsburgh Courier*, while not downplaying the importance of the other three, stressed Leon's singular importance to the Eagles labeling him as "the formidable right hander" and underscoring his hitting prowess. Rated by both the daily and weekly press, the article continued, as "superior to the much publicized Satchel Paige," the loss of Day would substantially hamper the Eagles' pursuit of the Negro National League pennant. Unfazed by the controversy but less than pleased with four of his starters holding out, Abe was sure the finances would work out, which they did. However, Day wasn't himself in 1938 and couldn't repeat his 1937 performance.[4]

Sore Arm Holds Day Back

But things looked promising as the 1938 season started. Day opened the season in what appeared to be his usual spectacular form, shutting out the Pittsburgh Crawfords 1–0 in early May at Ruppert Stadium though he "pitched in agony after the 5th inning." Earlier in the month, the *Brooklyn Eagle* had reinforced the *Courier*'s assessment of Day, touting Leon as "Satchel Paige's nearest pitching rival." It was, nevertheless, downhill for Day after his opening day performance. Three weeks later Abe, retaking the team's managerial duties from Bell in 1937 in addition to his duties as chief scout, pulled Day before the first inning was over in a game against the Homestead Grays. Buck Leonard and Vic Harris had each tagged him for a four-bagger. His last outing in 1938 came in a ninth inning relief appearance against the Bushwicks. The first Bushwick batter tapped Day's easy throw back at him. Day threw the runner out and walked to the dugout. By mid–June, Day was reported "being out with a bad arm." By early July, noted sportswriter Wendell Smith of the *Pittsburgh Courier* informed his readers that "ace pitcher Leon Day has been laid up with a sore arm." His name was conspicuously absent from news accounts of games and box scores for the rest of the season. Injuries to fellow Eagles Willie Wells and Terris McDuffie didn't help the Eagles' cause. The team ended the first half tied with the Pittsburgh Crawfords for third place.[5]

With Day out for the rest of the 1938 season, the Eagles struggled, losing more games than they won and finishing in fifth place for the second half in what was now a six-team league. Only the New York Black Yankees had a worse record.[6] The Eagles' pitching staff was further diminished with the release of McDuffie in August. The press cited his "temperament" as the reason. Temperamental he was, but in fact, Abe had learned of a romantic relationship between McDuffie and Effa and instances of McDuffie mistreating her including an episode when he kicked her in Grand Central Station. On a bus ride from Newark to Pittsburgh, Abe was overheard saying, "When I get there I'm going to trade that son-of-a-bitch to Posey" (Cumberland Posey, owner of the Homestead Grays). Abe did get rid of McDuffie but not to the Grays. Abe traded the talented but mercurial hurler to the New York Black Yankees for rookie pitcher Jimmy "Slim" Johnson whose career lasted only five years[7] but had recently won two impressive games against the Grays. At the same time, Abe again relinquished his managerial duties, turning them over to Dick "King Richard" Lundy who had previously managed the Brooklyn Eagles for a short stint and was rated as an excellent shortstop in his playing days.[8]

By December both Abe and Gus Greenlee had given up on trying to sign Paige. Paige's status, Greenlee said, "is strictly up to the Eagles management." "There's no question that Paige would help our team materially," Abe, now thoroughly fed up with Paige's antics, told a reporter for the *Chicago Defender*. "We can't let even a twirler so good as Paige ruin our league."[9]

Day Back on Top

For the rest of the 1938 season and the off season, Day became his own physical therapist doing exercises to loosen and strengthen his arm. He held two flat irons in his right hand and waved them in a circular motion alongside his body. It worked. Come spring training in 1939 in Daytona Beach, Florida, he told Riley, "I tossed and never felt nothing and then I started to throw hard, really cutting loose, and I never had any more arm trouble until I got out of the army eight years later."[10] With his right arm feeling better by opening day, Leon gave it a game try. Leon had been working out, albeit cautiously, at Lundy's insistence. "Should he come around sufficiently," Lundy told the *Courier*, "he will be one of the most dangerous pitchers in the Negro National League."[11]

Chapter 6. Cuba and a Career Pause

Day's arm came around, enough so that Abe decided against sending Leon to Detroit for treatment. At first Lundy used the right-hander sparingly in early spring exhibition games. What he saw convinced him that Leon was once again one of the most feared pitchers in the game.[12] Leon gave his arm its first serious test on the Eagles' trek north in Macon, Georgia, against the Atlanta Black Crackers, defending champions of the Negro American League, composed of teams in the Midwest. Leon easily went the distance in the second game of a doubleheader subduing the Crackers 8–5 while striking out eight.[13]

Once the season started, Lundy's prediction proved true. In his first start, Day blanked the Stars 1–0 as part of a four-game Eagles win streak. Day helped his cause by singling in Fred Wilson, an outfielder who hit .327 in 1939 but made few friends by his frequent use of a switchblade knife to drive home his point. Leon shut out the Stars 4–0 in their next meeting. He struck out four and allowed only five hits. In early July, Day set down the Homestead Grays 6–2 in the first game of a doubleheader at Ruppert Stadium. He gave up only five hits but yielded eight walks which were tempered by his six strikeouts. The split enabled the Eagles to retain their first-place standing.[14]

In late July the Eagles split another doubleheader, this one against the Baltimore Elite Giants in Washington, D.C.'s Griffith Stadium. Day, in the words of a reporter for the *Afro-American*, "covered himself in glory" by leading the Newark nine to a 4–2 win in the opener. He went the distance, pitched scoreless ball for the first eight innings, slammed two triples, both deep into center field, scored a run by beating an outfielder's throw to the plate following a sacrifice fly ball by Willie Wells, and pinch ran for Biz Mackey, an eventual Hall of Fame catcher and later mentor to a 15-year-old rookie with the Baltimore Elite Giants, Roy Campanella. Day's performance won high praise from Abe. "Leon Day," the Eagles' owner told Art Carter, longtime sportswriter for the *Afro-American*, "is the greatest in the business. Day has speed, throws a deceptive curve, and uses his brains in the box. He can sock the apple and is perhaps the best fielding pitcher in the Negro National League." The *Afro-American* informed its readers that "Day had covered himself with glory."[15]

The Eagles' good fortune was not to last. August 1939 was unkind to both Day his team. Injuries, including Irvin with a bad hand and Fred Wilson suffering a spiked ankle, forced manager Dick Lundy, who had replaced Bell, to revise the lineup putting some players in unfamiliar positions. Mackey went from catcher to first base; Mule Suttles went from first base to right field; outfielder Ed Stone went to third. Day lost the first game of a doubleheader against the Stars, which put an end to his streak of seven consecutive wins. The Stars won the second game. Meanwhile, the Baltimore Elite Giants, with the help of an infusion of players from the Atlanta Black Crackers, landed in first place for the second half. The Eagles slipped to second place.[16]

This year, 1939, the moguls, for reasons undisclosed, instead of pairing the winners of the first and second halves for the Negro National League championship, as was the usual procedure, decided on two five-game series to determine which teams would contend for the league title. Perhaps the extra games with the lure of additional revenue influenced their decision. Based on total wins for the season, the first-place Homestead Grays were paired against the fourth-place Philadelphia Stars while the second-place Newark Eagles took on the third-place Elites.

Day started the first game of the 1939 Elite Giants–Eagles series. By the sixth inning the Giants had scored 9 of their eventual 11 runs. Day had walked five, struck out only one batter, and hit another. Bob Evans relieved him. Leon did not play in the series' remaining games.[17] The Grays and Elites each won their series, leaving the Eagles in their dust.[18] Even though the Eagles lost, Cum Posey held Day in high regard. As he had done since 1924, Cum Posey picked the eight best position players and the three best pitchers for his "dream team" for the season just finished. Posey named the diminutive right-hander, along with Hilton Smith of the Kansas City Monarchs and Roy Partlow to his January 1940 annual "dream team."

Of Day, Posey said, "Leon Day of Newark regained his arm in 1939 and was the mainstay of the Newark pitching staff." He is fast with a sharp curve, good control and plenty of nerve. Posey considered Smith 1939's best pitcher and Partlow as the most consistent hurler.[19]

Puerto Bound Once More

After the disappointing loss to the Giants, the hard-throwing 23-year-old again joined the migration of Negro Leaguers who, for the

Chapter 6. Cuba and a Career Pause

1939–40 season, answered the lures of higher pay and warmer climates offered in the Caribbean and Latin America. Day again signed with the Aguadilla Sharks of the Puerto Rican League.

In a game that started at 7:00 a.m. on a cold October morning, he shutout the Santurce Crabbers. The first three batters to face him struck out, putting Day on his way to a 6–0 victory. On January 7, 1940, he faced the same team, Santurce, and its hurler Bill Byrd of the Baltimore Elite Giants, a master of the spitball. The score was tied at one apiece in the fourth. For the next 14 innings neither team scored in a classic pitchers' duel. Umpires called the game due to darkness. When not pitching for the Sharks, Day, as he did in the States, played second base or center field posting a more than respectable .330 batting average.[20]

He enjoyed the 56-game season, telling Thomas E. Van Hyning, U.S. correspondent for the Puerto Rico Professional Baseball Hall of Fame, 1991–96, "Aguadilla paid me $20.00 a week.... It was a lot of fun living on the beach."[21]

His enjoyment was no secret to the people in Aguadilla, a poor community located in the northwest corner of Puerto Rico. As a youngster Victor M. Calderon, author of *The Wager Nobody Cared to Win*, an account of his struggle with attention-deficit hyperactivity disorder, described his fond memories of Leon. The town hired Leon and catcher Johnny Hayes, who had a 17-year career in the Negro Leagues, eight of them with the New York Black Yankees,[22] and filled out the 1939–40 team with local players. "The kids," Calderon said, "emulated all he did. We walked like him, copied his perpetual smile and his manner of throwing. We used his basket-style catch. He was a model citizen, didn't drink or smoke." Calderon and his father often shared meals with Day at Calderon's uncle's restaurant, the Garden Paradise.[23]

During that winter season, Day recalled, "there were good rivalries—Satchel Paige and I had a few duels." Day recalled one in particular that stuck in his craw. Paige was on the best team on the island, the Guayamas. The Sharks were among the worst. In one game between the two teams, with Day and Paige on their respective mounds, the Sharks led by one run and were one out away from beating the Guayamas. The Sharks' first baseman, a native Puerto Rican who Leon said was called Suscio, misplayed a ground ball hit his way, allowing two Guayamans to score and win the game by one run. "And I had him *beat*," Day lamented to Riley in an interview many years later.[24]

The first page of Leon Day's first contract with the Aguadilla Sharks, which paid him $25 a week for the 1939–40 winter season. That's $5 more than he remembered in his conversation with James Riley (courtesy Robert Edward Auction House).

Chapter 6. Cuba and a Career Pause

After it became clear the Sharks had no chance at the pennant, he jumped Aguadilla to join Eagle teammate Ray Dandridge in Venezuela. "We broke up the league down there," he told Riley. "I had won 12 and lost one. Our team, Vargas, was running away with the league."[25]

A new crop of rookies and returning veterans, including Day and Dandridge, who were expected back from Venezuela in time for spring training, held this year in Savannah, Georgia. Ray Dandridge, who had jumped the Eagles in 1939 to play in South America, appeared in Newark in April 1940. The *Pittsburgh Courier* noted that "hopes are that he will remain." He didn't. He took Day with him to Mexico.[26]

Chapter 7

Mexico Beckons

DAY AND DANDRIDGE did return to the States, but neither donned an Eagle uniform that year. The Mexican League had offered each man $350 a month, twice what the Manleys paid them. Long gone were the days of youthful exuberance when Leon jumped at his first chance at pro ball saying he'd play for nothing. Both men caught a plane to Mexico, joined the Veracruz team, and with the help of fellow "jumpers" Willie Wells and Josh Gibson, took the 1940 pennant by 15 games.[1]

Day had a good season. On the mound he went 6–0, four of them complete games, and struck out 29 batters in 67 innings. At the plate he hit a respectable .298.[2] Only after the 1940 summer Mexican season was over and Day played in the 1940–41 winter season in Puerto Rico, again for the Aguadilla Sharks, did he return to the States with the intention of staying.

Mexico was attractive to many players either for an entire summer season or just the winter season. In 1940, 63 Negro Leaguers, representing about 20 percent of all players in the Negro National League and the Negro American League combined, played winter ball in Mexico. Many were the best players including Josh Gibson, Cool Papa Bell, Willie Wells, and Hilton Smith in addition to Day and Dandridge. Money was a major motivator. In an interview with the *Baltimore Sun*, Day told reporter Roch Eric Kubatko, "You couldn't make enough money during the summer. If you didn't go away in the winter, you had to get a job."[3]

Dandridge, the Eagles' third baseman, and Day were making $150 a month in 1940 with the Manleys, who had said no to a request for a $25-a-month raise. Dandridge tried again, showing Effa $350 in cash and telling her, "Well, Mrs. Manley, this is the money they've given me to come play with them. If you can give me the same amount, I won't go."[4] Effa demurred. She knew she couldn't win a bidding war with the Mexican League president Jorge Pasquel who'd offered both players $350 a month plus expenses for themselves and their family.[5]

Chapter 7. Mexico Beckons

Other players fared as well or better in Latin America. Josh Gibson, for instance, earned $800 a month plus expenses for three and a half months in Venezuela playing only on weekends.[6]

Jorge Pasquel

The driving force in Mexican baseball was Jorge Pasquel. As one of Mexico's wealthiest and most influential people in the 1930s and '40s, Jorge presided over the family business, Pasquel Hermanos, Mexico's leading brokerage house as well as a holding company for investments and real estate. He was also the country's leading importer of liquor. A handsome, physically fit, and intelligent businessman who provided financial backing to Mexico's president Miguel Alemán Valdés, he was out to prove that a Mexican league was as good as the National and American Leagues and, by extension, that Mexico and the United States were on equal footing. To that end, he created a six-team summer league and in 1940 started stocking it with Negro Leaguers to whom he paid handsome salaries. National and American League players would follow in a few seasons.

Pasquel offered players more than money. He invited them to dinners he sponsored, encouraged them to bring their families at his expense, provided them with a housing allowance or spacious apartments in prime locations with maid service such as a six-room apartment overlooking Mexico City's Chapultepec Park, the equivalent of New York's Central Park, clothing, and cars. At times he resorted to illegal means by, for instance, stuffing Black players into car trunks to get them across the Texas-Mexico border clandestinely. Paperwork and work permits could be attended to later.

Jorge spared no effort to get his way. A salary dispute between Dandridge and Pasquel sent Dandridge on his way back to the States. As the train Dandridge had boarded in Mexico City neared Monterrey, the surprised third baseman saw a contingent of the Mexican army stop the train. The soldiers asked him to step off. Pasquel had decided to meet Dandridge's salary demands after all. The two developed a close relationship thereafter. So close, in fact, that when Bill Veeck, president of the Cleveland Indians, initiated several meetings with Dandridge in 1947 to discuss a possible contract with the Cleveland Indians,

Dandridge declined to consider the idea. He committed to continue playing for Pasquel in the summer Mexican League. Dandridge soon had a new house in Newark compliments of his Mexican employer.[7]

Jumping: An Established Practice

"Jumpers" such as Dandridge had long incensed team owners. The players knew it but realized they held the upper hand. In an early effort to stop jumpers, the moguls branded them "outlaws." After several contentious discussions during an early January 1941 meeting, they adopted a rule allowing the "outlaws" who wished to return to the Negro National League to sign a contract by May 1, 1941, committing them to stay with the league throughout their career and pay a $100 fine. Those who didn't sign would face a three-year suspension. A five-year suspension awaited any player who jumped after May 1. The pronouncements proved to be empty threats. Players continued to jump. Owners feared significant loss of paying spectators if they kept star players out of action for three to five years. They realized frustration had gotten the best of them and leveled only minor sanctions on returning "outlaws." In 1941, Day was the first to sign and pay the fine before May 1. His signing was considered by the *New York Age* to be "the big news of the week." He rejoined the Eagles for spring training in Daytona Beach, Florida. Two other Eagles, Monte Irvin, the Eagles' center fielder, and "Bus" Clarkson, a hard-hitting shortstop, soon followed suit.[8]

Some players enjoyed the extra money south of the border but missed the States. Art Carter, a sportswriter for the *Afro-American*, opined in January 1941 that many "jumpers" realized they had made a mistake leaving friends in the country and didn't particularly like the food or living conditions in Latin America.[9] Lennie Pearson, an Eagles first baseman and outfielder, cited loneliness as the reason players returned home. "Players like it down here," he said, "but they're eager to get home.... It is so lonely. The people are very nice, but we can't speak their language. The food is very good.... I imagine if I could speak Spanish, I wouldn't be so lonely."[10]

Monte Irvin and Willie Wells were two not quite so eager to return. Irvin found Mexicans to be more accepting of Blacks than Americans and, in one instance, more accepting than Puerto Ricans. Day, Irvin,

Chapter 7. Mexico Beckons

and several other players lived on the second floor of the Hotel Bonair in San Juan, Puerto Rico. Momma Seta ran a brothel on the first floor but wouldn't let the players avail themselves of her offerings. "Momma Seta, why can't we go downstairs?" Irvin asked her one evening. With a smile and rubbing his hand, she replied, "Wrong color."

"In Mexico," Irvin said during the 1941–42 winter season, "they had wonderful night clubs. You could dance all night; proposition a woman, and there's no problem; first time I really felt free. It took two or three weeks to get used to the regime back in the States." Irvin returned to Mexico for the entire 1942 season. He enjoyed the extra money, $500 a month salary and $200 a month for expenses, as well as the acceptance. He said he "had a great year in Mexico. I was having fun. It was really terrific down there. I could have run for mayor."

Wells gave *Pittsburgh Courier* journalist Wendell Smith, who had gone to Veracruz, Mexico, to interview him, his assessment of the role of race in encouraging players to disregard the pleadings of their owners and play in Latin America. "I was branded a Negro in the States," he told Smith while getting a haircut. "Well, in Mexico I am a man. I will encounter no restrictions of any kind because of my race. Not only do I get more money here, but I live like a king."[11]

CHAPTER 8

Strides Toward Integration

WHILE DAY, WELLS, and other players were plying their trade in Latin America, Jim Crow was alive and well both in Newark and the U.S. military. The Manleys encountered him head on upon their arrival in Newark. Blacks, as we have seen, were largely confined to the Third Ward. Many women found jobs in the garment industry. Men looked to meat packing, leather tanning, and tool and die-making trades for jobs. Some Black entrepreneurs owned beauty parlors, candy stores, and small grocery stores. Few made substantial incomes. Many said they relied on "mother wit"—inborn instincts to survive.[1]

In one instance in 1940, Jim Crow took the personage of a ticket clerk at Newark City's Pennsylvania Station. Mrs. Letteria May Dalton—a nationally known educator; longtime teacher of handicapped pupils of both races in Lima, Ohio; wife of physician Dr. A.A. Dalton; and a graduate of Columbia University—asked a clerk for a ticket to Lima. The clerk called the station's reservation service to ask about a ticket for "a colored lady." Mrs. Dalton took exception to the term. The clerk said, "We have a special coach for your people." She lodged a complaint with C.H. Mathews, Jr., the line's passenger traffic manager. Mathews apologized in a letter to her, stating, "It is my intention to have this matter thoroughly investigated with the employees at Newark station to determine the name of the ticket seller involved and you may be assured that corrective action will be taken." He further stated, "The railroad maintains a non-discrimination policy." No evidence of corrective action could be found.[2]

Jim Crow also struck an ugly, race-based blow in 1941 in Cranbury, New Jersey, forty-three miles south of Newark. Ten white men dragged nine Black potato pickers from their shacks at midnight, forcing them to strip naked, lie on the ground with their hands taped behind them, and submit to beatings with rubber hoses. Amid the pickers' cries the men threatened to rape the lone woman in the group. Then they covered the pickers with white paint, kept their clothes, and forced them to walk three miles back to their shacks in the field from which they had been driven. A local hospital refused to treat their injuries. An all-white district court jury of nine men and three women quickly took a more sympathetic view. They deliberated nine minutes on May 10, 1940, before awarding $9,000 in damages to the pickers. Nine of the ten men assailants, who ranged in ages from 18 to 24, threw themselves on the mercy of the court. They walked away with suspended sentences of two to three years. The tenth member of the mob, a minor, escaped prosecution altogether.[3]

The Ballpark: A Haven

One place where Jim Crow was banished was the Negro Leagues ballparks. Stanley Glenn, a catcher for the Philadelphia Stars from 1944 to 1950, said, "Negro Leagues baseball was a great happening. The ballpark was one place you could vent. There were so few places to go. Only black-owned restaurants could you go to. Philadelphia, Newark, Baltimore, it was all the same. It was the number one place to go after church. And we had open seating. At least 20 percent of the fans were white. They sat anywhere. We never had that crap. Ladies came dressed in their Sunday best; high-heeled shoes, silk stockings, long-sleeved gloves, and hats on their heads. They'd sit there in the 90-degree heat. Men came in their Sunday suits complete with tie, hat, and shined shoes."[4]

Effa Manley echoed a similar sentiment in 1946. The war had created many jobs for Blacks, which allowed more to buy tickets to her games, but "the important thing," she wrote to a friend, "is large crowds of Negroes have somewhere to go for healthy entertainment. Up to the baseball start, you must admit there was not a lot of entertainment for the average working man."[5]

The push for full equality of Blacks in the army and the burgeoning defense industries gained momentum in Newark. Despite the defense of a segregated army by its highest-ranking officers, calls for an end to discrimination in the army came from many voices as the war continued. One of the loudest was that of prominent Black jurist William H. Hastie, dean of Howard University's Law School in 1939, who would go on to become the first Black governor of the Virgin Islands and be appointed by President Harry S. Truman in 1949 as a judge to the United States Circuit of Appeals for the Third District, the highest legal position held by a Black man at that time.

During the early years of the war, Hastie served as an aide to Secretary of War Henry L. Stimson. He resigned the post in 1943 in protest "of the reactionary policies and discriminatory practices of the Army Air Force." "The simple fact is," he said after two segregated training facilities were completed over his objections, "the air command does not want Negro pilots ... mingling with other personnel which as a service pilot is a must in carrying out his various missions."[6]

Hastie's responsibilities also included investigating complaints of segregation in defense industries. One such complaint brought him to Newark in December 1942 to investigate the U.S. Office of Dependency Benefits which employed 3,000 "colored" and 10,000 whites. Hastie toured the agency, housed in Newark's ten-story Prudential Life Building. He found no evidence of segregation and said so in his final report. He'd been duped. The agency went to great lengths to hide their segregated practices. Just hours before his arrival, supervisors were ordered to assign some "colored" workers to all-white units and some whites to menial jobs usually performed by Blacks while Hastie was in the building. A request by a "colored" employee to meet with Hastie to explain the duplicity was denied.[7] Employees, especially the "colored," were not duped by Hastie's report. "Bill Hastie can say anything he wants," said one, "but we know for a positive fact that these crackers are doing everything they can to get us out and into some sort of Jim Crow setup." Hastie was not pleased. The situation no doubt hastened his resignation.[8]

Another voice for integration in Newark was that of the sixth annual convention of New Jersey's Congress of Industrial Organizations (CIO) in 1943. The convention, to no avail, asked President Roosevelt to end the army's Jim Crow policies.[9]

Some progress, however, could be seen. A rare step forward in an effort to banish discrimination occurred when the Fair Employment Practice Committee (FEPC) was established on June 25, 1941, by President Roosevelt's Executive Order 8802. The order banned discrimination in defense industries that received government contracts.

FDR issued the order reluctantly. Faced with the distinct and embarrassing possibility of 100,000 people marching down Pennsyl-

Chapter 8. Strides Toward Integration

vania Avenue in the nation's capital to demand equality in the workplace under the leadership of civil rights and trade union leader A. Philip Randolph, Roosevelt agreed to issue the order if the march was called off. Randolph agreed to the deal. Some supporters of the march had not gotten the word that it had been called off. A few days after FDR issued his executive order, an editorial appeared in the *Chicago Defender* declaring, "If the 'March on Washington' does nothing else, it will convince white America that the American black man had decided henceforth and forever to abandon the timid role of Uncle-Tomism in the struggle for social justice."[10]

The FEPC was responsible for some changes in New York and New Jersey. Under its auspices representatives from 12 industrial plants in the New York and New Jersey area were called on to answer charges of discrimination against Blacks and Jews. Newark's Tite Flex Metal Hose Company was among them. The committee found 8 of the 12 companies, including Tite Flex Metal Company, guilty and ordered the eight "to cease and desist."[11]

Newark's public school system, while not segregated, employed few Black teachers—eight to be exact. Mayor Vincent J. Murphy appointed William R. Jackson, a Black YMCA executive, to the school board on July 4, 1942, the body's first Black member. Jackson's first move was to hire more Black teachers.[12]

Toward the end of World War II, six U.S. representatives from both parties signed a statement in July 1945 written by the National Negro Congress calling for full military equality. "At the same time, in an interview with the *Chicago Defender*, Captain Hugh N. Mulzac, a navy officer aboard the carrier U.S.S. Booker T. Washington, wondered if the army could win the confidence of the Chinese and the Indians and others when it practices discrimination against dark-skinned people in its own ranks."[13]

A. Philip Randolph forcibly brought the concern to the attention of a Senate Armed Forces Committee hearing in April 1948. He said, "If we are to continue to have a Jim Crow army, I will advise Negroes not to fight." Senator Wayne Morse (D–OR) interrupted the applause from the mixed audience to suggest such an act "could be treason." "Not treason," Randolph replied. "Civil disobedience."[14]

The issue had caught the attention of President Truman who, on July 26, 1948, signed Executive Order 9981, creating the President's

53

Committee on Equality of Treatment and Opportunity in the Armed Services. The order mandated the desegregation of the U.S. military.[15]

Segregation had the effect of putting most Black soldiers in support roles during World War II. Toward the end of the war, however, several all-Black units assumed combat duties. They performed with honor and distinction. Examples include the famed "Red Tails" who learned their craft at the segregated Tuskegee Army Airfield, near Alabama's Tuskegee Institute founded by Booker T. Washington in 1881 to train teachers, hence the name Tuskegee Airmen. These aviators flew over 15,000 sorties while earning more than 850 medals. The 761st Tank Battalion, better known as the Black Panthers, was another example. Their commanding officer, General George S. Patton, told them, "I don't care what color you are as long as you're here to kill Germans." That they were. They fought for 183 continuous days including the Battle of the Bulge and the Battle of the Rhine while earning 11 Silver Stars, 69 Bronze Stars, 300 Purple Hearts, and 1 Medal of Honor to Sgt. Warren G.H. Crecy.

Integration on the field of battle took another step forward near the end of the war. Some Black infantrymen volunteered to leave their units to fight with white soldiers. Most whites were initially "apprehensive, reluctant, and disliked" the idea, but those attitudes turned positive once they fought alongside the "tan Yanks." Lt. Millard G. Durham, commander of A Company of the 310th Regiment, said of them in May 1945, "The colored troops, in all engagements, proved to be as courageous and aggressive as the veterans of any other company." The results of 250 interviews with white soldiers in integrated units conducted in June 1945 yielded similar changes in attitudes, but the report to Stimson, in his second term as secretary of war, summarizing the interviews, was suppressed for six months. It would take until November 1954 for the army to report it was fully integrated.[16]

More Progress in New Jersey

A constitutional convention, held at Rutgers University in New Brunswick, from June 12 to September 10, 1947, updated the state's 103-year-old constitution.[17] A Bill of Rights amendment, the first to be enacted by any state and sponsored by the convention's only "colored"

Chapter 8. Strides Toward Integration

member, Oliver Randolph, outlawed segregation in the public schools and the state militia. The amendment read, "No person shall be denied the enjoyment of any civil or military rights, nor be segregated in the militia or in the public schools, because of religious principles, race, color, ancestry, or national origin." "Colored" voters, both Republican and Democratic, contributed substantially, the *Afro-American* reported, to passage by "a thumping majority of more than 472,000 votes."[18]

Implementation, however, was slow. A report by the New Jersey Division Against Discrimination submitted to John L. Bustard, state commissioner of education, in June 1948 declared that none of New Jersey's 52 school districts had taken any action. Thirty-seven were making plans. The remaining districts had no plans underway.[19] The issue was still alive and well in March 1962, eight years after the landmark *Brown v. Board of Education* unanimous U.S. Supreme Court decision which overturned the 1898 Supreme Court's *Plessy v. Ferguson* decision mandating a "separate but equal" doctrine. In another move, Newark's board of education, in a 5–1 vote, dropped the long-standing requirement that students attend high schools in their residential area. Many lived in predominately Black areas resulting in de facto segregation. In return, attorneys representing students agreed to drop a federal court suit against the board charging de facto segregation. Similar suits led by National Association for the Advancement of Colored People (NAACP) attorneys were underway in Trenton, Jersey City, and Montclair.[20]

A Jim Crow preference for segregation by some in Jersey's hospitality industry was expressed by a motel owner. In a survey conducted on 185 motels in 1955 by the State Department of Education Division Against Discrimination, the owner said, "We don't rent to Negroes. We don't allow them in town. The only ones who come to town are those brought in by summer visitors. One Negro bought a place here 40 years ago. He didn't get to live in it. It burned down before he moved in." The town was Somers Point, 100 miles south of Newark.[21]

Chapter 9

Day Vacates the Mound

DAY'S ARMY SERVICE, in a segregated unit, wouldn't begin until the fall of 1943. Until then, he would remain stateside. In early spring 1941, Day joined the Eagles in Daytona Beach, Florida, for spring training. The Eagles welcomed him back with open arms. The *Chicago Defender*, as we have seen, hailed his return as "the big news of the week."[1]

His versatility, still intact, served him well as he struggled on the mound. "Biz" Mackey, in his fourth year as player-manager for the Eagles, gave Day the ball on opening day. Unfortunately, as a writer for the *Afro-American* put it, "he did not fare especially well." Staked to a 4–0 lead over the Cuban Stars in the first inning, Day had to be relieved by Manning in the sixth after giving up four runs. The Cubans won the game 10–7. Outfielder Russell Awkard was inducted into the army the next day, leaving a hole in the "outer pastures." After failing to finish a game a few days later, Day left the pitching rotation to replace Awkard in the outfield and filled in at second and third base when needed.[2]

Abe had put together a moderately good pitching staff to make up for Day's absence from the mound. Max Manning in his fourth year with the Eagles could keep his fastball and curveball low but struggled with power hitters. Florida native Jimmy Hill had won eight and lost two in 1940. Haywood "Big Train" Cozart had hurled two workman-like but nondescript seasons for the Manleys. Len Hooker, a right-hander, had mastered the knuckleball. James Brown, whom Eagles former manager Dick Lundy called "one of the best pitchers I've ever seen," showed a great deal of promise but kept deserting the Eagles to see his new wife in Sharpsburg, North Carolina.[3]

Although no longer pitching, Leon's contributions continued at a high level. Ten days into his center field position, Day led the Eagles into first place by pacing the team's doubleheader win over the Philadelphia Stars 5–2 and 5–4 in Newark's Ruppert Stadium in late May. Day drove in three of the runs with a triple in the first game, and another

Chapter 9. Day Vacates the Mound

three-base knock in the second brought in one. The *New York Amsterdam Star-News* credited Day with "doing particularly well."[4] During an early June game, Day manned second base in an exhibition game against the Bushwicks. A writer for the *Afro-American* noted that Jimmy Hill was now the team's "ace" albeit "a left-hander." Day continued playing every day as either an infielder or outfielder while pitching but occasionally. In a mid–June game against the New York Cubans, Day split his time between the mound and center field. While on the mound, he struck out ten. His triple and two singles contributed to the Eagles' 24–7 walloping administered to the island boys on Island Park in Harrisburg, Pennsylvania.[5] By this time his batting average had reached .377, good for sixth place among Negro National League hitters. The end of July found the former mound ace at second base for both games of a Saturday doubleheader against the Baltimore Elite Giants. His triple in the first game brought home one run, but it was not enough to avoid a loss to the Giants, 7–5. He fattened his batting average and bolstered the Eagles' win with two doubles in the second game won by the Eagles 4–1.[6]

Both teams met again for a Sunday doubleheader, this time in Baltimore's Oriole Park. Day was still at second and continuing to swing a fearsome bat. In game one, he accounted for seven Newark runs by banging out three doubles, a four-bagger, and crossing the plate twice as the Eagles trounced the Giants 17–8.[7] In early August, Manley's nine tightened their tenuous grip on first place. They squeaked by the St. Louis Stars of the Negro American League in the first game of a Sunday doubleheader at Ruppert Stadium 4–3. The Eagles ran circles around the Stars in the second, 11–0. Second baseman Day scored five runs and hammered out five hits to keep his batting average at an enviable .361. The *Afro-American* cited the Eagles as "the hottest club in the Negro National League." Day's feats in the field and at the plate now classified him as a position player and a "slugger" for a *New York Age* reporter. The scribe credited Eagles manager "Biz" Mackey with "putting together a great team of young players with trio of sluggers in Monte Irvin, shortstop, Leon Day, second baseman, and Len Pierson [*sic*], left fielder."[8]

As the season wore on, Day and teammates, notably Monte Irvin, Lennie Pearson, Jimmy Hill, and Max Manning, had earned the affection of their fans. As many as 14,000 now filled the seats in Ruppert Stadium.[9] As beloved a team as they were, they finished in third place behind the league-leading Homestead Grays and the Baltimore Elite Giants much to Abe's frustration and disappointment.[10]

On the last day of this disappointing season, August 31, 1941, Effa, in a successful attempt to boost attendance, sponsored a program of three competitive events for the Eagles' players and their opponents, the Baltimore Elite Giants, at Ruppert Field. She called it Borican Day in honor of John Borican, Black, born in Bridgeton, New Jersey, and an athlete of national renown. In 1941 he was the first athlete to be crowned national champion in both the decathlon and pentathlon. The 28-year-old also held the American record in the 660, 880, 800, and 1,000 meter races. In November *Life* magazine tagged him as the greatest athlete since Jim Thorpe. In addition to being an athlete of exceptional ability, Borican was the answer to *New York Amsterdam Star-News* sportswriter Dan Burley's search "for guys who could win yet give the sportswriters something to write about outside of cold figures with a few adjectives thrown in." "He's chesty," Burley wrote, "carefree, and doesn't hide his attraction to the fairer sex."[11] The sprinter died a little more than a year later on January 4, 1943, of a mysterious form of pernicious anemia at the age of 29.[12]

Eagle players took all three events. While Borican looked on from the stands, Day, in full uniform, won the 100 yard dash in 11.1 seconds. Monte Irvin took the honors in the throwing contest. Catcher Charlie Parks made the most accurate throw to second base. Once play got underway the Eagles as a team fared less well, losing to the Giants 7–2.[13]

Back Again to Puerto Rico

Once the season ended Day quickly joined teammates Willie Wells, Ray Dandridge, Monte Irvin, Lennie Pearson, and 19 other Negro National League players returning to the Puerto Rico Winter Baseball League for the 1941–42 winter season. By early February Raymond Brown of the Homestead Grays, who would later pitch a perfect game against the Chicago American Giants in 1945 and one of five players designated as surefire major leaguers by the *Pittsburgh Courier*; Bill Byrd of the Elite Giants; and Day, with a much-improved arm, ranked as the league's standout pitchers. Day posted a respectable 10–7 record from the mound and belted the ball for a .360 average, including two

Chapter 9. Day Vacates the Mound

homers. The season lasted 22 weeks with only two games played each week, giving players and their wives and families time to enjoy the island's amenities, including horse racing. To allow those spectators who wanted to both see a game and place bets at their favorite racetrack, Sunday games started at 10:00 a.m. Those who were not interested in the races could take in the 3:00 p.m. Sunday game.[14]

The 1941–42 season would be Day's last with the Sharks. In his most recent four seasons in Puerto Rico he compiled 503 strikeouts, 35 wins against 28 losses, and an earned run average of 2.63 over the course of 571 innings. The only pitcher to come close to Day's strikeout total was Terín Pizarro, a native of the island and the dominant pitcher in Puerto Rico between the late '50s and the early '60s. Day's salary had improved from $20 a week to $50 a week.

Day became an icon with Puerto Ricans both on and off the field. They called him "El Caballero del Box," gentleman of the box. Leon indulged in the native food including barbecued goat with rice and beans and chicken and rice. His only complaint was occasional seasickness experienced on the steamships that ferried him and other players between the States and San Juan. "I got seasick," he said, adding, "the food would fly from the tables. The ocean was rough."[15]

Not only did Day experience rough seas, but the dark clouds of war contributed to his unease. By January 1942, the United States was at war with Japan and the Axis powers. Some wondered if baseball should be halted. Major League Baseball commissioner Kenesaw Mountain Landis sent a letter to President Roosevelt asking his opinion. FDR responded with what has become known as "the green light letter," saying major league baseball, and by inference Negro Leagues baseball, would be good for the morale of workers and sanctioned its continuance. Congress agreed.[16]

Of immediate concern to Day and his Eagle teammates playing in Puerto Rico—Willie Wells, Ray Dandridge, Bus Clarkson, Ed Stone, and Monte Irvin—was getting safely back to the States after the 1941–42 winter season. The Japanese attack on Pearl Harbor found the players in Ponce, Puerto Rico. "I never will forget it," Day told James Riley. "I wanted to fly back but they wouldn't let us fly, and they [Germans] were sinking ships out there in the Atlantic." German submarines were patrolling the waters between the island and the United States. Flying was out of the question because tickets were not issued to civilians.

Leon Day

Liga Semi-Profesional de Base-Ball de Puerto Rico
(PUERTO RICO SEMI-PRO BASE-BALL LEAGUE)
Box 2467, S. J. - Tel. 3201,
San Juan, Puerto Rico

PLAYER'S CONTRACT

Parties: The _____ BASE-BALL CLUB, hereinafter called the Club, and _____ of _____ hereinafter called the Player.

Description: The Club is a member of the LIGA SEMI-PROFESIONAL DE BASE-BALL DE PUERTO RICO (Puerto Rico Semi-Pro Base-Ball League), and, as such, and together with the other members of the League, forms a part of the Constitution thereof. The purpose of these agreements and regulations is to offer to the public baseball in which order, efficiency and discipline shall be assured by means of a clear definition of the relations between the Club and the Player and between one club and another.

Agreement: In accordance with the facts above stated, the parties hereto execute the following agreement:

Employment: 1.—The Club contracts the services of the Player to play baseball during the 194_-194_ season, including pre-series and post-series games, if any are played, and the Player agrees to render his services efficiently and loyally.

Salary: 2.—For the above mentioned services, the Club will pay the Player the sum of _____ dollars per week ($ _____) which he shall begin to earn as soon as the Club starts training by playing pre-series games, and which he shall continue to earn until the Club has played all the games necessary to close the Regular Series, play-off games, if any are played, and the Final Series games, if the Club should enter the Finals.

Loyalty: 3.—The Player shall serve the Club, or any other Club to which he may be assigned, in accordance with the regulations of the League, with loyalty, and he binds himself to observe good moral conduct and to carry out his duties faithfully and in a sportsmanlike manner.

Bar: 4.—The Player agrees that he can not directly nor indirectly form a part of the Board of Directors of the League or of the Board of Directors of any Club affiliated to the League.

Services: 5.—The Player agrees that during the term of this contract he shall only play baseball with the Club, and that he can not, without the written consent of the Club, take part in any boxing matches or exhibitions, wrestling, pancratium, football, basketball, or any other sports.

Assignment: 6.—In case this contract is tranfered to another club, the Player, upon receiving notice from the assignee club, shall present himself at the place, day and hour mentioned in said notice, and, if he fails to do so, he shall have no right to receive compensation from the day that he was notified of his transfer.

Rescission: 7.—Upon ten days written notice to the Player, this contract may be rescinded at any time that the Club so decides.

Conditions: 8.—The Player accepts as a part of this contract, those reasonable conditions which the Club may require and which have the approval of the President of the League.

The first page of Day's 1941–42 winter season contract with the Aguadilla Sharks, which rewarded his play in previous winter seasons with a hefty raise from $25 a week for his first season with the team to $60 a week (courtesy Robert Edward Auction House).

Chapter 9. Day Vacates the Mound

Fortunately, all arrived safely to Richmond, Virginia, for spring training to prepare for what looked to be a promising 1942 season.[17]

Safely back home, Day was back on the mound. In an early and successful test of his arm, he threw for three innings against the Washington Hilldales, an independent Black team, in the Eagles' first contest of the year played in late April 1942 in Portsmouth, Virginia. He shut out the Hilldales 3–0 while fanning seven.[18]

Day would continue to pitch in 1942 while still playing other positions. In an exhibition doubleheader against the Homestead Grays in late April, for instance, the Eagles won both games in front of 6,000 spectators in D.C.'s Griffith Stadium. Day held down first base.[19] In May he alternated between center field and second base.[20]

Posing with a bat in the deck circle (circa 1941), Day reminds us he could hit with authority as well as strike batters out with a blazing fastball and hard-breaking curve (courtesy the National Baseball Hall of Fame and Museum, Cooperstown, New York).

A popular slate of games was Sunday afternoon doubleheaders featuring four teams in Yankee Stadium and the Polo Grounds where crowds of 10,000–20,000 were common. Day took the mound in the first game of such a doubleheader in early June 1942. As 17,000 spectators looked on, he went the distance, held the New York Cubans to six scattered hits, and smashed a double to deep left field as the Eagles won easily 8–3.[21] That performance convinced Willie Wells, who had replaced "Biz" Mackey as the team's player-manager, to put Day back in the pitching rotation and minimize his infield and outfield duties. Wells' decision sat well with the *Pittsburgh Courier* which anointed the right-hander as the "core of the club" and noted Day's return to the mound as the centerpiece of a strengthened Eagles team.[22]

The change seemed questionable at first as the Eagles promptly lost a doubleheader on their home field, Ruppert Stadium, to the New York Black Yankees. Day lost the opener. The Eagles overcame their double defeats and made a serious bid for the first-half pennant by whipping the perennial champs, the Homestead Grays, three games in a row. In Pittsburgh's Forbes Field on a Saturday doubleheader in late June, the Eagles prevailed 6–2 and 11–1. In game one the day before Day went the distance and neutralized the bats of Grays sluggers Josh Gibson, Buck Leonard, and Sam Bankhead by either fanning them or popping them up. Even though Wells saw Leon as primarily a pitcher, the right-hander's bat was still an asset. Day manned left field for the second game contributing two singles and scoring a run.

A week later in Washington's Griffith Stadium, the Eagles took the Grays' measure once again, 6–5, but it took 14 innings to do so. Day played the entire game in center field connecting with a single and a double in seven trips to the plate. In a mid–July doubleheader against the Philadelphia Stars, Leon pitched the Eagles to a 6–2 win in the first contest. "It was," the *Philadelphia Tribune* reported, "just too much Day for the boys from Quakertown."[23]

The second game, however, marked the beginning of the end of the Eagles' pennant hopes. Former Eagles pitcher Terris McDuffie and company "annihilated" the men from Newark 10–0. The Grays went on to sweep Wells' roster in four straight games. The first entertained 4,500 fans in Newport News' Builder's Stadium, a record for that park. Upward of 3,000 turned out for the last three games in Norfolk, Virginia. Later, the Eagles suffered an 8–4 loss to the Baltimore Elite Giants in Yankee Stadium before 12,000. Day made only a brief appearance. The Giants' win clinched the first-half pennant. Cum Posey, in his capacity as secretary of the Negro National League, announced that the owners had decided the season would not be played in halves but as a complete schedule, meaning there would be no champion until season's end.[24]

Newark's struggle through the second half was interspersed with moments of brilliance. The first was when Day, holding down left field, and Willie Wells combined for two doubles in the 14th inning as the

Chapter 9. Day Vacates the Mound

Eagles slipped past the Grays 6–5 in late June. Day's "masterful performance" in shutting out the Bushwicks and ending their nine-game winning streak came two weeks later in a mid–July game.[25] Day's brightest moment came in late July when the "mighty mite" threw a one-hitter at the Elite Giants. His heroics snapped the Giants' seven-game win streak 8–1. Only two Eagle errors stood in the way of a shutout. He struck out 18 batters. He was in full command of his curve and fastball.

Afro-American sportswriter Art Carter and Cum Posey both called the 18 whiffs a Negro National League record, which it was. The Negro Leagues record, however, was set by Alvin "Bubba" Gipson, Sr., on August 28, 1943. Under the lights against the Philadelphia Stars on their home field at 44th Street and Parkside Avenue, Gipson, a journeyman hurler of modest talent throwing for the Birmingham Black Barons in the Negro American League, had the game of his life. He set down 20 Stars on strikeouts. Fans poured out of the stands seeking autographs and patting him on the back.[26]

Three of the six Negro National League teams—Grays, Eagles, and Elites—battled each other down the stretch through August and early September. On the 1942 season's last weekend in early September, the Grays grabbed the flag by downing the Philadelphia Stars in three straight games. The Elites and the Stars finished in second and third place, respectively. Manley's Eagles landed in fourth place. The Grays would face the Negro American League's Kansas City Monarchs for a World Series playoff in September.[27]

Even though the Eagles failed in their quest for the flag, Day and Eagle teammates Ed Stone and Lennie Pearson, a hard-hitting first baseman who developed a close relationship with Effa Manley during his 12 years with the Eagles (1937–48), would have a hand in the series. The Philadelphia Stars' Bus Clarkson, a college graduate who began his career with Oscar Charleston and the Pittsburgh Crawfords before joining the Stars, joined them. Down three games to none to the Monarchs, Grays owner Cum Posey contacted the four players. With the blessing of Eagles owner Abe Manley and Stars owner Ed Bolden, a shy and modest man who preferred working in the background, they traveled by bus from Newark to Kansas City. When asked why he thought the Grays had selected him, Day, in a rare lack of modesty, said, "I guess they picked me to go against Satchel [Paige, who was scheduled to start the game for the Monarchs] because they thought I could beat him." They were right.

The Grays won 4–1 behind Day's 12 strikeouts while yielding only one walk and five hits. The Grays tagged Satchel Paige for nine hits, five of them by the "ringers."

After the game Monarchs secretary William "Dizzy" Dismukes, a pitcher of note before moving from the mound to the Monarchs' front office, promised a protest. The protest baffled Posey. Tom Baird, the Monarchs' general manager, Posey said, had told him just the week before that it would be OK for the Grays to use the four players to compensate for the loss of four Grays. Two players, second baseman Matt Carlisle and right fielder David Whatley, had been drafted. Pitcher Roy Partlow was sidelined with boils under his pitching arm. Shortstop Sammy Bankhead had suffered a broken arm two weeks earlier. The protest was made, and the game disallowed. "I beat Satchel out there in Kansas," Day later proudly told Riley. Monarch's first baseman Buck O'Neil remembered the game and Day's performance well. "Leon," O'Neil told Riley, "struck the bat out of our hands. We didn't do nothing on him, really. He threw the ball right by us." A disappointed Leon Day later told Riley, "After I beat him [Paige] they had an argument about it. We were supposed to go to Philadelphia to play the next game, but they weren't going to let me play with them anymore." The Monarchs wrapped up the series the next day in Philadelphia, while the four "ringers" took the train back to Newark with tickets paid for by the Monarchs. A month later Day learned Posey had named Paige and himself to Posey's 1942 "dream team." "We think Leon Day was the best pitcher in Negro baseball," Posey explained and continued, "He was a great pitcher throughout the year despite being used as a pitcher, outfielder, and infielder."[28]

Chapter 10

Pathways to the National and American Leagues

WHILE DAY WAS having a memorable 1942 season keeping the Eagles in contention, white baseball flirted, somewhat seriously, with the prospect of admitting "colored" players to its ranks. The issue flared into public view when Leo "The Lip" Durocher, a Hall of Fame shortstop with a mercurial temper and, at the time, player-manager for the Brooklyn Dodgers, told a reporter in July 1942 that Kenesaw Mountain Landis, commissioner of the National and American Leagues from 1920 to 1945 and generally considered the man who kept Blacks out of the National and American Leagues, was responsible for the banning of Blacks in the National and American Leagues. Landis countered with a statement denying Durocher's claim. Landis famously added, "There is and has been no rule in baseball barring Negro players from the big show."[1]

Landis' pronouncement sparked a firestorm. Larry S. MacPhail, Brooklyn Dodger president, who had an up-and-down relationship with Durocher, exploded in an interview over lunch at Toots Shor's Restaurant on Broadway in New York City. "There is," MacPhail asserted, "an unwritten law against colored players in the National and American League. And any statement that there is no agreement, formal or informal, barring colored men from playing organized baseball is 100% hypocrisy."[2] Sadly, MacPhail had it right.

Queries to white owners by the *Cleveland Call and Post* on the matter yielded only four responses. Clark Griffith, owner of the Washington Senators, said in part, "It is my belief we should have white baseball leagues and colored baseball leagues." Alva Bradley of the Cleveland Indians said he "stood with Landis, and that the Indians would consider players of the Negro race." William Benswanger of the Pittsburgh Pirates said, "In our opinion there is no bar against Negroes in baseball."

Powel Crosley, Jr., owner of the Cincinnati Reds, said, "As far as I know Judge Landis is entirely correct." The *Call and Post* concluded, "There is not much hope."[3]

But perhaps there was a glimmer. William E. Benswanger, president of the Pittsburgh Pirates since 1932, an accomplished pianist and a director of the Pittsburgh Symphony, authorized the *Pittsburgh Courier* to identify four "colored" players of National and American League caliber. They, Benswanger promised, would be given a tryout with the Bucs. After surveying leading sportswriters of Black papers, ballplayers, managers, and owners for suggestions, Wendell Smith, *Courier* sportswriter and energetic advocate for integrating the National and American Leagues, chose four. His picks, in addition to Day, were Josh Gibson, legendary home run hitter and catcher for the Homestead Grays; Willie Wells, Newark Eagles shortstop; and Sam Bankhead, infielder for the Homestead Grays.

Smith lauded Benswanger for "risking the wrath of his associates for an ideal which has been contrary to the general pattern of the exclusive sport in which he operates." Bob Rice, head of the Pirates' farm system and baseball schools, Benswanger said, would personally conduct the tryouts. Alva Bradley, a wealthy Cleveland businessman and owner of the Cleveland Indians, made a similar pledge to give three members of the Cleveland Buckeyes a tryout with the Indians: player (infielder)–manager Parnell Woods, center fielder Samuel Jethroe, and pitcher Eugene Bremer. Bradley would later sell the club to Bill Veeck in 1946 who integrated the American League when he signed Larry Doby in 1947.[4]

Philadelphia Phillies manager Hans Lobert invited Baltimore Elite Giants catcher Roy Campanella, last year's Most Valuable Player in the Negro National League, to Shibe Park, the Phillies' home field in Campanella's home city. Campanella wowed Lobert with his drives into the faraway bleacher seats. "You're okeh, Son," Lobert told the slugger. "Sit tight and you'll hear from me soon."[5]

American and National League scouts were in the stands for some Negro Leagues games. A doubleheader between the Eagles and Stars in Buffalo on July 18, 1942, attracted scouts from six major league teams—the Reds, Tigers, Red Sox, Braves, Athletics, and Phillies. They were in the stands checking out five players, including Eagles shortstop Willie Wells. The Stars manhandled the Eagles in game one of a doubleheader,

Chapter 10. Pathways to the National and American Leagues

20–5. In the midst of the debacle, Wells displayed his usual talents at short, connected for a homer, but did not receive an offer then or later.[6]

Nothing came of any of the promises. Smith need not have praised Benswanger so effusively. His bold offer went unfulfilled. Campanella never heard back from the Phillies. After seeing the three Buckeyes in action during just one game, Alva announced, "Frankly, they are not big league material. Why? Not one of them got a hit, and the pitcher, Bremer, was knocked out of the box. They just don't stack up."[7] Sports editor Lem Graves, Jr., of the *New Journal and Guide*, a Black weekly in Norfolk, Virginia, was disappointed but not surprised. Following Landis' comments and the promises of tryouts, Graves spoke with several Homestead Grays players. All favored integration of the National and American Leagues, "but," he continued, "they're not doing any handstands. They've been given the run-around too long."[8] American and National League integration would have to await Jackie Robinson's and Larry Doby's appearances in a Brooklyn Dodger and Cleveland Indian uniform, respectively, in 1947. As *Afro-American* sports columnist Sam Lacy, a perpetual and powerful advocate for Blacks in the National and American Leagues and one of the first African American members of the Baseball Writers' Association of America, pointed out in his April 25, 1959, column in the *Afro-American*, "Sam Lacy's from A to Z," the Red Sox had not even invited a player of color to spring training before inviting Green in 1959.

Sportswriters Weigh In

The exclusion of Blacks from the National and American Leagues had infuriated Black sportswriters for years. *New Journal and Guide* reporter Edgar T. Rouzeau in 1939 proposed an "annual all-star interracial baseball series between picked stars from the colored leagues and luminaries from the major leagues." Such a series, Rouzeau thought, would reduce whites' opposition to Blacks in the National and American Leagues. Day was among those Negro Leaguers Rouzeau nominated to play for the colored team.[9] The series never took place. Jay Don Davis, a sportswriter for the same paper, suggested in 1942 that Landis could be baseball's Abraham Lincoln if "he removed the evil racial barrier." Davis went on to say, "Bronze chronicles have waged a relentless fight against it for a quarter of a century."[10] Wendell Smith, first Black reporter to work for a daily paper, said a week before the Negro Leagues' 1942 all-star game, "If the National and American League are looking for sepia material they'll find it at the East-West Game." "The majority of the stars," he continued, "in the battle are big leaguers. Only color has kept them out." Smith named 11 players in particular "plus a few others" worthy of the National and American Leagues. Smith's nominations included the four he recommended to Benswanger. Others were Satchel Paige and fellow pitcher on the Monarchs Hilton Smith, infielder Pat Patterson, pitcher Eugene Smith, infielder Ted Strong, pitcher Verdel Matthis, and outfielder Willard Brown. "These men," Smith said, "play big-league ball."[11]

Another plea for integrating the game came from Herb March, a representative of the CIO's Steel Workers Organizing Committee. March wanted to deliver his comments to a joint meeting of American and National League owners in December. Landis turned him down because March had not given 30 days' notice. March's point, had he been allowed to voice it, was that "Negroes fighting shoulder to shoulder with white troops and working with white men in the war plants should be given a chance to play ball with them."[12] A year later in December 1943, Wendell Smith, joined by publishers of major Black newspapers—John Sengstacke of the *Chicago Defender*, Ira Lewis of the *Pittsburgh Courier*, and Howard Murphy of the *Afro-American*—along with Paul Robeson, celebrated actor, singer, football player, and activist, addressed the same gathering. They left after their remarks were over.

Their remarks for including Blacks in the National and American Leagues, received high marks from the assembled moguls. When asked after the meeting if any actions were taken, Landis replied, "It was taken under consideration."[13]

"Consideration" was all advocates for Blacks in the National and American Leagues would get from Landis. They, nevertheless, kept pressing. Two new thrusts continued the fight. The first sprang into action two weeks after Smith's sentiments appeared in the *Pittsburgh Courier* on August 15, 1942. William O. Walker, editor of the *Cleveland Call and Post*, a leading Black weekly, and president of the National Negro Newspapers Publishers Association, whose membership included the *Pittsburgh Courier*, *Chicago Defender*, and *Afro-American* as well as hundreds of smaller papers, called for the formation of committees in

Chapter 10. Pathways to the National and American Leagues

each city with a National or American League team. Walker charged each committee "to do all in its power to bring club owners in each city around to signing Negro baseball players." Cleveland led the way. Frank Lausche, Cleveland's mayor and former semipro ballplayer, Frances P. Bolton, the first woman from Ohio elected to Congress, and attorney John Shackelford, former Negro Leagues player from 1924 to 1930, were among those invited to join Cleveland's committee.[14] At about the same time, William T. Andrews, an African American New York State Democratic assemblyman, formed the Citizens' Committee to End Discrimination. The committee, Andrews said, "would demand," at the 1943 annual winter meeting of big league club owners, "that the national American pastime be continued by pooling the outstanding colored players with the available league players in the selection of new teams." More than 70 Black and white prominent citizens including academics, writers, labor leaders, NAACP officials, and community leaders signed on. Nothing could be found about the committee's activities.[15]

The Black press kept up the pressure. Sportswriters took pride and pleasure in reporting instances of Black clubs beating National and American League aggregations. Such victories demonstrated that Negro Leagues players and teams were on a par with or better than some of their cohorts of paler complexion. Examples included the Cuban Stars taking three of five games from the Brooklyn Dodgers, a "colored" all-star team headed by Paige beating a similar team of whites headed up by Dizzy Dean, star pitcher for the St. Louis Cardinals, and the fact that Paige had faced teams of the National or American League eight times without a loss.[16]

Day enjoyed the contests against white teams, especially those when the Black teams won, which was often. "We used to play harder against them," Day told baseball writer Donn Rogosin, "than we did against ourselves. We weren't allowed to play with them, but by beating them we proved that we could have."[17]

Did He or Didn't He?

As the campaigns to integrate the National and American Leagues swirled on, an oft repeated attempt to actually do so may have taken place: Bill Veeck's plan to buy the moribund Philadelphia Phillies after the 1942 season. The team finished dead last in the eight-team National League, 62½ games behind the pennant-winning St. Louis Cardinals. Not only would Veeck buy the team, the rumor continued, but in what surely would be an earth-shattering move, he would stock it entirely with Negro Leaguers such as Satchel Paige, Monte Irvin, Roy Campanella, Luke Easter, and Josh Gibson. Had Landis' quip about having no objection to an all-Black team inspired Veeck? We'll never know, but Veeck's plan, the story goes, was thwarted by Landis and National League president Ford Frick. Veeck never bought the Phillies, but his interest in doing so has been the subject of hot debate ever since.

In the 1998 article that initiated the debate, "A Baseball Myth Exploded: Bill Veeck and the 1943 Sale of the Phillies," the three Society for American Baseball Research (SABR) authors Larry Gerlach, David Jordan, and John Rossi contended that their exhaustive review of both the white and Black press of the day made no mention of such a plan. The trio found the lack of mention both deafening and telling. Perhaps they overlooked a 1954 *Philadelphia Tribune* article quoting Abe Saperstein, founder of the Harlem Globetrotters and an active and controversial figure in Negro Leagues baseball, as saying Veeck intended to both buy the team and replace the white players with Negro Leagues stars.[18] Nonetheless, the three claimed Veeck created the story to enhance his 1962 well-received autobiography, *Veeck as in Wreck*. The three added that Veeck failed to publicly discuss the matter and that he gave inconsistent accounts of the plan later in life. The authors concluded "that he had a singularly cavalier attitude toward the details of this story." They continued, "We must face the fact that Bill Veeck falsified the historical record. This is unfortunate. His actual role in advancing the integration of major league baseball is admirable and can stand on its own merit."[19] Veeck integrated the American League by signing Larry Doby (1947) and Satchel Paige (1948) to Cleveland Indians contracts.

Prominent baseball historian Jules Tygiel took issue with Gerlach et al. In 2006 in a SABR article titled simply "Phillies," Tygiel, after summarizing *A Baseball Myth Exploded*, presented firm evidence of newspaper articles and public statements by Veeck himself about the plan years before the appearance of Veeck's autobiography. Tygiel noted that his findings fall short of absolving Veeck but do raise questions about the trio's conclusions and "lends greater credence to Veeck's original story." Tygiel characterized the threesome's conclusions as "a rush to judgment" and cautioned other writers on the perils of "relying on an absence of evidence and overreaching one's resources in drawing conclusions."[20]

One for whom Veeck's original story stands on solid ground is the eminent and prolific baseball writer Paul Dickson. In his 2012 biography of Veeck, *Bill Veeck: Baseball's Greatest Maverick*, Dickson states, "During the three years I researched this biography I came to the conclusion that Bill Veeck was telling the truth." To support his claim, Dickson cites instances of Veeck's interest in the Phillies appearing in print as early as 1942, examples of Veeck's public statements made long before 1962 describing his interest in and efforts made toward buying the Phillies, testaments to Veeck's veracity from family members who recalled Veeck discussing the plan frequently at home, and fellow baseball writer Jonathan Eig's statement in his book *Opening Day* (2007) that for Veeck, it would have been "a typical move—rushed, radical, and revolutionary. Turning to Negro Leaguers to re-stock the Phillies seemed just like the sort of thing he would do."[21] Veeck was after all, as Dickson's subtitle makes clear, baseball's greatest maverick.

Whether Day figured in Veeck's plan is not known, but he should have. *New Journal and Guide* sportswriter Peter Suskind certainly thought so in June 1943. "If ever there was a more perfect time," Suskind wrote, "for big league moguls to practice what they've been whispering now is the time and Leon Day is the man.... He's way over and above those guys who are drawing in fabulous baseball salaries."[22]

1943

The year 1942 saw much talk but no progress toward integrating the American and National Leagues. The Negro Leagues continued apace. Day continued to draw attention. Sportswriters expected much of him as the 1943 season got underway. The *New York Amsterdam News'* coverage of the Eagles' spring training, held this year in nearby Trenton, New Jersey, due to a federal government gas rationing program, noted, "Leon Day is generally conceded by most experts as the best hurler in Negro baseball."[23] Cum Posey, whose 35-year career (1911–46) in the Negro Leagues including positions of player, manager, officer, owner,

Leon Day

and secretary, all with the Homestead Grays, called the Eagles star "the best colored pitcher of all time."[24]

Day didn't disappoint, at least initially. In his first 1943 outing, against the white, Class B minor league farm team of the Phillies, the Trenton Packers of the Inter-State League, Leon faced all nine batters in the game's last three innings and struck out six as the Eagles romped 12–3.[25] A week later he went 8⅓ innings against the powerful Grays giving up only seven hits and fanning five. Jimmy Hill relieved him with the score tied 2–2 and took the loss as the Grays pushed across three runs in the tenth inning.[26] As exhibition games gave way to league games, Leon, holding down center field when not pitching, maintained his contributions at the plate doubling home one of the four Eagles runs in their victory over the Philadelphia Stars in the Star's home opener. Day pitched the Eagles to a 9–1 blowout of the Stars two days later in the Eagles' home opener. Leon limited the Stars to one run and collected two of the Eagles' 13 hits.[27]

It wasn't, however, all smooth sailing for "the mighty mite." In late May in the first night game at Griffith Stadium, the Grays, behind ace pitcher John Wright who, behind Jackie Robinson, would become the second Black player signed by Branch Rickey, had their way with Day, the league's strikeout king at the time. The Grays dethroned the king and his court 6–0. Day gave up eight hits in six frames before being relieved by rookie Jake Elam whose career lasted just one season. On the first Sunday in June, the New York Cubans lambasted the Eagles 11–1 before 11,000 spectators in the Polo Grounds. Day started but was nicked for a four-run rally in the second inning when the boys from the island got to him for a double, two singles, and two walks. Leon took over center field for the game's duration where his bat also failed him as he went 0 for 5 at the plate.[28]

Day ran into another buzz saw before a hometown crowd of 8,000 at Ruppert Stadium three weeks later. The Grays' barrage of hits in the second inning ushered him back to center field. In a mid–August game, again against the Grays, Day and the Eagles came up short, 9–5. Day did have one good game against the Black Yankees in late July. He came on in relief of Jimmy Hill in the sixth inning of the first game of a four-team doubleheader, a popular format during the 1940s held in Yankee Stadium and in the Polo Grounds. After walking two Yankees with no outs, Leon settled down and struck out the next three on the way to a 6–4

Chapter 10. Pathways to the National and American Leagues

Eagles win. The Grays downed the Stars 14–4 in the second game on their way to another National Negro League pennant.[29]

Even though Day wasn't having his best season, he hadn't lost his luster with fans voting on players for the upcoming East-West game, the Negro League's equivalent to the National and American Leagues' annual all-star game. By the end of July, Day led all pitchers in the voting for a pitching position with the East squad.[30]

A month before the East-West game, the Washington Homestead Grays, who now split their home games between Pittsburgh's Forbes Field and D.C.'s Griffith Stadium, and the Bushwicks squared off on Independence Day. The matchup was not new. The Grays had beaten the Bushwicks twice earlier in the season, but the game's location was new. This was the first Black-white encounter to occur in Griffith Stadium owned by Clark Griffith, a staunch opponent of Blacks in the National and American Leagues but a willing recipient of rental fees for his ballpark regardless of the participants' complexions. Before 10,000 spectators, the Grays prevailed once again, 11–3.[31]

CHAPTER 11

From Ruppert Stadium to Utah Beach

WORLD WAR II was taking players away from teams as the '43 season wore on. Some were drafted. Some volunteered. Some, in place of either option, took jobs in the mushrooming defense industries which were ramping up production of ships, tanks, rifles, ammunition, uniforms, and other items needed to support the war effort. According to a list compiled by Negro Leagues historian Larry Lester, 111 Negro Leaguers served in World War II, 14 of them Newark Eagles.[1] Five Eagles—pitcher Max Manning, infielder Clarence Israel, catcher Charles Parks, and outfielders Monte Irving and Charles Thompson—were the first of the Eagles to wear army khaki. Day would soon join them but not before participating in a three-game exhibition series in late September.[2]

The right-hander appeared in all three games between a team of Negro National League all-stars and the Negro National Leagues' pennant winners, the Grays, who were waiting for the Birmingham Black Barons and Chicago Giants to decide which Negro American League team would oppose them in the upcoming Negro Leagues World Series. In game one Leon held down the keystone sack and rapped out three singles in a losing cause as the All-Stars fell to the Grays 2–1. Game two saw him on the mound in what would be his last pitching appearance for two and a half years. Wildness cost him a win. He gave up a mere four hits but walked in the winning run in the seventh inning giving the Grays another 2–1 victory. In game three he played his last game before being drafted, which the Grays narrowly won 8–7, at second base.[3]

Had he not been called by the army, Day would have joined a team being assembled by Tom Wilson, owner of the Baltimore Elite Giants, to play in the 1943–44 California Winter League based in San Diego. It was the league's 23rd season. Wilson's team, called the Baltimore Elite Giants, consisted of Negro National League all-stars. News reports said

Wilson had signed Day, who Wilson's assistant Vernon Green claimed was faster than Satchel Paige was in his day. The six-team league consisted of the Giants, the Homestead Grays, two California teams, and two service teams. Day's absence disappointed Wilson who agreed with Green's assessment of Day.[4]

Day Joins a Segregated Army

On September 1, 1943, in Baltimore, Maryland, Day reported for his physical. Leon served two and half years, most notably as a member of the Allied Invasion Force, code-named Operation Overlord, that stormed the Normandy beaches on D-Day, June 6, 1944. Military historian Cornelius Ryan cited that day "as the day the battle began that ended Hitler's insane gamble to dominate the world."[5]

Day's trip to Normandy started on November 12, 1940, when he registered for the draft at age 24, two months after the Selective Training and Service Act became law. The act initiated the first peacetime draft in the nation's history. All males between 21 and 45 were required to sign up. The government established a lottery to determine who would serve.[6] Army units were segregated at the beginning of the war and would remain so until 1945 when some mixed units were introduced to the battlefield. Typically white officers commanded Black troops who were assigned to noncombat support roles such as construction, maintenance, and truck driving.

A few days after Pearl Harbor, December 7, 1941, senior army officials left no doubt as to the army's stance on segregation. Army chief of staff General George Marshall, in a speech to 20 members of the national Black press who paid their own way to attend a two-day War Department conference in Washington, D.C., said the army would continue what the *Chicago Defender* described as "its undemocratic policy of segregation." Marshall, citing an urgent meeting with President Roosevelt, left it to Colonel E.R. Householder to justify the policy to an increasingly irate audience. "The army did not create discrimination," Householder told the group. "It [the army] is made up," he continued, "of citizens who have pronounced ideas about Negroes and the army can do nothing to change it." He added, "The army is not a sociological laboratory. Experiments to meet the demands of the champions of every race would endanger the efficiency of the organization." Brigadier General B.O. Davis, the first African American general in the U.S. military, accused the assembled journalists and others like them of "sowing discontent in the minds of the soldiers."[7]

As a result, Jim Crow flourished in army training posts. Separate barracks were built so that distance or natural barriers prevented the mixing of Black and white service men and women. Other posts where both Black and white troops were stationed featured separate reception centers, theaters, guesthouses, clubs, toilets, and drinking fountains. The army's policy resulted in New Jersey draft boards being ordered in the spring of 1941 to skip over the names of "colored" men in two draft calls and draft only whites to meet their quotas. White draftees resented the order as they would have more of a chance to be drafted. A White House spokesman denied that the order violated the draft act's provision that "men shall be selected in an impartial manner ... and that there shall be no discrimination against any person on account of race or color."[8]

Day's Army Service

In late September 1943, Day reported to Fort Dix, 16 miles south of Trenton, New Jersey.[9] From Fort Dix a troop train took him to Camp Gordon Johnston, a 155,000-acre training installation in coastal Franklin County, Florida, in the town of Carrabelle, 54 miles south of Tallahassee on the Gulf of Mexico. There, the 816th, 817th, and 818th Amphibious Truck Companies were formed. Day was assigned to the 818th. The companies consisted of motorized amphibious vehicles, technically known as DUKWs, but commonly referred to as a "Duck." They transported men and supplies from ships to land.

The short-lived camp (1942–46) served as an amphibious warfare training center. Its coastal environment, being similar to the Normandy beaches, helped Day's all-Black company of 173 soldiers train for D-Day.[10]

For most troops the trip was their first away from home. They came from the four corners of the country; they took a train to a regional processing center where, after spending a night or two, boarded another train for the trip to Florida. Upon arrival they found their wooden barracks

Chapter 11. From Ruppert Stadium to Utah Beach

lacked flooring. Entertainment possibilities consisted of the PX, a barbershop, and a few small shops. Officers and enlistees found the camp short on luxuries but long on demanding training activities under the hot Florida sun.[11]

Day after day, after an early breakfast, the men trained on the DUKWs. Built by General Motors, Inc., the six-wheel vehicle weighed 7.5 tons, operated at 6.4 mph in the water and up to 50 mph on land. It measured 31 feet long, 8'8" feet high with a fold-up canvas top and a windshield. The term "DUKW" was GM's manufacturing code: "D" stood for 1942, "U" for amphibious, "K" for all-wheel drive, and "W" for dual-wheel drive.[12]

DUKW training lasted from 8:00 a.m. to 6:00 p.m., followed by dinner and then, on some evenings, a 5- to 12-mile hike with a rifle and rucksack. Other nights were devoted to learning French. On March 14, 1944, the three companies left for New Brunswick, New Jersey. From there, they traveled by troop carrier to Liverpool, England, and then by train to Basingstoke for final preparations.

The DUKWs would prove their worth, not only on D-Day but in Asia and Africa as well. The army, however, had initially rejected the proposal for the DUKW. Only when an early model that just happened to be near a Coast Guard vessel that went aground near Provincetown, Massachusetts, saved the lives of the vessel's seven-man crew did the army accept the proposal. There were 21,147 built. First appearing at Guadalcanal in late 1942, the DUKW made its first European appearance in Sicily, Italy, in July 1943. "Ducks" saw service in England, France, Australia, the Soviet Union, and after World War II, in the Korean War.[13] Between the end of World War II and the start of the Korean conflict, the army used them as recruiting aids. A recruiting caravan toured towns in Michigan, for instance, in September 1946. At each stop potential recruits were treated to free military films in the evening, a sound truck playing popular songs, and a ride in a DUKW. Anyone wanting a ride "will be welcome to do so," the announcement read.[14]

The cumbersome-looking vehicle caught the attention of the UK prime minister Winston Churchill. He described the vehicle to the House of Commons in 1944 "as a heavy lorry which goes at between 40 and 50 miles per hour ... and can plunge into the water and swim out for miles in quite choppy weather returning with a load of several tons, coming ashore and coming off wherever it is specially needed."[15]

In a more poetic vein, W.P. Lambertson, columnist for the *Fairview Enterprise* in Fairview, Kansas, said of the DUKW, "It is one of the most remarkable performers of the war.... It rides through the waves, not on them, always staying upright and meets the shore as interruptedly as the daylight meets the dawn."[16]

Day drove a DUKW loaded with food, fuel, and ammunition between one of the more than 5,000 ships anchored in the English Channel and Utah Beach where Allied infantrymen continued to fight the Germans in the days after D-Day. The soldiers gave their DUKWs such nicknames as "Cup Cake," "Shoo Shoo Baby," "Sea Hawk," "Sea Lion," and "Boogie Woogie." Ollie Stewart, a war correspondent for the *Afro-American*, noted that such duty could be dangerous. He took a ride on one. "The channel," he reported, "was rough on Sunday as we ploughed out to a Liberty Ship for a load of rations. Spray covered me and my life jacket as we ploughed a mile and a half where the ship was anchored. We banged the side of the ship and rocked perilously as the ship's derrick lowered fifty cases at a time into our dukw. It was raining and the slightest miscalculation would have dumped us all into the channel. Finally we headed back to land meeting a steady stream of similar craft bucking the waves." DUKWs on their way from the beach to the ships often carried German POWs.[17]

Day learned firsthand about the dangers. He first drove a "DUCK" onto Utah Beach on June 12, 1944, six days after the initial landing. He was, in his words, "scared to death." "When we landed," he told Riley, "we were pretty close to the action because we could hear the small arms fire." Several nights later when he again drove his "Duck" onto Utah Beach, he would have cause to be both alarmed and defiant. His ammunition-loaded "Duck" was lit up by German planes "dropping flares and lighting the beach up so bright you could have read a newspaper." Realizing he could be an easy target, he slammed on the brakes, jumped off his "DUCK," and dived into a foxhole occupied by a white military policeman (MP). The startled soldier yelled, "Who's driving that duck out there?" Day yelled back, "I am." "What's it got on it?" asked the MP. "Ammunition," Day answered. "Move that duck from out in front of this hole," the MP hollered. "Go out there and move it your own damn self," Day shot back. Neither man moved.[18]

The DUKW units stayed at Normandy until late August 1944, by which time the Allies, at a great cost of life and limb, finally had the

Chapter 11. From Ruppert Stadium to Utah Beach

The amphibian "Duck," formally known as a DUKW, like the one Day most likely drove from ships in the English Channel to Utah Beach where the battle raged for days after the Allies' initial landing on D-Day, June 6, 1944. Fortunately, Leon survived his dangerous duty without a scratch (author's collection).

Germans in retreat through France and Belgium trying to reach Germany. DUKW drivers traded in their DUKWs for 2.5-ton 6 × 6 cargo trucks and joined the famed Red Ball Express. While no documentation could be found to prove Day participated, it seems highly likely that he did. In any event the express brought well-deserved accolades to those who kept supplies flowing to Patton's troops, 70 percent of whom were Black.

"Red Ball" was a railroad term for "priority freight." Born on August 24, 1944, the express was a motorized transportation network that had clear sailing from the Normandy beaches and ocean port cities in northern France to "dump sites," where the fast-moving Allied front welcomed their arrival. Damaged rail lines, jammed roads, disabled vehicles blocking the way, drivers getting lost, and convoys kidnapped severely hampered efforts to get supplies where they were needed. To speed up deliveries a two-road network, meticulously improved and

The Red Ball Express in action in the fall of 1944. A soldier directs the convoy of trucks that carried tons of supplies to General George Patton's fast-moving troops. More than 70 percent of the drivers were Black and earned well-deserved praise from General Dwight Eisenhower and some white newspapers for their round-the-clock work (author's collection).

maintained, was commandeered on French soil running initially from Saint-Lô in Normandy to Chartres, 54 miles southwest of Paris, and later extended to Soissons. Only Red Ball trucks and other vehicles, mostly jeeps and trailers, could use the route. Each vehicle and the route itself were marked with an identifying red ball.[19]

The roundtrip route stretched almost 500 miles. The trucks carried supplies: ammunition, food, plane parts, medicine, troops, PX items, and clothing to the First and Third Armies rapidly pursuing the Nazis. Two men manned each truck. One drove. The other slept. Returning vehicles carried captured German food and clothing for captured German POWs and any captured items deemed worthy of use. Organized in convoys with a speed limit of 25 miles per hour, the drivers drove nonstop day and night, rain or shine, with only periodic ten-minute rest stops. The trip was hazardous. A German attack from the ground

Chapter 11. From Ruppert Stadium to Utah Beach

or air in the form of exploding German artillery shells or sniper fire could, and often did, occur at any time. Some trucks were armed with 50-caliber machine guns. Each driver carried a carbine.

Blacks, until the very end of the war, were typically assigned non-combat support roles out of the ill-founded belief that Blacks lacked the capabilities for combat. The Red Ball Express became the most legendary of all Black support activities. The express, Black historians Edna Green Medford and Michael Frazier said, "proved the worth and valor of the Black soldier." In the short span of four months 412,193 tons had been moved by 140 truck companies. On an average day, 899 trucks were rolling. Allied Supreme Commander General Dwight D. Eisenhower praised their work. "He wants you to know," said an aide, General E.S. Hughes, "the part you are playing is vital. His [Ike's] message is for every man engaged in this vast project. The troops at the front could not do without you." Members of the white press added their plaudits in January 1945. *Time* magazine gave a description of the Red Ball Express. The *Cincinnati Inquirer*, in a rare statement of praise for Blacks in a white daily, said of the Negro soldiers, "Many of them drove 2½ ton trucks with one ton trailers; others loaded and unloaded cargo; still others kept the equipment serviced and repaired. All together they helped achieve an almost impossible total of military transport when speed was essential."[20]

Repaired and improved rail lines brought a halt to the Red Ball Express on November 16, 1944. The express returned to public view when Universal Studios made the movie *The Red Ball Express* in 1952. Budd Boetticher, an American film director best known for low-budget westerns in the 1950s starring Randolph Scott, directed the film. The Department of the Army, in an effort to downplay the vital role played by Blacks, insisted that "race relations be modified and that the positive angle be emphasized," Boetticher said in 1979. "The army," he continued, "wouldn't let us tell the truth about the black troops because the government figured they were expendable."[21]

Chapter 12

Baseball and the War

REGARDLESS OF THE Department of the Army's opinion about Black soldiers, they made a major contribution to the Allied victory in Europe. Germany surrendered on May 7, 1945, six months after the demise of the Red Ball Express. With the war in Europe over, thousands of GIs had few official duties to do as they awaited orders to return home. Since about 200,000 had participated in informal baseball games during the war, the sport seemed a productive way to occupy veterans' energies. Why not a World Series of sorts?

To find the two best service teams, a series of regional tournaments were held. General Patton tasked Harry "The Hat" Walker, a decorated combat veteran and an outfielder for the St. Louis Cardinals before the war, to put together a Germany-based league composed of teams from Patton's Third Army, including a team of his own, the "Red Circlers." The name derived from the unit's distinctive shoulder patch. The team had traversed Europe by bus but found the going difficult after D-Day because much of the infrastructure had been destroyed. A spare B-52 solved that problem allowing the Red Circlers to take on all comers with greater ease. In addition to Walker, the Red Circlers included National Leaguers Johnny Wyrostek (Phillies), Benny Zientara (Reds), Ken Heinzelman (Pirates), and several promising minor leaguers from the American Association and International Leagues. The biggest star was a lanky, six-foot six-inch right-handed pitcher with a mean side-arm delivery who had only three innings under his belt with the Cincinnati Reds before the war, but whom everyone could see was going places: Ewell "The Whip" Blackwell. He did go places after the war as a starter for the Reds and a member of six National League all-star rosters, 1946–51.

Two teams emerged as the best: the Red Circlers and the France-based, awkwardly named, Overseas Invasion Service Expedition (OISE). They would determine the championship of the European theater of operations. The improvised series of five games took place in early September 1945.

The Red Circlers were the heavy favorites given the number of National Leaguers on the team. The OISE All-Stars consisted mostly of minor leaguers and college players. Only two had any National or American League experience, both so-so pitchers. Russ Bauers won 29 games while losing the same number for the Pirates between 1936 and 1941, and "Subway" Sam Nahem managed ten wins and eight losses in three seasons with the Dodgers, Cardinals, and Phillies.

To attract as large a crowd as possible, a spacious venue was needed. What better site than Stadion der Hitlerjugend, the Hitler Youth Stadium, in Nuremberg, Germany, where Hitler, Goebbels, and other Nazi leaders had once preached Aryan supremacy to thousands of exuberant Germans. Now, German POWs built temporary wooden stands to accommodate an expected huge crowd and painted over swastikas in the arena renamed Soldiers Field. The irony became even more pronounced when it was discovered that two players for the OISE All-Stars were Black: Leon Day and outfielder Willard "Home Run" Brown, a cleanup hitting outfielder from Shreveport, Louisiana, who had played for the Kansas City Monarchs when they dominated the Negro American League, 1937–42. All other players on both teams were white. Although whites and Blacks had played informally among each other during the war, this would be the highest profile series of games in which both Blacks and whites competed.[1]

Thousands (estimates vary from 50,000 to 150,000) of servicemen of all ranks from generals to privates cheered, drank beer and Coke, gobbled peanuts, gambled, and soaked up the rays. The American flag was raised while a bugle corps played the national anthem to start the first game. Armed Forces Radio carried the games to service members around the globe.

To no one's surprise the Red Circlers took game one on September 2, 1945, the same day Japan surrendered. The next day in game two, Day led the OISE All-Stars to a close victory, 2–1. He struck out ten, one more than the Whip had managed in game one, while giving up only four hits. Two of the strikeouts were by Harry Walker, a .300 hitter for the St. Louis Cardinals in 1942 and 1943. The right-hander pitched shutout ball through the eighth inning, outdueling the opposition's hurlers Ole Olson and former Pittsburgh Pirate pitcher Ken

The Overseas Invasion Service All-Star team (shown here in September 1945) that upset the favored Red Circlers to win the European theater of operations "World Series." Leon Day is in the bottom row, far right (next to Willard Brown). Other players unidentified (author's collection).

Heintzelman. Willard Brown, the only other Black player for the OISE nine, connected for four hits, including three doubles. Tony Jaros, a first baseman from the University of Minnesota, led the white OISE batters with three doubles. Before the game *Afro-American* sportswriter Ollie Stewart said, "Day must be thinking something like the following as he took the mound. The World Series will be opening in the United States this week. If I was not in the Army, I still couldn't play in the World Series-because they say a colored man isn't good enough. Well, I'll just show them a thing or two." "So," Stewart concluded, "Leon Day showed them a thing or two or three."[2]

With the series tied at one game apiece, the teams flew to Reims, France, for the next two games. They were played just a few kilometers from a small schoolhouse that had served as General Eisenhower's command center and where German officers had signed the surrender papers. The OISE All-Stars took game three but lost the fourth capped by a two-run homer off Day by Walker that spurred the Third Army

Chapter 12. Baseball and the War

nine to a 5–0 win. Day was not the pitcher in this game that he had been in game two. Even though he went the distance, he gave up four runs on six hits in the first 3⅔ innings.

The Germany–based team won the coin toss to decide the location of the fifth and deciding game. Back in Nuremberg, Blackwell started and held a slim 1–0 lead until the seventh when Day and Brown turned the tide. Sent in as a pinch runner in the seventh, Day stole second and third and dashed home on a short flyball to left field. In the eighth inning, Brown's double to deep center field drove in the winning run for the OISE's stunning upset victory. Back in France the All-Stars were treated to a parade and a steak and champagne–laden banquet compliments of Brigadier General Charles Thrasher. In contrast to the many restaurants in the States where Day and Brown could not have broken bread with their OISE teammates, all enjoyed themselves with gusto.[3]

Day's and Brown's performances prompted *Afro-American* writer Ollie Stewart to predict that "big league moguls will be even more frightened of sepia ball players when all the war veterans get back. They have made the white boys look bad in every important game over here." Stewart also put in a plug for dropping the color bar when the veterans return. "Mixed teams," he observed, "are creating good will among the GIs, which is one reason why we fought the war, after all."[4]

Chapter 13

Racial Tensions at Home

WHILE BLACK MEN were fighting and dying for America overseas, racial conflicts, many of which existed before the war, kept bubbling to the surface in Newark. Individuals' responses to discrimination varied. Some took an activist stance. Six Black women walked off their jobs in August 1943 at the Newark-based American Transformer Company complaining that white women with less experience and skill were assigned much better jobs at higher pay. Supervisors turned a deaf ear to their complaints. They told the women to quit if they were dissatisfied. They did just that.

After receiving a multitude of complaints, officials at the National Housing Agency announced "the definite possibility" of new housing in Newark for Blacks in the defense industries and living in Newark. Their promise offered little by way of immediate relief to the 86 percent of Blacks in Newark the agency found to be living in "overcrowded or poor housing."

Heated discussions between Blacks and whites about whether to integrate the new Sojourner Truth YWCA ended with the facility being open to all. The New Jersey Congress of Industrial Organizations Council continued, to no avail, to lobby President Roosevelt to integrate the armed forces by executive order.

Black playwright Hughes Allison's play, "*It's Midnight Over Newark*, vividly portrayed Newark's tax-supported City Hospital's ban against Black physicians and other concerns such as prostitution and inadequate housing." Allison said the play's purpose "was to put race discrimination right on the stage where the general public can see it gnawing at the very foundations of democracy."[1]

Despite being well received by both Blacks and whites, the play had no impact on the hospital's board of directors. They issued a statement saying, "The ban [on hiring Black physicians] will remain unchanged." Earlier in 1940, an editorial in the *Afro-American* criticized a proposal

Chapter 13. Racial Tensions at Home

to create a Newark city hospital that would serve only Blacks. Citing a New Jersey state law that outlawed discrimination in public facilities, the paper said, "A separate hospital is not the answer ... any more than separate schools or parks would be. Let the campaign [to integrate existing hospitals] be waged with vigor whether it takes one year or ten."[2]

Five years earlier a six-person interracial committee seeking to integrate the staff of the Newark City Hospital was rebuffed in no uncertain terms by its board chairman, Dr. C. O'Crowley. "The presence of Race doctors on staff would disrupt that staff and this is not the time to make a protest against the policy of this city-owned hospital in refusing to admit Race physicians," O'Crowley told the committee.[3]

Many parks in New Jersey were segregated. One in particular, Olympic Park in Irvington, saw in 1939 an opportunity to make some money by hosting the Essex County (which contained Newark) Flag Day Committee's annual parade. The committee was on the verge of accepting park manager Henry Gunther's offer until committee member James H. Lindsay announced that "no colored veterans would take part because the park is segregated." Several members confronted Gunther. He offered to lift the racial ban but for the day of the parade only, share 10 percent of the revenue with the committee, and donate $150 to cover printing costs. At an earlier meeting the committee had agreed that the celebration would not be held where discrimination based on race, creed, or color is enforced. The group declined Gunther's offer.[4]

Not only parks but many New Jersey beaches were segregated. Virginia Flowers, an African American young woman and socialite, light-skinned enough to "pass," outfoxed the Long Beach mayor and council in 1939. She bought seven badges for darker-skinned African American women giving them access to the three "whites"-only beaches—#1, #2, and #4 in Long Beach, 93 miles south of Newark. The mayor and council had previously confined Blacks to beach #3. Following complaints by white bathers about Blacks now bathing on the all-white beaches, Mrs. Ollie Bullock filed suit in New Jersey's supreme court to have the segregation ordinance declared unconstitutional. Seeing defeat looming, Long Beach's mayor and city commissioners proposed to drop the segregation policy for Long Beach if Mrs. Bullock dropped her complaint. Mrs. Bullock refused. A ruling by the New Jersey supreme court would apply as well to other New Jersey beaches, including Atlantic City, Asbury Park, and Cape May. Judge Perskie then ruled the policy unconstitutional on the grounds that the officials "did not want members of the black race to intermingle with members of the white race." New Jersey beaches were now legally integrated, but whites' animosity toward Blacks were little affected.[5]

Prior to Perskie's ruling the publicity surrounding Long Beach's segregation policy prompted hundreds of people to patronize other beaches such as those at Belmar, about a mile away. Establishments along the Belmar boardwalk, however, were another story. Most served "colored" patrons in separate cups and dishes. "Colored" moviegoers were forced to sit on one side in theaters. A swank club at Asbury Park beach, Cuba's Spanish Tavern, had seen its patronage change from mostly all Black to predominantly white. While Blacks were not banned from the club, they were not encouraged to come. As one said, "It has become something like the Cotton Club in New York. You can go there but you're not too welcome."[6]

Energetic moviegoers at Newark's Savoy Theater foiled ticket sellers' and ushers' attempts to enforce the Jim Crow requirement that Blacks sit in the balcony or in the orchestra's one segregated row. Enduring the ticket seller's reminders, Black patrons darted into the center of the orchestra knowing the ticket seller would push a button alerting ushers that the patrons should be diverted to the balcony or the orchestra's one row designated for Blacks. The Black patrons dared the ushers to do anything about their presence and patiently stayed put. The manager's only recourse was to call the police, which rarely happened unless a fracas broke out.[7]

An approach employed by some whites emphasized caution and patience on the part of Blacks while whites pleaded their case. The instance of a Black chauffeur and his employer, New Jersey's governor at the time, Charles Edison, son of the inventor, serves as an example. "Most of your problems," Edison told a reporter for the *Afro-American* in 1943, "come from people who are in a hurry." To make his point, he told of his Black chauffeur being denied lodging at a resort where he had driven the governor. "The boy," Edison said, "did not raise hell, but I was indignant." Edison conveyed his feelings to the resort's

Chapter 13. Racial Tensions at Home

administrators. They promised "to make provisions for such emergencies." Edison took their response as "a victory," adding, "if the boy [actually a young man] had insisted on his rights, he would have only antagonized people."[8]

Chapter 14

He's Back and Rarin' to Go

While conflicts over segregation and integration were flaring in New Jersey and elsewhere, Day was serving two and a half years of army duty overseas. He received an honorable discharge at Fort Dix in March 1946. But before he could again don an Eagles uniform, Jim Crow gave him an ugly welcome home. Dressed in his army uniform and on his last leg home from World War II, Day strode out of Newark's Pennsylvania railroad station. He headed straight to the cab stand. After opening the door and getting in the back seat, he heard the cabbie snarl, "Get outta my cab. I don't take any niggers." "You mammy tappy [Day's term for an expletive of the highest order]," Leon shot back. "There I was over there ducking bullets for you, and you *are* gonna take me somewhere, maybe the police station." Fearing Day's anger, the cabbie relented and drove him the 11 miles to his home. As he got out of the cab, Day threw the fare on the ground and told the driver, "You get your mammy tappy ass out of the car and pick it up." The driver did.[1]

An encounter with a customs agent in Miami, Florida, after returning from winter ball again brought Day face-to-face with Jim Crow. The agent threw Day's clothes all over the floor. "He wanted me to say something," Day said. "Then he could lock me up or beat me up or something. If you were black, you were wrong. You just had to grin and bear it."[2]

He lost little time in signing with the Eagles upon his return from Europe. Even though he had played well in the army all-star games in Europe, many wondered if his absence from Negro Leagues competition had taken its toll. Day responded as only Day could. On opening day against the Philadelphia Stars at Ruppert Field on May 5, 1946, the army veteran threw a spectacular no-hit, no-run game for a 2–0 shutout, one of only two opening day no-hitters. The other was Cleveland Indians Bob Feller's April 16, 1940, game against the Chicago White Sox. Only three Stars reached first base against Day: two on errors by shortstop William Felder (an infielder of modest talent filling in for Willie Wells

Chapter 14. He's Back and Rarin' to Go

who split the 1946 season between the New York Black Yankees and the Baltimore Elite Giants) and one on a walk. A vivid memory of the game for Leon was striking out Oscar Charleston, considered by many the best Negro Leagues player ever. "He was the manager," Day boasted to Hines. "He came in to pinch hit," Day continued. "I pitched against him that one time. Struck him out!"

The nifty right-hander left the field on the shoulders of his teammates with an ear-to-ear smile. Also smiling was Effa Manley. "It really was a beauty," she wrote four days later to Art Carter, sportswriter for the *Afro-American*. "The last man up," she continued, "was a pinch hitter, Henry McHenry, a pitcher who was called the Stars' veteran ace. Day blazed three fastballs over the heart of the plate. McHenry whiffed on each one. Went down swinging! Can you imagine what a thrill that was?"[3]

As spectacular as Day's performance looked to observers, he didn't consider it one of his best games. His arm was hurting. "My arm never was what it was before I went into the army. My arm never felt right even on opening day," he explained to Riley. His pain started in the fifth inning, but Day stayed in the game. In his usual low-key vein, he explained his no-hitter by saying, "I had good control and a good defense."[4]

The game was memorable for another reason. On a seemingly close call at the plate in the sixth inning, umpire Peter Strauch (white) called Eagles base runner and star second baseman Larry Doby safe. Stars catcher Bill Cash thought otherwise. He had a point. A photo in the March 11 edition of the *New York Amsterdam News* showed Cash putting the tag on Doby before his outstretched hand touched the plate. The photo was of no use to Cash at the time. Cash dropped Strauch to the ground with a single punch. Stars player/manager Homer Curry went "berserk," sprinted to the plate from his position in right field and kicked Strauch while he was down. The benches emptied. A contingent of spectators, some white and some Black, spilled on to the field. Someone called the police. Both mounted officers and foot patrolmen took 30 minutes to subdue the conflagration. Both Cash and Curry refused to leave the game after being given the thumb. Newark police officers did the honors of escorting both men from the field. Day, meanwhile, calmly watched the fracas from the Eagles' dugout before taking the mound in the seventh to continue his no-hitter.

Umpire bashing was not new, but Effa thought there might have been a racial twist to this episode. In a letter three days later to Eddie Gottlieb, a white entrepreneur who promoted and booked games as well as assigned umpires to games, she questioned "whether white umpires should continue to work games for the colored teams." Gottlieb chose not to answer her, but the event prompted team owners to start protecting umpires. In a groundbreaking move they fined Cash $50 and suspended him for three games. Further assaults would bring a fine of $100 and a ten-game suspension. Curry escaped punishment perhaps because he apologized to Strauch after the game. While they were at it, the moguls issued meaningless five-year suspensions to eight players, including Eagles Dandridge and McDuffie, for jumping to Mexico.[5]

A week after his no-hitter, sore arm and all, the diminutive right-hander went the distance against the New York Black Yankees in Newark's Ruppert Stadium. After giving up two runs and five hits in the first three innings, he pitched shutout ball the rest of the way, allowing only three base hits, for an 8–2 victory. Day contributed from the plate as well as the mound, lacing two singles into the outfield in three at bats.[6]

The Race Heats Up

After a month of play, the Eagles and New York Cubans were deadlocked for first place in the six-team Negro National League. In late May, Day held the New York Black Yankees scoreless for seven innings before 15,000 spectators in the first game of a Yankee Stadium Sunday doubleheader. The Yankee bats came to life in the eighth bringing in three runs to cop the game and negate Day's performance. Several days later he beat the Stars 9–2 at Philadelphia Phillies and Athletics Shibe Park. Day contributed two singles. The Eagles lost their next few games falling to fourth place. They rebounded by taking two doubleheaders from the Cubans. In game one of the first doubleheader, "the stocky right-hander" limited the Cubans to one run and four hits in a 7–1 victory. Several of those runs scored in front of 14,000 in the Polo Grounds resulted from Day's perfect day at the plate with a walk and three singles. Two games taken from the Grays, including a 16–2 trouncing with Day on the mound, and two shutouts of the Stars vaulted the Eagles back into first place by the end of the season's first half.

Chapter 14. He's Back and Rarin' to Go

Their late surge was deemed "the most sensational drive in the history of the Negro National League."[7] Day's performances earned him the accolade from journalist Wendell Smith as "the Mighty Mite of the mound ... the best pitcher in either league."[8] Could this be the season Abe Manley had longed for—a World Series win for the Eagles?

The odds looked good. The first-half winners lost only 9 of the 32 league games played in the second half. In addition to a solid pitching staff, Eagles position players were hitting at a prodigious clip. Outfielder and shortstop Monty Irvin was cruising along at .384. Third baseman Pat Patterson connected at a .364 pace. Infielders Lennie Pearson and Larry Doby were flirting with .350 in mid-July 1946.[9] The hitters kept hitting, and Day and crew kept pitching. Day was singled out in July by Wendell Smith "as the best pitcher in either league." By early August the Eagles were nestled in first place for the season's second half. Day, now on the far side of 29, had recorded 83 strikeouts in 14 games to lead all Negro National League hurlers. He fanned another 10 Homestead Grays, to up his total to 93, in a 15-inning game in D.C.'s Griffith Stadium on August 11. With the score tied 7–7 at the end of the ninth, Day outlasted the Grays' relief pitcher Bob Thurman by pitching shutout ball for the next six frames. Seeing he wasn't getting any offensive help, he smacked a walk-off homer over the left field wall in the top of the 15th to win the game.[10]

Several days later, he took particular pleasure in beating Satchel Paige and the Kansas City Monarchs 7–4 at Ruppert Field in a mid–August encounter. Day tired in the fourth inning, but by that time he had gone two for two at the plate and scored two runs. Circus catches by Eagles outfielders Bob Harvey and Johnny Davis and hits off Paige by Patterson and Irving, in addition to Day's, sealed the win.[11] Enough wins followed to give the Eagles the second-half championship. The Eagles finished 13.5 games ahead of the New York Cubans, followed by the Elite Giants, Homestead Grays, Philadelphia Stars, and the New York Black Yankees.[12]

Abe and Effa were ecstatic. Not only were they on their way to a World Series, but mushrooming attendance at games enabled by job growth spawned by the war's industrial organizations had fattened their coffers for the third season in a row. Prior to 1944, Abe's losses, according to his figures, since 1935, had grown to $100,000 (equivalent to $12.3 million in 2024 dollars). No wonder he had startled other owners with a threat, never carried out, to leave the Negro National League in 1943.[13]

A World Series at Last

While the Eagles were dominating the Negro National League, the Kansas City Monarchs were doing the same in the Negro American League. The 1946 Negro World Series between the two teams opened on September 17 in the Polo Grounds before 19,423 fans. Ruppert Stadium was occupied that night by the Newark Bears. *New Journal and Guide* sportswriter Lem Graves, Jr., predicted an Eagles win in six games. The Eagles' "potent bats" and the "clever hurling of Max Manning, Leon Day, and Rufus Lewis should," Graves continued, "decide the argument in Newark's favor in spite of the unquestioned brilliance of Satchel Paige."[14]

As expected, Day took the mound for the Eagles in game one. Not only had his stellar pitching, 11 league wins to 4 losses, contributed to the Eagles' success, but he was the team's leading hitter connecting for a .431 average with 58 at bats in 24 games. Uncharacteristic wildness on Day's part resulted in several Monarch walks and hits in the first inning, but spectacular plays by Irvin, Doby, and Pearson limited the damage to just one Monarch run. Day lasted until the fifth inning holding the Monarchs scoreless. Rufus Lewis, a native of Hattiesburg, Mississippi, had won six while losing only one game for the Eagles, relieved Leon. He held the Monarchs to just one more run, but that was enough to give the Kansas City nine a 2–1 victory.

The teams played game two again at night in Ruppert Stadium, where World Heavyweight Boxing Champion Joe Louis, in town for a bout against the Italian challenger Tami Mauriello, which Louis won easily the previous night in Yankee Stadium, threw out the ceremonial first ball. Thanks to four singles off Satchel Paige, two Monarch errors, Doby's 400-foot, two-run shot over the right field fence off starter Hilton Smith, who hailed from Giddings, Texas, and was considered by many to be as good as Paige, the Eagles overcame a 4–1 deficit to win the game 7–4. Games three and four were played at the Monarchs' home field, Blues Stadium. With 15 runs and 21 hits, the Monarchs prevailed in game three. The Eagles easily took game four behind 14 hits and 8 runs to the Monarch's 1 run.

Then it was on to Chicago's Comiskey Park. Eagles hurler Max Manning and the Monarchs' Hilton Smith both went the distance. Smith and the Monarchs won the game 4–1. Down three games to two,

Chapter 14. He's Back and Rarin' to Go

An unused bleacher ticket to game one of the 1946 Negro Leagues World Series between the Newark Eagles and the Kansas City Monarchs. Day started the game but did not finish it (courtesy Huggins and Scott Auction House, Lot 688, summer 2004).

Biz Mackey, Eagles manager once again, gave the ball to Leon for game six at Ruppert Stadium. Day again suffered control problems, had to be relieved but stayed in the game in center field where he robbed Buck O'Neil of a potential game-winning triple with an over-the-shoulder catch on the dead run.[15]

Day's catch remained a vivid memory for O'Neil. "As I rounded first," he recounted in his 1996 biography, *I Was Right on Time*, "I began thinking I might have an inside the park homer. Leon Day, however, was on his horse.... I don't know how he did it, but he ran that ball down and made an amazing catch, better even than the one Willie Mays made on Vic Wertz in the 1954 World Series. Everyone on our bench just stood there, their mouths hanging open. Leon Day had saved the day for Newark."[16]

Lenial Hooker, a Stanford, North Carolina, native who had mastered the knuckleball, relieved Day. The hard-luck right-hander spent his entire Negro Leagues career, 1940–48, with the Eagles losing many a one-run game. Nonetheless, he maneuvered the Eagles to a 9–7 victory helped by two round-trippers off the bat of Monte Irvin.[17]

The seventh and deciding game took place in Ruppert Stadium on September 29, 1946, under partly cloudy skies with temperatures

in the mid–'60s. Day's contribution came not from the mound but from another running, over-the-shoulder catch in deep left center field of a ball slammed again by Buck O'Neil in the third inning. Rufus Lewis went the distance for the Manleys' team. John Ford Smith, a former army lieutenant, not related to teammate and eventual Hall of Fame Monarchs pitcher Hilton Smith, did the same for the Monarchs. The outcome was in doubt until the top of the ninth when the Monarchs, behind 3–2, had the tying and winning runs on second and third base with two outs. Effa Manley, watching from the grandstand with head down, eyes closed, arms crossed, unable to watch the action on the field, heard what she described as "the sickening sound of a bat hitting a ball." Monarchs third baseman Herb Souell caused the sound with a pop-up to Eagles first baseman Lennie Pearson. Effa sighed with relief. Cheering well-wishers surrounded her. The Eagles were finally champions of the Negro Leagues.

Things might have turned out

Left: **Pictured here is a World Series ring presented to each member of the World Champion 1946 Newark Eagles. This ring was presented to Cecil Cole, a right-handed pitcher whose only season in Negro Leagues baseball was 1946 (courtesy Hunt Auctions, Lot 760, March 7 and 8, 2008).**

Chapter 14. He's Back and Rarin' to Go

differently had Hilton Smith and Satchel Paige been available for game seven. Both had jumped the Kansas City team for Satchel Paige's All-Stars for the start of a historic nationwide barnstorming tour of Negro Leagues stars against the Cleveland Indians' Hall of Fame pitcher Bob Feller's team of players from the National and American Leagues.[18]

Along with the championship had come another profitable year for the Manleys. Attendance had been stronger than ever. With their profits the Manleys gave each player a ring with an intricately designed Eagle and an inset solitary .45 carat diamond on top. They bought the team a new Stratoliner bus for $15,000 that sat 23 people much more comfortably than did the old bus which often broke down between cities. "Newark Eagles Baseball Club" proudly graced each side of the team's new transport.

Chapter 15

Uneven Progress in Race Relations

THE PAIGE-FELLER GAMES, in addition to adding to players' incomes, demonstrated that Blacks and whites, both as players and spectators, could get along just fine, at least north of the Mason-Dixon Line. Feller's team was all white. Paige's team was all Black. Both had players of exceptional talent. Feller's players included four eventual Hall of Famers—himself, Bob Lemon, Stan Musial, and Phil Rizzuto—plus first baseman Mickey Vernon, who had won the 1946 American League batting crown. Paige's team featured two Hall of Famers—himself and Hilton Smith—and standout players such as Max Manning and Buck O'Neil. Had it not been for his sore arm, Day would have undoubtedly been on Paige's team. Jackie Robinson played the first three games for Paige's all-stars but left to form his own barnstorming team that included Monte Irvin, Roy Campanella, and Larry Doby, all three future Hall of Famers.

As Feller put it after the tour, "We played on equal terms. They didn't train like we did, but they were no better or no worse than the best major leaguers." Feller's all-stars went 11–5 against Paige's. No games were scheduled south of the Mason-Dixon Line in deference to the hostility expected from many whites who might strenuously object to Blacks and whites on the same field. Black spectators, however, did join white spectators in large numbers to see "the games between the races" without any reported incidents occurring on the field or in the stands as exemplified by the mixed-race crowd of 27,403 at an October 6 game at Yankee Stadium where Paige's all-stars shut out Feller's 4–0.[1]

A novel feature of the tour was the mode of transportation. Each team used a DC-3 that Feller had rented from the Flying Tigers Airline. "Bob Feller All-Stars" graced both sides of the fuselage of one while "Satchel Paige All-Stars" appeared on the other.

Chapter 15. Uneven Progress in Race Relations

Flying had been used only sparingly in the past and was considered so dangerous that some owners paid their stars to stay home. Tom Yawkey paid Ted Williams $10,000 to fish rather than fly. Detroit Tigers owner Spike Briggs shelled out the same amount to southpaw Hal Newhouser to stay home. The lefty had averaged 27 wins in the previous three seasons.²

The wisdom of the decision to play the games north of the Mason-Dixon Line became apparent during the Eagles' 1946 southern barnstorming tour in their new bus. As the bus passed a truck in Mississippi, they heard a white farmer call out, "Golly, look at the jigaboos." "Your mother didn't think so last night," Lennie Pearson yelled back through an open window. "We almost killed him," Irvin recalled. "Let 'em say whatever they want," Irvin told Pearson. Mackey stepped to the window and called out, "Ok. Anything you say." Mackey, Irvin, and the others wanted to prevent the farmers alerting the Ku Klux Klan or state troopers to Pearson's remark.³

Newark Moves Forward

The year 1946 also saw signs of racial progress in New Jersey. On January 3, 1946, a contentious meeting of Newark's city commissioners resulted in the long-sought appointment of a Black physician to the City Hospital. Dr. Mae McCarroll joined the staff. A graduate of Fisk University, the Women's Medical College of Pennsylvania, and Columbia University, she had long fought for such an appointment. "I am pleased," she said, "to represent the beginning of greater opportunities for Negro physicians in our city." Thirty-eight years later, in 1984, she and a colleague, Dr. Aaron Haskin, were honored for their medical contribution to the city when the city's new health building was dedicated as the Haskin-McCarroll Building.

The year 1946 was also when the YMCA's camp in Andover, New Jersey, was opened to all boys. Black youngsters previously had been limited to the all-Black Camp Osceola outside of Trenton.

Other dents in Newark's segregated state included an increase in jobs for Blacks as switchboard operators, clerks, stenographers, installers, coin collectors, and technicians with the city's telephone company. A sorority started by 14 white girls at Upsala College, a private school

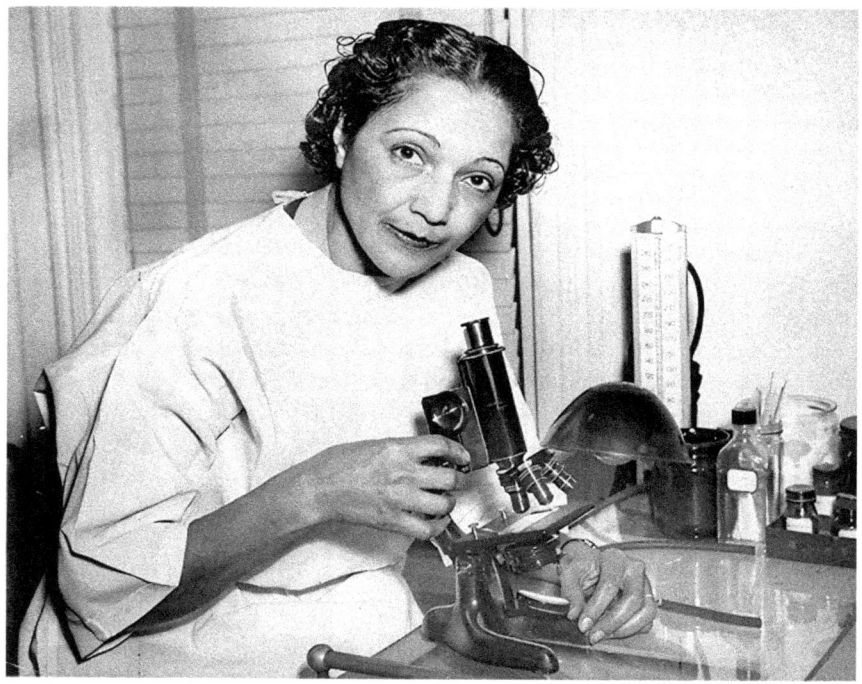

Dr. Mae McCarroll, the first Black physician appointed to Newark's City Hospital, at work (author's collection).

in East Orange, took as its mission abolishing discrimination in college sororities. A new state constitution included a clause banning discrimination in citizens' civil or military activities and in public schools. The *Philadelphia Tribune* hailed the statement as "a new emancipation clause." It took two days "of heated debate" for the clause to be approved by a 51–18 vote of convention delegates.[4]

The new clause took several years to have its desired effect. Pan Ye Woo, proprietor of the Far Eastern Restaurant in Newark's Third Ward, successfully appealed a judge's ruling in July 1948 that two customers were entitled to $100 each because they were refused service in a section reserved for whites and ordered into "a section set aside for colored patrons." Two years later, a waiter snatched menus from the hands of two Black customers, telling them they had to join the restaurant's club before they could be served. Asked how to join the club, the waiter said

Chapter 15. Uneven Progress in Race Relations

they'd have to see the manager. "Where is he?" the two asked. "He's out," the waiter replied. The two filed a complaint with the New Jersey Division Against Discrimination which ordered Pan Ye Woo to cease discriminating against Black patrons. The division ordered the owner to inform, by letter, those who had filed similar complaints that the club policy had been discontinued. At a December 1950 mass meeting of the Camden, New Jersey, NAACP chapter, Harold Lett of the division hailed the policy change as proof "the Civil Rights Law has teeth."[5]

Chapter 16

Two Seasons in Mexico

AFTER A TWO-AND-A-HALF-YEAR absence from Negro Leagues baseball, Day, in addition to his no-hit 1946 opening day masterpiece, had acquitted himself as the once-again ace of the Eagles' pitching staff. He posted the team's best pitching record for the 1946 campaign with 13 wins and only 2 losses. He garnered 109 strikeouts, 42 more than runner-up Max Manning's 67.[1] His wildness during the World Series, however, left some, including him, wondering if his arm was losing strength. He returned home after the series without any baseball plans.

An unexpected visit from Ray Dandridge put his wondering to rest. Jorge Pasquel had deputized Day's former teammate to sign players of his choosing for the Mexican League 1947 summer season. Day was first on Dandridge's list.

Leon demurred at first, saying, "I can't go down there. My arm is bad." "Come on down and make some of this money," Dandridge replied. Dandridge offered him $5,000. That, compared with the $2,400, $600 a month for four months, with the Eagles gave Day renewed confidence in his arm.[2] Leon and battery mate Leon Ruffin, who had a similar offer, first wanted to check with Effa to see if she'd match Pasquel's offer. "I can't pay that kind of money," she told them. When asked why she couldn't, she said, "If Mexico took Mickey Owens from Brooklyn, Feldman from the Giants, and Max Lanier from St. Louis, how do you expect me to keep them from taking Day and Ruffin from me?"[3] Leon left for Mexico the next day for what would be two summer seasons with the Mexico City Red Devils.

Shortly after arriving, Leon's doubts about his arm proved to be well founded. "I couldn't hardly throw a strike," he told Riley. "It looked like the plate moved on me. I could always throw a strike before, so I knew it was my arm. It had to be my arm." In an interview with William Marshall, researcher for the Louie B. Nunn Center for Oral History, University of Kentucky Libraries, Day said the atmosphere, being

Chapter 16. Two Seasons in Mexico

thinner at Mexico's higher elevation than Newark's was a problem for him. "It [his curveball] wouldn't break as much as it should you know and that's the air. A fast ball wouldn't hop."

Arm trouble and the atmosphere no doubt contributed to his mediocre performance on the mound. In 1947 he won 10 while losing 11 with one shutout to his credit. His arm caused him no problem at the plate in 1947. He pounded the ball for a hefty .359 average. The following year, with his arm still bothering him, he won eight and lost nine with an uncharacteristically high 4.34 earned run average while recording only 29 strikeouts. One victory was a 2–0 win over the first-place Monterrey Industriales bringing a halt to their six-game victory streak. His batting average fell almost 90 points to .270.[4] In the end, however, he was pleased he went, sore arm and all.[5]

In the middle of the 1947 season, a rare reference to Day's wife appeared in the press. An account of a letter received by the *Pittsburgh Courier* "from Boston's Doris and Norman Harris who are doing Mexico in the grand manner," noted that Mr. and Mrs. MacDaniels (*sic*) as well as Mr. and Mrs. Leon Day had attended a party at Mexico City's fashionable Hotel Calvin. The writer explained that "Mrs. MacDaniels' [*sic*] and Mrs. Day's hubbies are playing baseball." Mrs. McDaniels' hubby was Booker McDaniels, a right-handed power pitcher, who had occasional control problems during his six-year Negro Leagues career with the Monarchs.[6] Little else could be found about Mrs. Day or the Days' marriage.

Day enjoyed his quarters in Mexico City. "We had a beautiful apartment on Budapest Street," he told Marshall. He was a celebrity. "Don't care where you went," he told Marshall, "somebody knew you. Couldn't go in a bar and sit down you know.... You couldn't get away from it. You had to hide. They knew you."

Travel around Mexico was by bus, train, and plane. Day didn't like traveling by bus considering it "hazardous 'cause sometimes the buses would go over. We worried about the bus going over." Trains were known to slip off the rails on occasion including once pulling out of a stop in Guadalajara on the way to Mexico City. Day preferred flying. He and several players once managed to fly to Monterrey while the rest of the team left Mexico City the night before for the 600-mile train ride.[7]

Chapter 17

A Mixed Blessing

A LONG-AWAITED MOMENT for Black baseball's players, writers, and fans occurred on April 18, 1946, when Jackie Robinson took the field for the Montreal Royals, a Brooklyn Dodgers farm club, against the Jersey City Giants at the Giants' Roosevelt Stadium in Droyers Point in Jersey City. Robinson's was the first appearance of a Black player in "organized baseball" since the color bar had been established.

Typical of the many plaudits he received was one from James Malloy, director of the National Maritime Union. Malloy's telegram read, "Every time you sock the old apple it is a blow against Jim Crow and all its Fascist manifestations. Remember, we seamen are behind you."[1]

The next year, while Day was in Mexico, Robinson cracked the National League's color bar. His appearance at first base on opening day 1947 with the Brooklyn Dodgers led to major changes in the National and American Leagues, the Negro Leagues, and Pasquel's Mexican operation. Larry Doby, a teammate of Day with the Eagles, was the second player of color to crack the color bar when he signed with the Cleveland Indians in July 1947. Others, including Hank Aaron and Roy Campanella, soon followed.

Black fans started deserting Negro League parks for National and American League stadiums. Star Black players became more hesitant about jumping to the Mexican and other Latin American leagues. Monte Irvin, for instance, told Pasquel before the 1947 summer Cuban season began, he'd consider returning to Mexico but first wanted to see how Robinson would make out, and if more Negro Leaguers would be signed to National and American League contracts. A disbelieving Pasquel told Irvin, "I don't think that Jackie will make it. I don't think they're really sincere about bringing you guys into baseball." Irvin bet Pasquel $5 Jackie would be in the 1947 Dodger lineup. We know who won that wager.[2] As more Blacks appeared in National and American

Chapter 17. A Mixed Blessing

League uniforms, fewer up-and-coming stars of color like Irvin and Campanella opted for Latin American leagues.[3]

As the talent pool in Latin America grew thinner, the Negro Leagues continued to feel the financial pinch of fewer people in the stands. The six-team Negro National League dissolved in December 1948. The Eagles, New York Black Yankees, and the longtime champions Homestead-Washington Grays dropped out of the league. The remaining three Negro National League teams—New York Cubans, Elite Giants, and Philadelphia Stars—were absorbed by the Negro American League.[4] At the end of the 1948 season, two Houston businessmen, Dr. W.H. Young and Hugh Cherry, bought the Newark Eagles franchise including uniforms, gear, and the new Stratoliner bus. The two men moved the team to Houston, Texas.

Upon returning home from Mexico at the end of the 1948 summer season and learning of the sale, Day was none too pleased. "That was about the end of it," Leon told Riley years later. "They said they were gonna send me to Texas. I said I wasn't going to Texas. That was too far away from home. I didn't like the way the man talked saying I had to go. I told them I wasn't going and they traded me to the Elites [the Baltimore Elite Giants]." In return the Houston club got the Elites ace hurler Jonas "Lefty" Gaines who had just finished a successful ten-year stint with the Elite Giants. Leon was pleased with the trade. It allowed him to stay on the East Coast not far from his New Jersey home, return to the city where he grew up, and continue playing with a professional team—one that would do quite well in 1949, as it turned out.[5]

The Numbers Game

While the Baltimore Elite Giants would shine in the 1949 season, the same could not be said for many low-income Baltimore residents. Many jobs created to meet the needs of World War II had been eliminated in the four years since the end of the war. As a result, the "numbers games," for years a popular pursuit among both Blacks and whites, gained in popularity in the Queen City among those down on their luck. For a nickel or dime investment, big profits were possible. The odds ran as high as 500–1. A nickel bet could net a player $25. Whites controlled the games in South and East Baltimore while Blacks ran the games in Baltimore's Old West neighborhood. Referred to as "bankers," a game organizer could take in $3,000–$5,000 a day for a daily citywide take in 1947 of about $50,000. Today we know numbers games as state government-run lotteries such as Mega Millions and Powerball. In 1947 there was no government oversight. The games were illegal.

To play, one picked a three-digit number and bet the number with a "writer" who recorded it, gave the bettor a receipt, and gave the money and a copy of the receipt to a "pickup" man at a designated place and time. The pickup man took all monies and receipts to a banker's place of business. That could be an office, kitchen table, or dining room. "Lookout" men kept a careful watch for police, both uniformed and undercover. Bankers agreed to use the race results at an East Coast racetrack to determine the winning number. They noted the pari-mutuel payouts for the horses that finished 1–2–3 in a particular race. If, for instance, the payoffs were 26.30 for win, 29.70 for place, and 22.00 for show and the bankers agreed to use the number in the unit place, the winning number would be 692. Bets could be in any amount, though most were of the nickel and dime variety. The banker paid the winning player or players, if any, compensated his helpers, and pocketed what was left.

By one account, bankers were "ardent sports fans, who dressed flashily, carried wads of money, owned sporty automobiles, and threw money away on fast women." Retired Old West entrepreneur Clarence Brown described the risks, which were substantial. "You could get locked up," he said in 2006. "You only wrote numbers for people you thought you knew. No whites—they were undercover police. Then they put a Negro on the police force and they'd bust you. It was a $500.00 fine for the first time and $1,000 for twice."[6]

Day's Last Negro Leagues Stop, Baltimore

Day avoided the temptation of games of chance and stuck to baseball. By May 1949, the now 33-year-old was a Baltimore Elite (pronounced "Ee-lite") Giant. Popularly known as "the well-traveled Elite Giants," the team's arrival in Baltimore in the spring of 1938 marked the end of a long search for a dependable fan base and financial stability. Before Baltimore, the team's stops had included Nashville, Tennessee; Columbus, Ohio; Detroit, Michigan; and Washington, D.C. Initiated on

Chapter 17. A Mixed Blessing

January 7, 1921, at a meeting of team officials in Nashville, Tennessee's Elite Pool Room, 38-year-old president and owner Thomas "Smiling Tom" T. Wilson had renamed the Nashville Standard Giants, a semipro team he had founded in 1918, the Nashville Elite Giants. The name "Giants" indicated, in the vernacular of the day, that it was a "colored" team.[7]

No longer touted in the press as a team's ace hurler, younger hurlers now laid claim to that title, but still a sturdy performer, Day was included in a listing of several Elite "first-string mounds men." He shared the Elite Giants spotlight with Joe Black, who would soon be a Brooklyn Dodger, Bob Romby, a hard-hitting first baseman as well as the team's only left-handed pitcher, and pitchers Bill Byrd, Al Wilmore, Leroy Ferrell, and Sylvester Rodgers.[8]

Although he pitched infrequently, Day still swung a bat with authority. He connected for a ninth-inning game-winning homer against the Chicago American Giants in game one of a mid–June Sunday doubleheader. Elites manager Jesse "Hoss" Walker, who had assumed the Elites' managerial reins in 1948 after a steady if not spectacular career as an infielder with several teams, had substituted Day in center field that day for Henry Kimbro, a talented outfielder who played 13 seasons with the Giants, had sprained his ankle.[9] Day's bat was again the deciding factor in a 13–12 win in a late–August game against the Stars at Bugle Field. Inserted as a pinch hitter in the seventh inning with the tying and winning runs on base, Leon came through with a bloop single into right field scoring both runners. Playing third base in a game against the Birmingham Black Barons, Leon laid down "a clever bunt" to score starting pitcher Al Wilmore from third and later in the game drove Wilmore in again with a clean single to left field.[10]

Day's pitching had its ups and downs when he did take the mound in 1949. Four hits by the Indianapolis Clowns in the fourth inning of an early May game sent him to the bench. A week later he showed off his familiar form going the distance to beat the Philadelphia Stars 3–2 while connecting for two of the Giants' seven hits. In early June, Memphis Red Sox pitcher Jim Hutchinson, near the end of an 11-year career with the Sox, outpitched Day for the win. Day lost a squeaker 1–0 against the Birmingham Black Barons. Barons catcher Lloyd "Pepper" Bassett's solo homer was the difference. Bassett carried the nickname "Rocking Chair" for his habit of catching several innings seated in a rocking chair. In another June game, Day came through in spectacular fashion with a solo ninth-inning game-winning 352-foot homer to break a 3–3 tie to give pitcher Bill Byrd a 4–3 win.[11]

The rest of the Elites played superbly. The Giants finished first in both halves of the 1949 season to win the newly formed Eastern Division's title of the Negro American League. The Kansas City Monarchs, the Western Division entry, bested the Chicago American Giants in a five-game playoff series to take the Western Division title. Monarchs owner Tom Baird, however, withdrew his team from the series due to injuries to star players and the loss of two players to the National and American Leagues. Baird's decision left the Chicago American Giants to face the Baltimore Elite Giants in the World Series.

Games one and two were scheduled for September 16 and 17 in Baltimore. Richmond, Virginia, later changed to Norfolk, Virginia, and Chicago's Comiskey Park would host games three and four. Additional games would be scheduled as needed. The *Black Dispatch* of Oklahoma City gave the Baltimore Giants the edge, citing the fact that five starters were hitting over .300. The paper listed Leon, batting .271, as a utility player.[12]

The *Black Dispatch*'s prediction was spot-on. The Baltimore Giants swept the Chicago American Giants in four straight games 9–1, 5–4, 8–4, and 4–2. Leon's contribution in the final game was a decisive two-run double to right center–scoring Lennie Pearson and Butch Davis.[13]

While the Elite players were elated, little public enthusiasm was displayed in Baltimore. There were no parades or celebrity-laced trophy presentations. Only the players lived it up after the final game. First baseman Clinton "Butch" McCord remembered, "Some had some beer. We didn't throw the beer on each other. We drank the beer. I drank OJ [orange juice]." Leon Day's name didn't appear in the press accounts of the series.[14]

Beginning of the End

For those rooting for Black players to be welcomed to the National and American Leagues, 1949 was a banner year. As of October 1, 1949, Jackie Robinson, in his third year with the Dodgers, led the National

Chapter 17. A Mixed Blessing

League in batting and stolen bases. Sam Jethroe, initially with the Dodgers' Montreal Royals farm club, was signed by the Boston Braves with whom he won the Rookie of the Year Award in 1950. Hank Thompson and Monte Irvin patrolled the New York Giants' outfield. Larry Doby, Luke Easter, and Satchel Paige were wearing Cleveland Indians uniforms. Other former Negro Leaguers, including the Elites' Joe Black and Junior Gilliam, were soon to be in the minors on their way to the bigs. As an *Afro-American* writer put it, "we can look back at 1949 with pardonable pride. It was really great."[15]

Great, yes, but also the not-so-faint rumblings of the death knell for the Negro Leagues. Attendance fell off precipitously as thousands of Black fans flocked to National and American League parks to see players who looked like them. Mike Royko of the *Chicago Daily News* captured Blacks' pride at those games in his description of the scene at Wrigley Field when the 1947 Brooklyn Dodgers, with Jackie Robinson on board, made their first trip to the Windy City. Royce saw "blacks coming by the thousands, pouring off the northbound Els and out of their cars. They didn't wear baseball game clothes. They had on church clothes and funeral clothes: suits, white shirts, ties, gleaming shoes, and straw hats. A tall, middle-age black man that sat next to me had a smile of almost painful joy on his face. He beat his palms together so hard they must have hurt."[16]

Not everyone, however, in Negro Leagues baseball looked at 1949 with pride. McCord bemoaned the plight encountered by Blacks attending those games. "You had black fans riding segregated trains, eating segregated sandwiches, and staying in segregated hotels. They sat," he continued, "in the bleachers 'cause they couldn't sit in the stands." Effa Manley was mad. After selling the Newark Eagles in 1948, she put her frustration and disapproval on public display. "Negro fans have deserted the Negro team because a few players get four cents more and the white teams have put their stamp of approval on them," she railed. Three hundred people, she feared, would lose their jobs. Adulation of Blacks in the National and American Leagues by Blacks was for Effa a sign of a Black inferiority complex that she had striven mightily to eradicate.[17]

During these turbulent times Leon was one of many Blacks who would play in the minor leagues but not make it to the show. When asked a week before he died if he regretted never donning a major league uniform, he replied, "You're crazy. I played in the Majors. I don't know if the white major leaguers could have played in our leagues."[18]

Integration in Baltimore

Integration was inching forward in Baltimore and its environs with much the same effect as that occurring in Negro Leagues baseball. Baltimore's Black professionals—doctors, teachers, lawyers, dentists, morticians, entrepreneurs, and entertainers—started moving to the suburbs, leaving behind the remains of what once had been a vibrant Black community, Old West. The York Hotel, home to many Elite Giants, disappeared. The Shake and Bake Family Fun Center took the spot where the Regent Theater, an entertainment centerpiece on Pennsylvania Avenue, once stood. Many sites that were earlier home to restaurants and clubs became public housing projects. A statue of jazz singer Billy Holiday, a Baltimore native, stands today on Pennsylvania Avenue near where the Royal Theater once stood as mute testimony to the neighborhood's illustrious past.[19]

Little progress toward integration in Maryland's or Baltimore's workplaces had occurred. Several legislatures in other states—New Mexico, New Jersey, Washington, and Rhode Island—had passed laws banning discrimination in the workplace. Connecticut, Illinois, Wisconsin, New York, and New Jersey had outlawed discrimination in their National Guard units. A resolution introduced by Albert L. Sklar, a Black member of the Maryland House of Delegates, to merely study discrimination in state agencies died a quiet death in the House Committee on Licensing Boards and Commissions.

Exceptions could be found in Baltimore if one looked hard for them. John Caitlin was granted a plumbing license in December 1949 by the State Board of Plumbing which had denied his earlier applications in 1941 and 1946. Caitlin gave as a reason for his success a change in the board's membership. In a similar vein, the Baltimore branch of the NAACP succeeded in getting William Holden a job as a bricklayer on a YMCA building under construction. Holden was previously denied the job.[20]

The 1948 Baltimore mayoral election saw Democrat Thomas D'Alessandro, Jr., father of future speaker of the U.S. House of

Chapter 17. A Mixed Blessing

Representatives Nancy Pelosi, defeat Republican mayor Theodore McKeldin, a civil rights advocate who broke new ground with his appointment of Blacks to key positions in the city. D'Alessandro pledged to continue McKeldin's work. In a speech to the Advertising Club of Baltimore, he called for an end to racial and religious intolerance.[21]

Racial intolerance had declined but not disappeared. A young Black boy was pulled from a line of children waiting to see Santa Claus. Whites violently opposed Blacks buying into their neighborhood even though the Supreme Court in *Shelley v. Kraemer*, in 1948, ruled 9–0 that restrictive real estate covenants preventing the sale of properties to minorities were unconstitutional.[22]

The court's ruling may have had a positive effect on race relations in the Fulton Avenue area of Old West. Whites and Blacks were living peaceably together a month after the court's ruling. Four years earlier, white residents had demanded that McKeldin put an end to the "block busting" caused by Black war workers and veterans buying homes in Fulton.[23]

Some downtown women's apparel stores refused to allow Blacks to try clothes on, a practice that lasted into the 1960s as Geraldine Day recalled. She said, "It was just what it was. You couldn't try on clothes. You could just buy them. Whites could do both. I'm a human being. My skin's a little darker, but they bleed just like I do, but it didn't make me want to kill somebody."[24]

A common attitude held by many whites toward Blacks was expressed by Matt Reinhold of Gallagher Realty Company. The lease on Bugle Field expired after the 1949 Giants' championship season ended. Powell was looking for a new park. Gallagher told Powell the company had a plot of land near Camden Yards, now home to the Baltimore Orioles, that "would be good enough for Negroes." Powell gave Reinhold the go-ahead to build a new facility named Westport Stadium. After seeing the finished product, Powell was less than pleased. "I can't find words to say how bad it was. It only looked like a baseball diamond. It had no infield grass, and a constant wind stirred up the grit."[25]

A more public expression of discrimination in baseball occurred when Baltimore's park board issued a ruling banning interracial play in the city's parks. By this time teams of all-Black players could occasionally use the city's facilities, but the board drew the line at games featuring players of both races. Just such a game was scheduled for April 27,

1950, at Baltimore's Herring Park. The game would feature an all-white Baltimore school team and one from York Junior College in Pennsylvania. Learning of the board's ban, officials of York Junior College (now York College of Pennsylvania) refused to keep their two Black players out of the game and canceled the affair. The "tan" players, shortstop Al Brown and left-handed hurler Ernie Hartzog, were pleased that teammates and school officials chose forfeiting the game over playing it without them.[26]

Baseball was not the only sport to feel the sting of discrimination in Baltimore in 1950. The National Catholic Intercollegiate Basketball Tournament, consisting of eight teams, had to find another city upon learning city hotels refused to accept Negro athletes. The *Chicago Defender* congratulated tournament officials for seeking another venue and sent "our worst wishes to the hotel operators of Baltimore."[27]

While segregation still reigned in Baltimore, instances of integration appeared elsewhere like young green shoots of vegetation on an arid land. The U.S. Naval Academy in Annapolis, Maryland, graduated its first Black cadet, Wesley A. Brown. The Pennsylvania Railroad ended its Jim Crow practices. The NAACP announced that 1 million Blacks had registered to vote in the South. U.S. Representative William Dawson of Chicago became the first Black to chair a congressional committee—the U.S. House Committee on Government Operations. Alabama's legislature ordered the unmasking of Ku Klux Klan members. The U.S. Department of Justice asked the Supreme Court to rule that segregation is discrimination, a successful harbinger of the court's unanimous 1954 decision, *Brown v. Board of Education*. State universities in Arkansas, Oklahoma, and Texas accepted a few "well-qualified" Black applicants to graduate programs. The Maryland court of appeals ruled that the University of Maryland must admit Baltimore's Esther McCready to its School of Nursing. In the world of baseball, the Brooklyn Dodgers with Jackie Robinson and Roy Campanella played white teams in the South but without the protests and canceled games that had marked previous such encounters. These, and similar events, in the words of *Chicago Defender* columnist Albert Barnett, show that "Negroes ... are slowly but surely breaking down the barriers of prejudice on many fronts."[28]

Chapter 18

More Baseball for Day

At age 33 and not ready for a "real job," he returned to Puerto Rico's winter league in the fall of 1949, this time in a Santurce Crabbers uniform. He pitched and played second base but, according to historian Thomas E. Van Hyning, "did not have his blazing stuff that he showed league fans in the late 1930's and early 1940's."[1] That would be his last appearance in Puerto Rico.

He returned to Baltimore in time for the 1950 Baltimore Elite Giants spring training held in Charlotte, North Carolina. Perhaps in silent acknowledgment of Van Hyning's observation, Day looked to win what the *Afro-American* called "a regular position instead of the once or twice a week duty as a hurler." His preferred "regular" positions had been second base and center field. At second he was facing stiff competition from James "Junior" Gilliam, a Nashville, Tennessee, native who broke into the Black leagues with the Nashville Black Vols at age 17 and hit .302 for the Elites in 1949. While Day was in Mexico for the 1947–48 seasons, Gilliam had replaced the Elites' starting second baseman Sammy T. Hughes at the keystone sack and with Tommy "Pee Wee" Butts, formerly of the Indianapolis ABCs and the Atlanta Black Crackers, and formed the league's best double-play combination. That left center field for Leon. He played several games there as an "outergardner," as outfielders were referred to, before being released, along with pitcher Bill Byrd, in mid–June 1950. "These fellows," Baltimore officials said, "were drawing salaries far in excess of their worth on the rapidly declining market of the day." Day's batting average had fallen to .190. His name rarely appeared in the press.[2] When it did, it was usually cited as just one of a cluster of hurlers. Wendell Smith, in a *Pittsburgh Courier* article describing the Elites' 1950 opening day roster, cited Day as one of nine pitchers who "form the hill crop."[3]

Oh, Canada

Leon quickly found an opportunity to continue playing, though the new location was over 1,200 miles from Newark, not quite as far away from home as the 1,600-mile trip to Houston would have been had he signed with the Houston Eagles. His opportunity came with the Manitoba-Dakota Baseball League, shortened to the ManDak League, based in Manitoba, Canada. The benefits were many.

The pay was better than that earned by the remaining Negro Leaguers. Salaries in the ManDak League ranged from $300 to $1,000 a month with each team limited to 16 players but no limit to the number of players from beyond Canada. A short season of 48 league games and a liberal mindset in Manitoba added to the appeal. "Negro Leagues players went to Canada," baseball writer Kyle McNary said, "where the seasons were short, the pay was good, and minds were liberal."[4]

Wilmer Fields, a star pitcher for the Homestead Grays for eight seasons (1940–42, 1946–50), agreed. "There was," he said, "no comparison between the treatment we received in Canada and the treatment we received in Latin America. In Canada, it was like a home away from home. In Latin American countries, everything was business. The Canadian people also wanted ballplayers that represented their city and their community off the field as well as on the field. It was a good feeling. The people there accepted my family with so much enthusiasm that our stay there was the finest we ever experienced anywhere but at our home."[5] Marvin Ligon, namesake of the barnstorming Ligon Colored All-Stars, who arrived in Canada driving a bus with Texas plates, in the '40s and '50s remembered, "We could stay in the hotels without any problems in Canada. A black face was somewhat unique out there on the prairies. We'd go into areas where they had never seen one, and so they were coming out to see the black faces as much as the baseball game."[6]

In addition to former Negro Leaguers, players came from the Pacific Coast League and top minor league clubs. Many of the Negro Leaguers, including four Hall of Famers—Day, Willie Wells, Satchel Paige (who made one three-inning appearance), and Ray Dandridge—were at or near the end of their careers. Barry Swanton, a lifelong resident of Winnipeg who attended many ManDak games as a youngster with his father and authored *The ManDak League*, fondly remembered the Negro Leaguers. "After the game," he said, "we would hang around

Chapter 18. More Baseball for Day

waiting for the players to come out so we could get their autographs. The ex–Negro Leaguers would always talk with us and sign autographs and not rush to get back to their hotels and rooming houses. My favorite was Leon Day. They always made time for us, and to this day, I remember that well." "The level of play," he said, "was similar to that in Class A or AA teams in organized baseball." Four of the five ManDak teams made the playoffs at season's end.[7] The league lasted from 1950 to 1957 when financial shortcomings caused the league to fold.

A liberal mindset in western Canada had preceded the ManDak League. A small group of Blacks who fled their Oklahoma homes in 1910 to escape racial discrimination found a Canadian welcome in the farming community of Athabasca, 870 miles northwest of Winnipeg in the neighboring province of Alberta. Athabasca was a small hamlet at the time of trappers, frontiersmen, and gold seekers. By 1950, the community numbered 400 people who had established a prosperous existence through growing wheat. Most farmers tilled 160 acres though some worked as many as 480 acres. Churches, schools, and a home for the aged had been built. Discrimination was a forgotten word. "We don't even know we are dark until we look in a glass," said one.[8]

The ManDak League was considered by many an "outlaw" league. It did not follow the provisions of any established professional baseball association. Rather, officials decided to adopt the constitution of the Southern Manitoba Baseball League. Players were allowed to, and often did without threats and fines from owners as was the case in the States, jump from team to team in a quest for higher pay and more playing time.

By the end of June 1950, Leon had joined former Negro Leaguers, notably Willie Wells; his son Willie Wells, Jr.; Andy Porter, one of the big three of the Elite Giants' pitching staff; Lyman Bostic, a solid-hitting first baseman who starred for the Chicago Giants and the Birmingham Black Barons; and Jimmy Newberry, former pitcher for the Birmingham Black Barons, on the Canadian ManDak League's Winnipeg Buffaloes, one of five teams in the newly formed league. The Minot Mallards were based in North Dakota. The Brandon Greys, Carmen Cardinals, and Winnipeg Elwood Giants, like the Buffaloes, were based in Manitoba. The Buffaloes were the only all-Black team.[9]

Stanley Zedd, white, of stocky build, and a sharp dresser, whose trademark cigar was ever-present, owned the Buffaloes. A colorful

The ManDak League's Winnipeg Buffaloes, the league's only all-Black team. This photograph was taken after Day joined the team, circa July 1950. Back row, from left: Smokey Harrison (trainer), Andy Porter, Taylor Smith, Joe Taylor, B. Haverstock (trainer). Middle row, from left: Leon Day, Johnny Britton, Samuel Hill, Jimmy Newberry, Lyman Bostic. Front row, from left: Percy Howard; Willie Wells, Jr.; Stanley Zedd (owner); Willie Wells, Sr. (manager); Jack Hector (club secretary); John Kennedy; Lomax Davis; Ernest Cantor. Front, Hutch Hutchinson (batboy) (courtesy attheplate.com).

Chapter 18. More Baseball for Day

figure, he was the kingpin of illegal gambling, crap games, and bookie operations in Winnipeg. A successful businessman, he owned the Margaret Rose Tea Room, an upscale restaurant. Police occasionally raided the gambling games. Zedd paid a small fine each time and was back in business the next night. Officers found Christmas turkeys delivered to them by a Zedd associate. One officer said of the owner, "He was a most honorable and generous criminal." He also sponsored several minor league hockey and baseball teams.[10]

The Buffaloes played their home games at Osborne Stadium which opened on May 19, 1932, with 4,000 permanent seats and subsequently expanded to 7,000 seats. Floodlights allowed for night games. A multisport facility, the stadium hosted softball, football, and soccer games in addition to ManDak League games. Barnstorming Negro Leagues teams used the stadium on their treks through Canada. A three-game series in July 1952 between the Memphis Red Sox and the Chicago American Giants played before 3,200 spectators was one example. The stadium was torn down in 1956 to make way for an insurance company's headquarters.[11]

Day had several memorable moments in Winnipeg. Shortly after arriving he teamed with player-manager Willie Wells in vehemently disagreeing with an umpire's call at first base. Both were ejected and fined, and the game was forfeited to the Mallards. In an early July game playing center field against the Brandon Greys, Day joined his teammates, in front of 1,000 shivering fans, in a barrage of 24 hits. Day had two doubles and two singles his first four times at bat. Left fielder Buster Davis slammed a homer, double, and a single good for five runs as the Buffaloes ran over the hapless Greys 22–6. On August 14, Leon showed his pitching prowess throwing a three-hit 9–0 shutout against the Minot Mallards. He struck out 11, walked only 1, gave up a mere 3 hits, and knocked in 3 runs with a bases-clearing double in the seventh inning. A reporter noted that Day, "one of the most versatile performers in the circuit, had the Mallards completely at his mercy."[12] Two weeks later he went 14 innings to finally subdue the same Mallards 12–9. He also stole a base. A week later, again against the Mallards, who no doubt were tired of facing him, Day gave up only five hits and drove home the winning run with a walk-off single in the bottom of the ninth to give the Buffaloes a 2–1 win and a two-game lead over the second-place Mallards. Manager Willie Wells assigned Day the fifth slot in the batting order, higher than a pitcher's traditional ninth position in the batting order.[13]

The Buffaloes took first place. Wells gave Day the ball in game one of a five-game championship series against the runner-up Brandon Greys in early September. Day struggled before a "far from full house" of 2,500 spectators at Osborne Field. After giving up three hits and six runs in 1⅔ innings and hitting a batter, Wells moved Day to second base and brought on Jimmy Newberry in relief. Day fared better at the plate, managing a double, a single, and two runs batted in. Newberry limited the Greys to just one more run while his mates, in a thrilling come-from-behind performance, plated nine scores to grab victory from certain defeat, 9–7. Newberry helped the Buffaloes win two more games to clinch the championship.[14]

Negro Leaguers were known to travel extensively as they changed teams. Newberry traveled farther than most. A native of Birmingham, Alabama, the owner of what he called his "dipsy-doodle" pitch, he arrived in Winnipeg after a nine-year career with his hometown Birmingham Black Barons. Although successful on the mound, excessive drinking contributed to a falling out with the Barons' president Tom Hayes. Failing to repay an advance from Hayes, Newberry jumped the Barons in June 1950 for the Buffaloes where he became the team's star pitcher. Hayes indefinitely suspended him from the Barons. The suspension mattered little to Newberry. After posting a 6–3 record with the Buffaloes in 1951, he jumped around the world to Japan for a year with the Hankyu Braves and an 11–10 record. Then it was back to the ManDak League and the Carmen Cardinals in 1953 with an unimpressive 5–10 record. He spent the next three years on five different minor league teams in the American Southwest.[15]

Leon started the fifth and deciding game of the 1950 championship series. He struck out eight, gave up six hits, hit no one, and walked none over the course of the 17 demanding innings it took for the Buffaloes to edge the Brandon Greys 1–0 for the ManDak League flag. The crowd, again only about 2,500, got its money worth and validated owner Zedd's preseason prediction that the Buffaloes "would roam and rule the prairies." At season's end, Day's won-loss record stood at 4–2. He stroked the ball for a .324 average and garnered a position on the *Winnipeg Tribune*'s all-star team as the utility player.[16]

The year 1951 found the aging right-hander back in Winnipeg. The

Chapter 18. More Baseball for Day

Buffaloes walloped the Brandon Greys 11–4 on opening day, May 19. Playing center field and garnering three hits good for three runs batted in, and a running catch of a ball destined for the center field fence, Day showed the fans he was still a first-rate player. A Saturday night crowd of 6,028 enjoyed the onslaught as well as the pregame ceremonies that included the awarding of last season's championship trophy to Zedd who introduced each Buffalo to the crowd.[17] A week later, Day was again ejected for arguing with an umpire's call in a game against the same Greys. On June 27, Leon, without challenging any umpire calls, went the distance against the Mallards throwing a 7–0 shutout and smashing a three-run homer over the left field wall.[18]

Although usually of mild demeanor, trouble came his way off the field when he and seven other Buffaloes were charged with disorderly conduct following an early morning "altercation." Each was fined $50 by the City of Winnipeg Police Court and an additional $50 by league officials. Another such charge, league officials warned the players, would result in a permanent suspension. There would be no more altercations or threats of suspension for Day. He would soon be off to another challenge and leave behind a 4–1 won-loss record and a batting average of .359 that included 3 homers and 20 runs batted in.[19]

Chapter 19

On to Organized Baseball

As Day and the other players were paying their fines, the rumor mill around the National and American Leagues had it that Bill Veeck, former owner of the Cleveland Indians among other franchises, was pursuing ownership of the American League St. Louis Browns. One of his first moves, the rumor continued, would be to sign Black players. After all Veeck, as owner of the Cleveland Indians, had previously signed players of color Larry Doby, Satchel Paige, Luke Easter, and Orestes (Minnie) Miñoso.

On July 4, 1951, Veeck, sporting a St. Louis Browns cap, confirmed part of the rumors. With the help of several financial backers, Veeck now owned the Browns. Days later, he met with Satchel Paige, then pitching for the Chicago American Giants of the American Negro Leagues and a previous employee of Veeck's Cleveland Indians. Paige denied any deal between the two at this time. He told a reporter for the *Philadelphia Tribune*, "I'm right here in the office with Mr. Veeck in Chicago and I should know about it." The reporter added, "A familiar look appeared in his [Paige's] eyes ... which usually indicates there is some truth in the statement."[1]

The scribe knew where of he spoke. Veeck convinced Paige to leave the Chicago Giants and sign with the Browns. Veeck then asked the Giants manager Winfield Welch, who held no ill will toward Veeck for taking Paige and was well thought of as a manager with a good eye for talent, to go to Canada and sign the best players there. The first player Welch signed was Leon Day.[2] In an interview in his YMCA room, Wells called Day "our bonus baby," saying he received an $800 signing bonus. Welch also signed four of Day's Buffalo teammates: pitcher James Newberry, infielders Johnny Kennedy and Charlie White, and outfielder Robert "Butch" Davis. Veeck said of them, "They are good players but far from major league uniforms right now." Only White made it to the National and American Leagues as a catcher for the Milwaukee Braves

Chapter 19. On to Organized Baseball

from 1954 to 1955. Veeck asked all to report to the (Toronto, Canada) Maple Leafs, a Triple A farm club of the Browns in the International League, but the Leafs signed only two, Day and White.

An article in the *Jacksonville (Illinois) Daily Journal* of July 11, 1951, announcing the players' departure from Winnipeg, displayed a bold, black line below the text saying, "Veeck didn't wait long to fulfill his promise [threat]."[3] Jacksonville, only 55 miles east of St. Louis, was no doubt the home of many listeners to broadcasts of the Brownies' games, not all of whom favored Black players.

The departure of the five Buffaloes was initially thought to be a devastating blow to the Buffaloes, but Zedd moved quickly to sign six replacement players from New Orleans, Baton Rouge, and Philadelphia to fill the void.[4] The replacements failed to help the Buffaloes to a second league championship. A disillusioned Zedd disbanded the team at the end of the 1951 season.[5]

The press, Black and white alike, took note of Day's and White's signing with the Leafs. Jim Vipond of Toronto's *Globe and Mail* devoted an entire column to the pair's arrival. He reminded his readers that he had argued for a year "that Negro players be acquired to help bolster a club hopelessly mired near the bottom of the second division."[6] Brief notices of the pair's signings appeared in papers in New York, Los Angeles, Kansas City, Philadelphia, and Chicago. Day was frequently misidentified in the press as "27-year-old 'Sonny' Day." He was actually 35 and never carried the nickname Sonny. He told Riley, "I went up about halfway through the season, and I didn't get to play much because they were trying to develop those young boys." When he did play, he was most often used as a relief pitcher.[7]

His first appearance in a Maple Leaf uniform came as a reliever in a scoreless, two-inning stint against the Buffalo Bisons on July 21, 1951.[8] He occasionally saw service in right and center field. One of his prominent offensive performances came in a July 23 game against the Syracuse Chiefs when, as a center fielder, he banged out three hits, including a double, to lead the Leafs to an 11–5 win.[9]

Day and White broke the Maple Leafs' color bar shortly after Jack Kent Cooke, the 40-year-old owner of newspapers and radio stations, had added the team to his stable of businesses on July 5, 1951. He put on promotions at Maple Leaf Stadium not unlike those masterfully produced and marketed by Bill Veeck. For the first game under his ownership, Cooke gave away sodas and hot dogs and hired a vocal quartet to entertain between innings. For other games, the new owner brought in actress Gloria DeHaven and musical comedian Victor Borge for appearances. After one of Borge's pregame performances, a foul ball hit him on his head as he sat in a field box. "See," the nonplussed comedian said, "I always use my head." In another promotion, Cooke hired a pole sitter who vowed to stay atop his perch until Toronto reached the first division.[10] How long the pole sitter sat is not known, but it could have been a while. The Leafs finished the 1951 season in fifth place in the eight-team league, an improvement over their seventh-place finish the year before. Cooke promised the ladies he'd give away nylons and washing machines "and do everything he can to make women fans because women control the purse strings."[11]

Cooke didn't ignore the more traditional attempts to attract fans by upgrading the roster. He soon signed a third African American, right-handed pitcher, Frank "Buster" Barnes, formerly of the Class A Muskegon (Michigan) Clippers.[12] The newly acquired pitcher put on a show for 5,400 fans when he allowed but four hits by the parent club St. Louis Browns in a 3–0 shutout in mid-August of 1951. The opposing pitcher, none other than Satchel Paige, went the distance and took the loss.[13] Unfortunately for Cooke, the contest was an exhibition game and didn't count in the standings. Barnes offered little help in league games, losing his only decision in two outings. He would have three "cups of coffee" with the parent club St. Louis Browns appearing in 15 innings over the course of the 1957, 1958, and 1960 seasons.[14]

After his time with the Leafs, Cooke moved to the States in 1961, acquired American citizenship, and among other investments, bought the Washington Redskins football team.[15]

Integration Gains in Toronto

Toronto presented a different mindset than the one in Winnipeg. At the same time that Day, White, and Barnes were integrating the Maple Leafs' roster, the legislature of Ontario, the Canadian province that is home to Toronto, was enacting laws outlawing discrimination in the workplace. Previous legislation had outlawed discrimination in advertising and real estate covenants, the latter designed to exclude

Chapter 19. On to Organized Baseball

minorities from purchasing land and homes. The new act focused on employment. It made discrimination "in respect to employment because of race, creed, color, nationality, ancestry, or place of origin" illegal. The legislation also established a process whereby a person could complain to the Ontario Labor Board where one's complaint would be heard and investigated. Ralph Matthews, a columnist for the *Cleveland Call and Post*, after pointedly noting that the voting power of Canada's "Negro" population is "infinitesimal" compared to that in America, suggested that Americans of all races "could go across the border and take a few lessons in the democratic process."[16]

Similar efforts were underway in the lower 48. President Harry S. Truman often and publicly stated his support for civil rights. He asked Congress in 1948 to fund and appoint a Fair Employment Practices Commission (FEPC). FDR had established a similar agency in 1941. The purpose of both was to address complaints of job discrimination. Congress reluctantly funded FDR's FEPC, which limped along until the end of World War II when two bills to make the committee permanent were defeated. The committee closed its doors in 1946 after having helped African Americans obtain 8 percent of defense industry jobs, up from 3 percent before the war. Southern senators objected to the committee's resurrection. Senator Richard B. Russell (D–GA), for instance, signaled a willingness to support anti–poll tax and anti-lynching legislation but adamantly opposed creation of another FEPC. Twenty years would elapse before the Equal Employment Opportunity Commission was established to fight discrimination at work.[17]

In the absence of federal support, some states and cities established antidiscrimination agencies. In one case involving National and American League baseball, the Philadelphia city council authorized a Fair Practices Employment Commission in 1950, headed by Dr. Frank S. Loescher, assistant professor of sociology at Temple University. Loescher thought the Phillies and Athletics to be fair game for investigation, saying both organizations were all white from top to bottom both on and off the field. All of the off-field personnel for both clubs—ticket sellers, ticket takers, ushers, refreshment sellers, and maintenance men—were white. He further noted that attendance went up substantially when teams with players of color came to Shibe Park in the City of Brotherly Love, thereby enhancing the coffers of each team. At the very least, Loescher said, the teams would have to explain their hiring practices in a public forum. No record of such an investigation could be found. Pitcher Bob Trice broke the color bar for the Athletics in 1953. John Kennedy followed suit for the Phillies five years later.[18]

On another front, the Supreme Court was hearing cases challenging the discriminatory practices of railroads. Blacks riding on lines of the Atlantic Coast Railroads, even those who purchased first-class tickets, were routinely forced to occupy seats reserved for "colored" patrons. Curtains were installed in dining cars to separate the races at mealtimes. In one particularly egregious case, seven women and one man with first-class tickets on a northbound Atlantic Coast Railroad train originating in Florida were forced to ride in the baggage car. The unheated car contained three coffins with remains, and the non-reclining seats were "excessively filthy, covered with grime, grease, and coal." The one toilet was "unsanitary, dirty, and repulsive." In November 1952, the Supreme Court ruled against such practices, defended by the railroad "as in keeping with the custom of the states in which the railroad operates."[19]

On the Decline

Day stayed with the Maple Leafs through the remainder of the 1951 season pitching in 14 games. In an August game, Leon, in a return to the Queen City, relieved starter Irvin Medlinger in the sixth inning as the Leafs suffered a 2–0 shutout at the hands of the International League Baltimore Orioles. Day pitched his first and only win for the Leafs against the Ottawa Little Giants in the second game of a doubleheader. Going the distance and locked in a 1–1 pitchers' duel with Pete Burnside, a 21-year-old southpaw with both promise and control problems. After several years in the minors, Burnside fashioned a pedestrian eight-year, 1955–63, career in the National and American Leagues winning 19 and losing 36. In this game, Day got the better of Burnside when in the seventh inning he singled in the winning run for a 2–1 victory. In his short stay with the Leafs, Leon batted .314 and had a 1–1 record on the mound.

He continued to play other positions. In a 10–2 loss to the Syracuse Chiefs, Leon started in right field, misplaying one ball, and then went to the mound in the fifth inning. He walked four, gave up four hits, and

Chapter 19. On to Organized Baseball

struck out just one. An earlier two-inning outing had been deemed "a respectable performance" by the Toronto papers.[20]

After Toronto, the right-hander opted for a warmer clime and more income. Leon signed on with Roy Campanella's All-Stars for a fall barnstorming tour of the South. Although Day never made the National and American Leagues, he got a good taste of life there playing with major leaguers Campanella, Monte Irvin, and Luke Easter, among others. In one game of note, he put in a stellar performance losing 1–0 in a pitching duel against Randy Gumpert of the Chicago White Sox pitching for Brooklyn Dodgers Gil Hodges' barnstormers. Day might have prevailed had Monte Irvin not been tagged out after straying too far from first base in the ninth inning with the bases loaded and Luke Easter due up.[21]

At the start of the 1952 season, after being released by the Maple Leafs, Day signed with the Eastern League's Class A Scranton (Pennsylvania) Miners, formerly a Boston Red Sox farm club; a New York businessman, Lou Baselice, purchased the Miners in the fall of 1951. Baselice struck up a working relationship with Veeck's St. Louis Browns, which no doubt led to Zack Taylor, the Browns' manager for the past four years, taking the Miners' managerial reins in 1952. Taylor's major claim to fame is implementing one of Veeck's best-known publicity stunts. It was Taylor who sent the midget, 3'7" Eddie Gaedel, to the plate on August 19, 1951, to lead off a game against the Detroit Tigers. Gaedel walked on four pitches, was replaced by a pinch runner, and was never heard from again.[22]

Taylor expressed satisfaction with most of his players as the 1952 season started. His biggest problem, he said, was pitching. Taylor named four of his hurlers "as showing the best form in the early going." Day was not among them. Day was included in a group of seven moundsmen that Taylor called "question marks."[23]

Used mostly as a reliever when pitching, the 36-year-old question mark gave some answers. On opening day in late April, he provided the margin of victory for the Miners with a run-scoring pinch-hit single in the tenth inning. Taking the mound in the ninth against the Williamsport Tigers with the bases loaded, he chalked up a save by retiring three in a row. In another game against the Tigers, he allowed but one hit in five innings of relief. The writer covering that game called Day "the Satchel Paige of Scranton." Another favorable comparison to Paige appeared in the *Sporting News* on June 25. The reporter noted,

"Leon Day," the 40-year-old Scranton hurler, is being referred to as "the Satchel Paige of the Eastern League. The right-handed Negro hurled 16⅔ relief innings [over several games], against Williamsport before yielding a run." The writer misstated Day's age—he was only 36—but he got the hurler's performance right. A two-inning appearance against the Reading Indians in which he yielded only "a scratch single" prompted this accolade from George Lyle, Jr., a sportswriter for the *Alabama Tribune* (Montgomery, Alabama): "He is still serving them up looking like peas to opposing batsmen.... Day ... won his own game with a single, 5–4." In a rare start, Day went the distance to notch a win against the Albany Senators.

Leon's age-tinted exploits earned him the moniker "Pappy" by a scribe for the *Plain Speaker* based in Hazelton, Pennsylvania. An article in the *Daily Gazette and Bulletin* (Williamsport, Pennsylvania) lauded "the old man of Scranton's mound staff" for his relief appearance which he ended by forcing the Williamsport Tigers' Jim Babcock to hit into a game-ending double play with the bases loaded before 775 spectators.

Things didn't always go his way. He walked in the winning run against the Binghamton Triplets in the eighth inning of a game, was the winning pitcher of record in a game against the Albany Senators, "although he toiled but one shaky stanza." In another game against the Senators, the usually dependable right-hander gave up two walks and hit a batter in the seventh inning before being relieved. More often than not, however, things did go his way. By late August, his won-lost record stood at 11–4. He encountered a bit of a slump from late August through the end of the season, finishing with a still-respectable 13–9 won-lost performance.[24]

Day was not the only Black member of the Miners. Right-hander Frank Barnes, ten years Day's junior, joined Leon for the 1952 season. A sportswriter for the *Daily Gazette and Bulletin* noted that Barnes "proved as troublesome to the Tigers as the Miner's other pitching ace Leon Day."[25]

After his release by the Miners and his winter days in Latin America behind him, Day signed up for another postseason hitch with Roy Campanella's All-Stars. The team again consisted of Black players like Monte Irvin, Harry "Suitcase" Simpson, Joe Black, Hank Thompson, George Crowe, and Larry Doby, as well as others from the minor leagues

Chapter 19. On to Organized Baseball

including the Minnesota State League, Canadian Provincial League, Pacific Coast League, and the Western International League.

Conditions in the South had evidently improved from those during the 1946 Paige-Feller tour. From early October to November 3, the All-Stars took on all comers, white and Black, in North Carolina, Tennessee, Alabama, Georgia, Arkansas, Mississippi, Louisiana, and Texas. High points for Day were a bases-loaded double to beat the Negro American League All-Stars 8–5 in a game in Shreveport, Louisiana, and teaming with Joe Black for a 6–0 shutout at Greenville, South Carolina. His four-bagger over the left field wall in the fourth inning gave Campy's nine a 2–0 lead.

Campanella's team outdrew the other four barnstorming teams active that fall. None of the four teams, managed by National and American League players Hal White, Eddie Lopat, Harry Walker, and Gene Bearden, attracted enough spectators to survive.[26]

Once Campanella's tour ended, Leon's thoughts turned back to Canada, but no team in the ManDak League expressed interest. Fortunately for Day, the Class A Edmonton (Washington) Eskimos of the Western International League in their first year of operation did. Eskimos general manager John Ducey announced the team had purchased Day's contract. After a short holdout for a higher salary, the Eskimos and Leon came to terms. In a sign of disrespect or ignorance, the *Lethbridge Herald* referred to him as "negro pitcher Leon Day."[27] In a May relief appearance shortly after he signed, he teamed with pitcher Larry Manler to give up nine hits to the Wenatchee Chiefs in a 4–0 loss.[23] Day went the distance in another game for a loss, his first as a starter, in early June.[29] In late June he was charged with his third loss after giving up four singles in the seventh inning to the Tri-City Braves. In between the June losses, he chalked up four wins as the "Eskies" went on what the local paper termed "a rampage."[30] He compiled a 5–5 won-lost record for the summer. In mid–August the Eskimos released him. The team disbanded a year later.[31]

Edmonton, where he was the only Black player on the team, was not as welcoming as Winnipeg and Toronto had been. He said of Winnipeg, "It was just as different as night and day in the United States. You could go any place you wanted." He said he was "treated alright" in Toronto. After a game in Edmonton, however, Day and a white teammate pitcher from Alabama, possibly Larry Manler, entered a bar across the street from the ballpark. Day told interviewer Marshall, "We get up to the bar, and he said 'give us two beers.'" "The bartender says, 'I can serve you but I can't serve him.'" Day's companion shot back, "What do mean you can't serve him?" "He," Day said, "was ready to fight," and I told him, "Come on, let's go." They left.[32]

The next year, 1954, the aging right-hander, now 38 and nearing the end of his remarkable career, returned to the ManDak League where he joined the Class A Brandon Greys for his last full season in professional baseball. He was used sparingly on the mound, at third base, and as a pinch hitter. He pitched only 11 innings, gave up 20 hits, and posted a 0–2 record. He could, however, still swing the bat. In 137 at bats, he connected for 45 hits, including one homer, three triples, and five doubles for a .328 average.[33]

Retirement

Day retired and returned home to Newark but still played occasionally in exhibition games. In the fall of 1955, for instance, he joined the Negro American League All-Stars consisting of such players as Pee Wee Butts, stellar shortstop for the Elite Giants, and Skeeter Watkins, who had played with Day in Newark and Canada. On October 16 in Norfolk, Virginia, they faced a barnstorming team of National and American League and minor league players, the Al Kaline All-Stars. Kaline's nine included Washington Senators first baseman Mickey Vernon and Baltimore Orioles Gus Triandros and Hal Smith. Kaline, a Baltimore native and eventual Hall of Fame outfielder with the Detroit Tigers, had just completed his second season in Detroit and had won the American League batting championship. The two teams faced off at Myers Field, home of the Norfolk Tars, a minor league affiliate of the New York Yankees. Nothing could be found about the game's outcome. Day may have also played with another Canadian team, the Winnipeg Goldeyes. In a card completed in his hand, he puts 1957 as his final year in baseball.[34]

Day's career generated considerable ink. He collected many articles about his play for a scrapbook. "I had a lot of scripts; you know write ups and such. I had a suitcase full," he told Riley. One in particular was dear to his heart. Written early in one season when "we had only played a few games," the clipping displayed his league-leading batting average—.450.

Chapter 19. On to Organized Baseball

> NAME: Leon Day
> BIRTH DATE: 10/30/16   PLACE: VA.
> POSITION PLAYED: Pitch, Infield, outfield
> DATES OF PLAYING DAYS: 1934 to 1957
> TEAMS PLAYED ON: Baltimore Black Sox Brooklyn Eagles; Newark Eagles-Elite Giants - Winnipeg Buffaloes-Toronto Maple Leafs - Puerto Rico - Mexico
> signature

A card completed by Leon Day. Note that he says his career lasted until 1957, three years beyond the generally accepted date of 1954. A July 6, 1992, article in *Sports Illustrated* notes he played for the Winnipeg Goldeyes in the Northern League after his time with the Washington Eskimos. He may have also included occasional exhibition games from 1955 to 1957. Note that he makes no mention of Cuba (courtesy Dr. Robert Hieronimus).

"I cut that one out. I wanted to keep that one, because I knew I wasn't going to be hitting .450 long." Unfortunately for Day and the history of Negro Leagues baseball, a fire in Newark destroyed the suitcase and its contents.[35]

CHAPTER 20

The East-West Games

"EXCEPT FOR A RADIO broadcast of a Joe Louis fight, this game was the biggest sporting event in black America," wrote Negro Leagues historian Larry Lester.[1] He was referring to the East-West All-Star game played in Chicago's Comiskey Park each August from 1933 to 1953. Two Black reporters, Roy Sparrow of the *Pittsburgh Sun Telegraph* and Bill Nunn of the *Pittsburgh Courier*, conceived the idea. They discussed it with Gus Greenlee who made two suggestions: the reporters contact Bob Cole, owner of the Chicago American Giants, about using the city's Comiskey Park, the same park that earlier in 1933 had hosted the National and American Leagues' first All-Star game. Greenlee also suggested that fans, rather than sportswriters, who selected the National and American League all-star rosters at the time, select the players by voting on ballots printed in newspapers. That way, Greenlee said, fans could experience a sense of personal involvement in the games. Cole agreed to both suggestions. The ballots were printed in weeklies throughout the country and returned to the *Pittsburgh Courier* or *Chicago Defender*. For the 1935 game, over 150,000 people in 13 states cast a ballot. Players for teams in the Negro American League receiving the most votes made up the West squad. The East squad fielded players with the most votes in the Negro National League.

"Chicago," Greenlee said explaining his choice of city, "was in the middle of the country, and people could get there from all over." The Illinois Central Railroad put on special coach cars along the New Orleans to Chicago route picking up fans along the way. The New York Central came in from the East. The Santa Fe Chief brought people in from Wichita and Kansas City. Many drove and a few flew in. The weekend of the game was cause for a citywide party. Hotels, bars, nightclubs, and restaurants did a land-office business. It was *the* weekend.[2]

The "Dream Classic," as the games became known, garnered so

Chapter 20. The East-West Games

much glamour and attention in the first two years that some eastern sportswriters lobbied for the game to rotate among other cities. Ed Harris, a sportswriter for the *Philadelphia Tribune*, pleaded in 1935, "Why can't the game be brought East? ... The fans here deserve a break as the Westerners have seen the game two years in succession." Harris got his wish, partially. The game continued each summer in Chicago, but a second game with the identical rosters as the Chicago game was added in five years; 1939 in New York's Yankee Stadium; 1942 in Cleveland's Municipal Stadium; 1946 in Washington, D.C.'s Griffith Stadium; 1947 in the Polo Grounds; and 1948 in Yankee Stadium.[3]

The inaugural East-West game took place Sunday afternoon on September 10, 1933. Those

Above: A copy of the ballot printed in Black newspapers across the country. Readers entered their choices for players to represent the East and West squads for the Negro Leagues annual All-Star Game. Gus Greenlee suggested fans, rather than sportswriters, nominate players as a way to give fans a personal stake in the games. This ballot is for the 1943 game won by the West 2–1. Satchel Paige, then with the Memphis Red Sox, was the winning pitcher (author's collection).

fortunate enough to be among the 20,000 spectators saw some of the greatest players, Black or white, ever to put on a uniform. Among them, all in one place, were Cool Papa Bell, Oscar Charleston, Biz Mackey, Josh Gibson, Jud Wilson, Judy Johnson, and Vic Harris for the East. The West squad countered with such luminaries as Turkey Stearnes; Willie Wells; Ted (Double Duty) Radcliffe; Mule Suttles; and Willie Foster, half brother of Rube Foster who is considered the father of Negro Leagues baseball. Willie, whose vote total led the list of pitchers, went the distance to lead the West to an 11–7 victory.[4] Although finishing fourth in the votes for pitcher and expected to start for the East, Satchel Paige declined the invitation. Nominally a member of the Pittsburgh Crawfords when not jumping to other teams, he chose to stay with the integrated independent team he was pitching for in Bismarck, North Dakota.[5]

Leon first took the East-West mound in the 1935 game. The 18-year-old finished sixth in votes cast for Negro National League pitchers. He had a rough go of it. "I was scared to death," Day told Riley. "There were over 50,000 people in that park. I was nervous because I hadn't ever seen that many people. It was just like I was in a daze or a trance." His nervousness showed. In four innings, the third to the seventh, he gave up six hits and four runs (only two earned) and struck out only three as the West beat the East 11–8.[6] The 1937 classic was more to his liking. If he was nervous, it didn't show this time. Called to the mound in the seventh inning with the game tied 2–2, Day pitched three shutout innings, struck out four, and gave up only one hit. He doubled and scored a run. His mates rallied for three runs to cement an East win, 7–2.[7]

Day appeared in both 1939 games. Forty thousand turned out for the Comiskey Park affair to see the West subdue the East 4–2 in spite of a spectacular performance by Leon. He entered the game in the seventh inning and held the West scoreless, but the damage had been done.[8] Seventeen thousand turned out three weeks later to see the East get even 10–2 in New York's Yankee Stadium. Day's contribution consisted of holding the West scoreless and hitless through the second to fourth innings.[9] Cleveland's Municipal Stadium hosted game two of the 1942 event witnessed by 11,000 paying customers who saw Paige, now with the Kansas City Monarchs, a western division team, reduced to coaching third base because of a sore arm suffered in that year's Chicago

Chapter 20. The East-West Games

game. Day pitched one scoreless inning as the East won 5–2. Proceeds from the game went to the Army and Navy Relief Fund.

Two days earlier on August 16, 1942, Day had one of his most satisfying games, emerging as the winning pitcher while Paige took the loss. Both Paige and Day took the mound in the seventh inning with the score tied 2–2. Each faced the best hitters from the opposing league. Paige went three innings, gave up five hits and three runs, and suffered the loss. Day pitched 2⅓ innings before 48,000 spectators in Comiskey Park, allowing no runs or hits while striking out five to lead the East to a 5–2 victory. The win was one of three Day had in four contests against Paige.[10]

Attendance at Comiskey Park for the 1943 game swelled to 51,000. Paige started and got the West off to a fast start pitching three no-run, no-hit innings. Those who followed Paige continued the shutout until the ninth inning when Buck Leonard hit a bases-empty homer for the East's only run. The West had produced two runs by the ninth, giving the West a 2–1 nail-biter of a victory. Day pitched one scoreless inning.

Columnist Lem Graves, Jr., of the *New Journal and Guide* thought Day's election to the East squad was based more on his reputation than his 1943 performance. More deserving than Day, in Graves' opinion, was Day's teammate Leniel Hooker who had won eight, including two over the Homestead Grays, and lost one. Calling the selection process "rotten" and acknowledging that Day "was one of the finest guys in the league," Graves nevertheless concluded, "he [Day] was selected on the basis of his former greatness. The kid is ailing this year and is not in there." Graves agreed with one J.L. Clark who had bemoaned in a letter to the columnist, "What does a guy have to do to get a call to the East-West game?"[11]

Day's last East-West game appearance came in the two 1946 games. The start of the first, played in Washington, D.C.'s Griffith Stadium, was delayed for 15 minutes while players for the West negotiated with the owners for a raise. Initially offered $50 for the game, players demanded and got $100. A similar "strike" had occurred at the 1944 game. That time, the East players demanded and got $200 with a promise from owners of no retaliations.

The East squad prevailed in the nation's capital 6–3, with Day pitching one inning. He was credited with the save. In Chicago before 46,000 people, the West won 4–1. Day again pitched one inning and gave up one hit.[12] In total, Day pitched 21⅓ East-West innings and recorded 23 strikeouts to become the most productive pitcher in East-West game history.[13]

Chapter 21

Post Career

THERE WERE FEW well-paying jobs in the 1950s for retired Negro Leaguers with a partial high school education. Fortunately, Day found "real jobs." Newark Eagles teammate Lennie Pearson owned a tavern in Newark, Lennie's Lounge, which Effa Manley helped him buy. Leon worked there as a bartender and at the Zipper Company as a substitute mail carrier. When former teammate George Giles heard Day was bartending, he commented again on Day's stature, saying, "A bartender! Can you picture Leon Day being a bartender? He couldn't even see over the bar."[1]

At the same time, Day managed to see well enough to tend bar at nearby Charlie's Lounge which was the more memorable of the two establishments for Day. There he met his future wife Geraldine Ingram, Gerry then. She often visited an aunt, grandparents, and a sister in the neighborhood of Charlie's tavern and would stop in occasionally.

Geraldine Ingram grew up in Wallace, North Carolina, as the seventh of nine children. The family lived in a house built by her maternal grandfather on land that supported enough corn, cotton, and tobacco so that the family didn't have to sharecrop. They raised chickens and bought only salt, pepper, and flour. Church picnics and barbecue pig roasts at harvest time were major pastimes. She played girls' basketball in high school, but that was the extent of her involvement in sports. None of her six brothers played any sports save for pickup basketball with a homemade hoop. Over several years her siblings all moved north to New York State or Newark. With two young babies, she decided to join her "baby sister" in Newark. Her older sister, also living in Newark, and baby sister, who was married and had a child, helped Geraldine settle in. She got her own apartment and a job in a factory making briefcases and suitcases. She and her sisters frequented clubs where she found gin "made me act silly." Eventually, the brothers left New York for Newark, and the grandparents—the last of the family to leave

Wallace—moved into an area in Newark called "the Neck" where her baby sister also lived. Geraldine would take a bus from her apartment to the Neck and visit Lennie's tavern "to get my beer" which she drank while visiting her sister before going home. She also visited her grandparents who lived nearby but never with any beer.[2]

On one visit to Charlie's tavern, she and Leon noticed each other. She took a friend along on her second visit. Both ordered Knotty Head gin, a Southern term for Seagram's gin. Leon served them and gave them both a second drink gratis. Her friend said to her, "That bartender keeps looking at you." On her third visit, she went alone. She remembered it "as kinda crowded and he jumped down to me. And we kept saying things we wouldn't say when we were sober." "Why you keep looking at me?" she asked him. "Why don't we just go and get it on?"[3]

Day was smitten. Soon after that, he asked her to dinner at the Grand Hotel. Several former Newark Eagle teammates were at the bar when they walked in. Some others were playing pool. "I didn't know they were ball players," she said later. "Well, look who robbed the cradle," one of the pool players remarked. The dinner was their first of many.[4]

Geraldine was 23 years younger than Leon. She liked older men. "I liked it that he was no young punk," she told *Sun* reporter Mike Klingaman. "Leon was old school," she continued. "He knew how to treat a lady, which is what I was looking for in a man." The die was cast. They struck up a relationship that would last until Leon's death.[5] They tied the knot on November 1, 1980, in Pigstown, Maryland, a community in southwest Baltimore that had once contained several slaughterhouses giving the neighborhood its name. Babe Ruth had been born in Pigstown 85 years earlier.[6]

Their relationship resulted in Geraldine learning to exercise more control over her temper. "I was young and wild when we first met. I liked to argue," Geraldine said. She was good at it. When she learned that more recently hired white and Vietnamese women made 25 cents more an hour than she did at an aircraft plant where she had worked in Newark, she "jumped in." The bosses listened. She and the other women in her situation got a 25-cent-an-hour raise.

Leon didn't like to argue. "When I'd get worked up," Geraldine said, "he'd leave the house and call a while later to ask, 'Are you alright now,' before he'd come back home. He toned me down." He told her, "I never heard my mother and father argue, but I knew they had disagreements."[7]

Chapter 21. Post Career

Geraldine's getting worked up went beyond their home. In May 1962, she drove a group of students to the Crystal Palace, a restaurant in La Plata, Maryland, fronting Route 301 that was not friendly to Blacks. The students, who formed a picket line with citizens of La Plata, were threatened with trespassing. Owners of nearby restaurants refused to serve them. A Crystal Palace employee drove his car back and forth through their line. A white reporter was told to leave "before you get hurt." Police made several arrests. A Crystal Palace employee let the air out of Geraldine's left front tire.[8]

Leon and Geraldine lived in Newark for a year when Leon moved to Baltimore to take a security guard job in Baltimore that his sister found for him. He worked as a security guard for several companies: Tragfer Bakery, Revere Brass and Copper, and Liberty Security Company. When Geraldine joined him in Charm City, she took a job as a forklift operator at Weyerhaeuser Paper in Dorsey, Maryland, south of Baltimore. There, she moved paper by-products from delivery trucks to a storage area, taking home $190 a week, less than the minimum wage. Even so, she enjoyed her job, but Leon's work concerned her. "All he had was a night stick," she said. "It's too dangerous," she told him. Even though finances were tight, she convinced him to quit working as a security guard. Leon found other ways to contribute to the family income, including signing autographs through the mail for a $10 fee and at card shows.[9]

Todd Bolton took him to baseball memorabilia shows where he made an extra $400–$500 a month.[10] Between the two of them, the Days managed to get by.

Reunions

At one of those shows held at the Meadowlands Hilton Hotel in Secaucus, New Jersey, and sponsored by the Negro Leagues Baseball Players Association to raise money for former players in early June 1992, Day talked history while he signed. With his grandson Leon at his side, Day wanted to set history right. He correctly insisted that Blacks had played in the National and American Leagues before Jackie Robinson. He told stories of the Walker brothers, catcher Moses Fleetwood and outfielder Weldy, who both played with the Toledo Blue Stockings, a

Leon Day

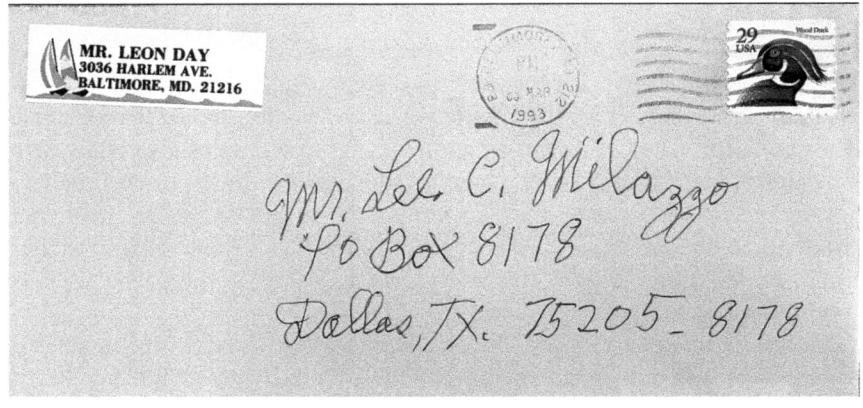

Top: Following his retirement from baseball, Day signed fans' autograph requests (which they sent by mail) for a $10 fee. Here is a hand-addressed envelope by Day to a fan just two years before his death. *Bottom:* A thoughtful handwritten note by Day to the same fan (both courtesy Dr. Robert Hieronimus).

Chapter 21. Post Career

member of the Northwestern League that had entered the American Association in 1884. The association was considered a major league at the time. At the same show, Gene Benson, former outfielder who played most of his 17-year career with the Philadelphia Stars, recalled the first Negro Leagues reunion. It took place in Ashland, Kentucky, but "those reunions," he said, "were never as spectacular as this one." In addition to Day and Benson, other players in attendance included Willie Mays, Walter "Buck" Leonard, Lester Lockett, Bob Harvey, Josh Johnson, Bert Simmons (former pitcher and outfielder for the Baltimore Elite Giants), and Monte Irvin. Among the attendees were Negro Leagues researcher Tom Kern and his daughter Emily. They remembered enjoying their conversation with the elder statesmen of the Negro Leagues. All expressed the hope that more people, especially Black youngsters, would take an interest in the Negro Leagues. Bert Simmons said, "If you ask an average Black kid who Josh Gibson was, he wouldn't know." Michael Simmons, a Chicago attorney and no relation to Bert who helped organize the show, was disappointed that the audience at the show was mostly white.[11]

Ashland Reunions

The first reunion that Benson mentioned took place 13 years earlier. Tom Stultz, publisher of the *Greenup County Sentinel* in northeastern Kentucky, thought Independence Day, 1979, would be a fine occasion to honor one of Black baseball's forgotten stars, Clint Thomas, and highlight Negro Leagues baseball. A native of Greenup and the proud owner of a 19-year Negro Leagues career (1920–38), he retired with a .300 plus batting average and the nickname "Hawk" for his sharp eye as a batter and speed and agility in the outfield and on the base baths. Thomas became known as the "Black Joe DiMaggio." The former Negro Leaguer had worked for the past 30 years as a custodian and staff supervisor in the West Virginia Department of Mines and the state senate.

With backing from sponsors of the Tri-State (Kentucky, West Virginia, and Ohio) Fair and Regatta to be held in Ashland, Kentucky, Stultz invited an elite group of retired Negro Leaguers, including Buck Leonard, James "Cool Papa" Bell, Judy Johnson, Ray Dandridge, and Leon Day, to join other retired stars Monte Irvin, Satchel Paige, Bob Feller (who had toured with Satchel in 1946), former baseball commissioner A.B.

"Happy" Chandler, Don Newcombe, Minnie Miñoso, and Roy Campanella for the festivities. The group gathered at the Greenup ballpark where little leaguers got autographs and posed for pictures with the players.[12]

The summer reunions in Ashland continued through 1984 when the funding ran out. The 1980 gathering drew 32 players, including Day and Thomas, and Effa Manley, who was the featured guest. Geraldine attended this reunion with Leon. She missed the first reunion because the organizer didn't have the money to pay her way. She offered to drive to the second reunion. Leon was skeptical of her ability behind the wheel, saying, "Drive? Don't you know that you've got to go through the mountains in West Virginia?" She insisted. Day contacted Bob Harvey, former Baltimore Elite Giant, who lived nearby. Harvey agreed to go along. Geraldine did all the driving. From then on, she accompanied Leon to most of his reunions and signings.[13]

Autographs and picture taking kicked off the 1980 affair at Ashland's Putnam Stadium. An evening banquet followed. Another autograph and photo session took place the next day. Chico Renfro, a retired Negro Leagues infielder and, at the time of the reunion, a sportscaster and sports director for Atlanta's WIGO radio station, emceed the reunion. Thinking something more permanent than reunions to honor the Negro Leagues and players would be appropriate, Renfro advanced the idea of a National Negro Baseball Hall of Fame. He suggested Ashland, Kentucky, as a site. "It's visionary just now," Renfro said, "but we have funding offers from the Philadelphia and Los Angeles areas."

Nothing came of Renfro's proposal, but the idea of Hall of Fame recognition for deserving Negro Leaguers would continue to gain support among admirers of the Negro Leagues and sputter along at Cooperstown. By the time of Day's induction, 15 years after the 1980 reunion, only 12 Negro League players' plaques could be found among the more than 200 plaques honoring National and American League players, umpires, and executives.[14]

A film company, Refocus Productions, from Westport, Connecticut, interviewed players and filmed the 1980 activities as part of a television documentary on life in the Negro Leagues. Two subsequent reunions each featured two players for special honors: Satchel Paige and Cool Papa Bell (1981) and Judy Johnson and Webster McDonald (1982). At the time of the final reunion, 1985, players and some collectors had donated enough memorabilia to warrant the formation of the Negro

Chapter 21. Post Career

Baseball Hall of History, a four-case display, an audiovisual show, and boxes of items and newspaper articles. The contents were acquired by the Hall of Fame in Cooperstown after the reunion which attracted 75 former players including Day.[15]

In a rare overture, the Hall of Fame officially recognized the Negro Leagues when it hosted a special reunion underwritten by the Southern Bell Telephone Company on June 20–21, 1991, at Cooperstown. Day, along with more than 60 other former players, attended. Hall of Fame president Ed Stack welcomed the group, saying, "The Hall of Fame is delighted to pay tribute to these pioneers of the game. They paved the way for Jackie Robinson and his successors to excel on major league playing fields. Eleven from their ranks have been officially inducted into the Hall of Fame." The players stayed overnight at the luxury Otesaga Hotel, toured the hall the next morning, and left for home in the afternoon.[16]

CHAPTER 22

Cooperstown Beckons

COOPERSTOWN WAS NOT the first Hall of Fame to honor Leon. On October 31, 1993, Day had been inducted into the Puerto Rican Professional Baseball Hall of Fame in Mayagüez along with four other former Negro Leagues players: Baltimore Elites catcher Luis Villodas, New York Cubans second baseman Carlos Manuel Santiago, Birmingham Black Barons shortstop Artie Wilson, and New York Cubans pitcher José Santiago. Day felt honored by the induction and by a similar induction into the Newark Hall of Fame, but he still eagerly awaited a call from Cooperstown.[1]

It had been a long road for the Days. Eligible for the hall since 1983, it would take five votes and 12 years for him to be elected. Day was ecstatic when his name first appeared on a Hall of Fame ballot in 1983. "I'm on the ballot," he blurted out to Geraldine, "to be elected to the Hall of Fame…. I'll be up there with the best, with the best. That's where the best goes up in Cooperstown to the Hall of Fame."[2] In the 1983, 1991, and 1992 elections, Day failed to garner the necessary 75 percent of the votes. The same held true in 1993, but he was just one tantalizing vote short, winning 11 of the 15 votes cast. Members of the 1993 Veterans Committee included former National and American League players Ted Williams, Roy Campanella, Stan Musial, Al Lopez, Monte Irvin, and John "Buck" O'Neil (the batting champion for the Negro American League in 1946 and the first Black coach, with the Chicago Cubs, in the National and American Leagues).

The Cubs hired O'Neil to keep an eye on recently signed Ernie Banks from the dugout. When two senior white coaches were ejected from a game, O'Neil was next in line to assume coaching duties at third base. Manager Charlie Grimm, however, called a pitching coach in from the bullpen, fearing O'Neil's appearance on the field would cost a white man his job. O'Neil was quoted in his biography as saying, "Not going out there that day was one of the few disappointments I've had in over sixty years in baseball."

Chapter 22. Cooperstown Beckons

The committee also included baseball writers, all from white dailies—Shirley Povich, Allen Lewis, Ernie Harwell, Bob Broeg, Jack Brickhouse, and Edgar Munzel—and former National and American League executives—Charles Segar, Gabe Paul, Joe L. Brown, and Buzzie Bavasi. Campanella, who certainly would have voted for Day, was ill that day, could not attend, and could not cast a ballot in absentia. He died shortly before the 1995 vote.[3]

Dr. Robert Hieronimus, a Baltimore-based author, activist, and leader of a campaign to see Day elected to the Hall of Fame, called the 1993 vote "a crusher" for Day. He wanted Campy to be the one who put him in the hall because, Hieronimus explained, "they were buddies, they were friends."[4]

Day knew the next vote was scheduled for March 7, 1995. He sensed it would be his last chance to regale in being counted among that rarefied group of baseball immortals. On the night of March 6, 1995, he dreamed that Hall of Fame board chairman Edward Stack had appeared in his room, told him of his election, and slipped the Hall of Fame ring on his finger. Saddened by reality after his call to Geraldine, he chatted with the nurses and signed autographs for them. Several hours later, Ed Stack called his home, told Geraldine of his election, and asked her to give Leon the good news. "No," she said, "I'd prefer for you to call and tell him." She gave him the hospital's phone number. When the phone rang in his room, Day was undergoing diagnostic tests in another part of the hospital.[5]

Day, though elated at the prospect of having a plaque in Cooperstown, dreaded the possibility of being denied yet again. Hieronimus, who had learned of Leon's election from Buck O'Neil earlier, knew of Day's fear and wanted to dispel it as soon as possible. He stationed himself outside the room where Day was undergoing tests. "You're in," Dr. Bob whispered in Day's ear as Day was rolled out of the lab on a gurney. Day's first reaction was, "No shit."[6]

Max Manning, meanwhile, answered Stack's call. "I'll tell him," Manning said to Stack. With a big smile on his face, the bespeckled Manning, chosen as the person to give Day the good news when he returned to his room, as the TV cameras rolled, said, "You made it, man." Day, not letting on that he already knew, said, "I'm ready to get up out of this bed. This has been in the back of my mind for a long time."[7]

The Hieronimus Campaign

Since 1987, when the last Negro Leaguer, Ray Dandridge, had been inducted in Cooperstown, pressure to induct more Negro Leaguers had been cascading against the hall from many sources. A major source was Dr. Bob Hieronimus, well-known Baltimore artist and activist, and his wife Zohara, a radio personality in the city. They initiated a campaign to get Day some visibility to enhance his chances of being elected to the hall. Day had been living in quiet retirement, first in Newark and later in Baltimore. Day's retirement started to brighten, however, in 1991 when the Hieronimuses entered the picture. "Many of these Negro Leaguers were impoverished," Hieronimus said at the time. "When I first met Leon," Dr. Bob continued, "he was in a little better economic state, but it was horrendous what he had to do to eke out a living."[8] The campaign soon got underway. White House visits were part of the campaign.

On February 19, at age 75 and 30 years into retirement, Day and other former players—Monte Irvin, Jimmy Crutchfield, and Josh Gibson, Jr. (son of the renowned slugger), as representatives of the Negro Leagues Baseball Players Association—met with President George H.W. Bush at the White House for lunch and a program in the East Room celebrating February 1991 as Black History Month. Irvin said afterward, "We were sitting in the front row and to see him call our names and get up and take a bow was simply outstanding." Day commented that "I had met a Cuban president and I had met a Mexican president, but that was the first time I had ever met an American president." Later, Leon joined eight other former players at a February 8, 1994, White House meeting with Vice President Al Gore that Dr. Bob also arranged.[9]

In between White House visits, the Hieronimuses' campaign picked up steam. Larry King interviewed Day on the Mutual Broadcasting System on March 3, 1992, drawing on questions supplied by Dr. Bob.[10] Dr. Bob invited other notable people and organizations in Baltimore to recognize Day. Maryland governor William Donald Schaefer proclaimed May 18, 1992, as Leon Day Day. During a 20-minute ceremony at the Maryland statehouse in Annapolis, the governor presented Leon with a key to the city.

Day, dressed in a pale-blue suit and Newark Eagles cap, after answering questions from Schaefer about his career, presented the governor with a replica Baltimore Elite Giants cap, a set of Negro Leagues baseball cards, and an illustrated book of Negro Leagues legends. "It was an honor for the governor to ask me down here. I really appreciate it," Leon said. Schaefer replied, "You've deserved a lot of recognition, and you're finally getting it."[11]

Sports Illustrated featured Leon in a short article in July. The national baseball card publishing organization, *Tuff Stuff*, published a four-page spread on him in its September 1992 issue. The Baltimore Orioles held a Leon Day Day on September 24, 1992, at their home ballpark, Camden Yards, in its first year in operation. The Hieronimuses placed a notice in the *Sun* touting the game as "Bravo Leon Day!!" They described Day as a "Future-Hall-of-Famer. Negro Leagues Baseball Star." Leon threw the honorary first pitch from the mound.[12]

A Rule Change

Day's election was not far off. A 1994 change in the Hall of Fame Veterans Committee's rules that allowed members to select four former baseball figures in place of the usual two, and increased emphasis on Negro Leaguers and 19th-century players helped. *Baltimore Sun* sportswriter John Steadman wrote, "The choice of Leon Day ... was a result of such a process."[13]

The hall's decision to emphasize Negro Leaguers was orchestrated by Buck O'Neil, a Veterans Committee member and outspoken advocate for inducting qualified Negro Leagues players. He thought many of the committee members, deeply committed to maintaining the hall's high standards, would not vote for players many had not seen and knew little about, making it hard if not impossible for a Negro Leagues candidate to receive the required 12 votes. O'Neil proposed an advisory group, under the supervision of the hall's vice president, Bill Guilfoyle, that would nominate a list of deserving Negro Leaguers and create a separate ballot containing those names for the committee to use to elect one—and only one—Negro Leagues player in each subsequent year.[14]

The advisory group selected seven players: Day; Willie Foster (known for his mastery of five pitches all delivered with the same motion); Willie Wells (called El Diablo, the Devil), the best shortstop in Black baseball in the '30s and '40s who amassed a batting average well over .300 during his 26-year career; "Bullet" Joe Rogan, a star pitcher and position player for the Kansas City Monarchs for 19 seasons who, like Day, used no windup; "Smokey" Joe Williams, considered by many the equal or better of Satchel Paige and ace pitcher for the 1931 Homestead Grays, considered by many the best Negro Leagues team ever; Norman "Turkey" Stearnes, slugger extraordinaire during his 20-year career; and Hilton Smith, known as "Satchel's backup" during his 13 seasons with the Monarchs. Smith would often relieve Paige after three innings and ably finish the game with an assortment of five pitches. All seven nominees were inducted at the rate of one a year, 1995–2001. Day was selected first, likely because he was the only one still living.[15]

Committee member and Hall of Famer Stan Musial thought Day and the others chosen by the Veterans Committee in 1995 were good choices. "There were a lot of candidates for us to consider, and I think we got four good ones," he said of the 1995 crop.

The Beat Goes On

Election of those seven did not, however, quell the Black media's drumbeat for more Negro Leaguers to be elected. Sam Lacy, a sports columnist for the *Afro-American* for over 50 years and one of the first African American members of the Baseball Writers' Association of America, devoted a column, a week before Day's induction, to criticizing the "tardiness" of Day's election. Lacy wrote in part, "The men who control the elections of Black nominees finally reached the conclusion that what should be done ... had to be done. From their exalted position, they suffered the little bird to sing."[16]

Day was only the 12th Negro Leaguer to earn induction into the hall. Satchel Paige, Monte Irvin, Josh Gibson, Buck Leonard, Ray Dandridge, James "Cool Papa" Bell, Oscar Charleston, John "Pop" Lloyd, Martín Dihigo, Judy Johnson, and Rube Foster preceded him.[17]

Induction Ceremony

Day had passed away before the ceremony at Cooperstown, but Geraldine attended. The ceremony began at 2:30 p.m. on a warm Sunday afternoon, July 30, 1995, under sunny skies.

Chapter 22. Cooperstown Beckons

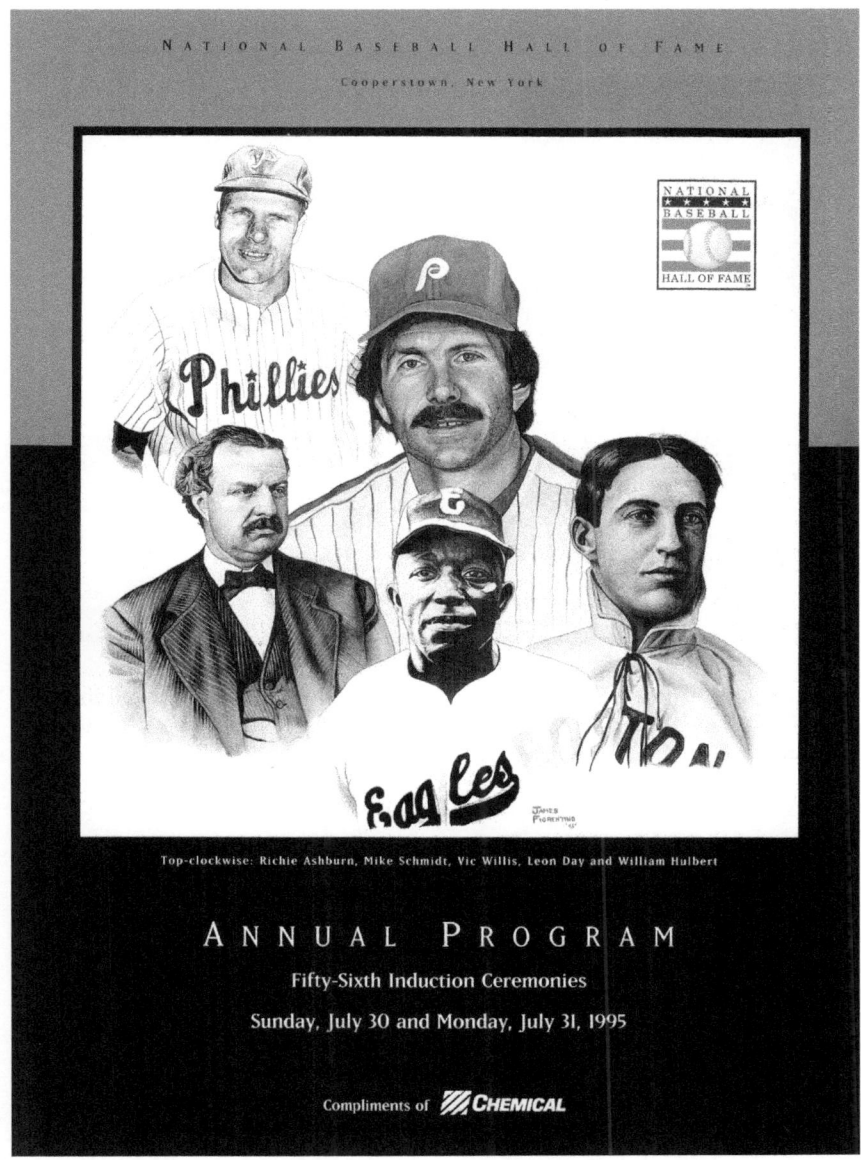

The cover for the 1995 Hall of Fame induction ceremony with Day's image front and center (courtesy Dr. Robert Hieronimus).

LEON DAY

Height: 5'9"   Weight: 170

Throws: Right   Bats: Right

Born: Oct. 30, 1916   Died: Mar. 13, 1995

INDUCTION DAY
JULY 30, 1995
COOPERSTOWN, NY

Baltimore Black Sox	1934
Brooklyn Eagles	1935
Newark Eagles	1936 - 1939
Venezuelan League	1940
Mexican League	1940
Newark Eagles	1941 - 1943
Military Service	1944 - 1945
Newark Eagles	1946
Mexican League	1947 - 1948
Baltimore Elite Giants	1949 - 1950
Minor Leagues	1950 - 1954

A page from the 1995 Hall of Fame induction booklet featuring Leon Day completing a pitch and providing a list of his teams (courtesy Dr. Robert Hieronimus).

Approximately 25,000 people attended. Some sat in folding chairs, but most sat on the grassy lawn of the Clark Sports Center. Included in the audience were thousands from Philadelphia who arrived in 200 chartered buses to show their support for Richie Ashburn and Mike Schmidt.[18] Previously elected Hall of Fame members sat in a section behind the podium from which Chairman of the Board Ed Stack introduced members of the Class of 1995. Following comments by several Hall of Fame officials, Bob Wolff gave the first acceptance speech after which he led the crowd in a rendition of "Take Me Out to the Ball Game" while he sang and strummed his ukulele. Geraldine was next up. Attired in a white dress with a white hat to match, she delivered a short and moving speech honoring her late husband (see Appendix A).[19]

His Hall of Fame plaque reads, "Leon Day, Negro Leagues 1934–1949: Used deceptive, no-wind up, short-arm delivery to compile impres-

Chapter 22. Cooperstown Beckons

Hall of Fame president Dave Marr (left) and Hall of Fame chairman of the board Ed Stack presenting Day's Hall of Fame plaque to his widow Geraldine at the July 1995 induction ceremony (courtesy the Baseball Hall of Fame and Museum, Cooperstown, New York).

sive single-season and career statistics during 10 years in Negro Leagues. Also played ball in Puerto Rico, Cuba, Venezuela, Mexico and Canada. Set Negro National League record in 1942 with 18 strikeouts in a game. Hurled no-hitter on opening day 1946 for Newark Eagles vs. Philadelphia Stars. Pitched in record 7 Negro Leagues all-star games."[20]

For reasons unknown, the emblem on his cap is an "A," which stands for the Aguadilla Sharks—Day had been a member of this Puerto Rican team. His is the only cap emblem on Hall of Fame players' plaques which is not that of a Negro or National or American League team.

Two days before Day's induction, a crowd of well-wishers had gathered outside Camden Yards Stadium to hear testimonials to Day's performance and character from dignitaries including Baltimore Orioles general manager Roland Hemond; Hall of Famer Frank Robinson, who had led the O's to pennants and World Series titles; former

Leon Day's Hall of Fame card. Note the "A" on his cap. It's for the Aguadilla Sharks and the only cap insignia on a Hall of Fame plaque that is not of a National, American, or Negro League team (courtesy Dr. Robert Hieronimus).

Negro Leagues players Ernest Burke and Gordon Hopkins, who shared their memories of Leon; *Baltimore Sun* sports reporter Brad Snyder, who had covered Day from the time of his election through his induction; and Baltimore mayor Kurt Schmoke, who proclaimed the day, July 28, 1995, "Leon Day Day." After his remarks, Mayor Schmoke then turned to Geraldine, who had earlier greeted the crowd, and said to her, "I'm going to ask you to do something you've never done before—join me in that cherry picker." When the picker reached the height of a cloth-covered street sign, Geraldine reached out and removed the cover to reveal a red-and-white street sign that read, "Leon Day Way." A portion of Camden Yards Street had been renamed in Leon's honor. Many in the crowd then joined Geraldine in boarding a Greyhound bus, partially paid for by the Orioles, with a banner on each side reading "Friends of Leon Day" for the trip to Cooperstown.[21]

An unfortunate turn of events occurred before the ceremony began. Twenty-three former Negro Leaguers, most of whom had played against Day and had never seen an induction ceremony, sat in the back of a five-and-dime store, J.J. Newberry's, adjacent to the Hall of Fame building, signing autographs and a lithograph of Day and Paige shaking hands in heaven. Paige had died in 1982. An hour before the ceremony, promised tickets had not arrived, no arrangements had been made to protect them from the sweltering heat (sitting unprotected on the lawn was not an option for the elderly group), and no transportation from J.J. Newberry's to the ceremony had been arranged. "These guys were under the impression they were going to see the ceremony," said a disappointed Stanley Glenn. To top it off, many had not been paid for their autographs. Manning refused his ticket in protest of the group's treatment. Some drove home before the ceremony started. Others stayed in Newberry's. Only seven former players, by virtue of being Geraldine's guests, made it to the ceremony.[22]

Other Honors

Cooperstown had been the pinnacle of recognition for Day, but he was honored a number of other times before and after his death as interest in the Negro Leagues picked up pace. The Friends of the National Afro-American Exhibition and Festival sponsored a program called "Baseball's Unsung Heroes" at Banneker Field in northwest Washington, D.C., on July 14, 1984. Among the honorees, in addition to Day, were Buck Leonard, Wilmer Fields, and Clarence (Half-Pint) Israel.[23]

The Atlanta Braves, with a contribution from the Southern Bell Telephone Company, sponsored a reunion of Negro League players in June 1989. Day was among 100 former players honored.[24]

In April 1990, Baltimore's Enoch Pratt Free Library sponsored a research conference that brought together former players, including Day, authors, and executives. The conference began work on a permanent Negro Leagues Library in the library's Afro-American collection. A call to the Pratt Library in January 2025 indicated such an archive does not now exist in the library.[25] On April 29, 1990, the Equitable Old-Timers Second Annual Baseball Series honored Day and other former players with an old-timers game in Baltimore.[26]

Baltimore Orioles president Larry Lucchino created a weeklong Fan Fest immediately preceding the July 13, 1993, All-Star Game held in Oriole Park. Among other attractions was the honoring of a group of Negro Leaguers who had received similar accolades on July 10 before a game between the Orioles and the White Sox. Day attended both events and was the subject of an interview by *Washington Post* reporter Gabby Richards. "I saw a lot of good ball players," he told Richards, "who weren't allowed to play in the major leagues. This is going to be great."[27]

Baltimore TV channels 53 and 32 (WNVT and WHMM) aired *Negro Leagues Baseball Minutes* in the fall of 1994. Producer-director Mary Lawrence, using interviews, photographs, and archival film footage, constructed segments featuring Leon and notable others including Satchel Paige, Josh Gibson, Larry Doby, Wilmer Fields, and Effa Manley. Group W Television produced *Not in Our League*, which featured Leon and Buck O'Neil. WHMM also broadcast a program on Southern black ballplayers, *Safe at Home Plate*, narrated by country singer and former player Charley Pride.[28] Before finding success as a singer, Pride had an on again, off again career as a pitcher for the Memphis Red Sox and the Birmingham Black Barons of the Negro American League from 1953 to 1958. By that time, the league, faced with the departure of star players to the National and American Leagues and ensuing financial pressure, had declined to minor league status. An indicator of the league's financial frailty was the unconfirmed story that Pride and another player were traded for a team bus.[29]

A special tribute was paid to Day at the Second Annual Negro Baseball League Celebration Awards ceremony held at the Marriott Marquis Hotel in Midtown Manhattan on December 1, 1995, nine months after his death. The gathering marked the 75th anniversary of Rube Foster's founding of the Negro National League. Legendary Grambling State University football coach Eddie Robinson emceed the event. He praised former Negro athletes of all sports, saying, "Without the dreams, sweat, and determination of all the former Negro athletes, African American players would be nowhere near where they are today in terms of their ability to succeed and achieve." Proceeds for the event went to benefit former Negro Leagues players, of which 160 were still alive, and the Negro Leagues Museum in Kansas City, Missouri.[30]

Events to honor Leon continued. Frederick Douglass High School, the school he forsook 65 years earlier because it didn't have a baseball team, awarded an honorary diploma posthumously on the afternoon of June 7, 1997, to its most famous dropout. Former teammates of Day and other former ballplayers attended.[31]

The land for Leon Day Park, consisting of 15 acres in West Balti-

Chapter 22. Cooperstown Beckons

A flyer to help raise funds for a statue of Leon Day to serve as a permanent tribute to the "Mighty Mite" (courtesy Dr. Robert Hieronimus).

more located just blocks from where Leon lived for 17 years, was dedicated in August 1997. Hundreds attended the ceremony, giving it the flavor of a block party. Geraldine, Mayor Kurt L. Schmoke, Orioles outfielder Eric Davis, the Oriole mascot, and a dozen former Negro Leaguers headlined the dedication. They extolled Day's play on the diamond and his character. Leroy "Toots" Ferrell, who played with Day in 1949–50, said of him, "He wasn't only a baseball player. He was a beautiful black man. I was only 19 when I met him. He was like a father figure to me." Thanks to two $100,000 donations, one from the Orioles and the other from a private, nonprofit conservation group, the Trust for Public Land, construction of a state-of-the-art diamond, fields for cricket, soccer, and football, a meeting room, and a picnic area got underway for completion in the spring.[32]

That same year, 1997, the Negro Leagues Baseball Museum opened in November in Kansas City, Missouri, at 18th and Vine, just blocks from the Paseo YMCA where Rube Foster organized the Negro National League in 1920. Among the displays was a 10,000-square-foot replica baseball diamond with lights, featuring life-size bronze statues of each Negro Leaguer in the Hall of Fame, save for Monte Irvin, when the statues were commissioned. "These statues," said Ed Steele who, with his wife Linda, led the design process, "represent the spirits of the Negro Leagues players. They're coming back to inspire people." Each valued at $30,000, the statues were displayed by position, though not in all cases in the position for which the player was best known. They depicted pitcher Satchel Paige, catcher Josh Gibson, batter Martín Dihigo, first baseman Buck Leonard, second baseman John Henry Lloyd, third baseman Ray Dandridge, shortstop Judy Johnson, left fielder Cool Papa Bell, center fielder Oscar Charleston, and right fielder Leon Day. Rube Foster was displayed as the manager.[33]

The interest in honoring Leon Day continues. As of this writing, Dr. Bob is leading a fundraising campaign to have a statue of Leon Day sculpted and displayed in Baltimore near Camden Yards.

Financial Pressures Face Geraldine

Geraldine left Cooperstown feeling uplifted in the belief that Leon had finally gained the recognition that he deserved and that she was

Chapter 22. Cooperstown Beckons

Leon Day and Teammates, Opening Day No-Hitter, 1946

Leon Day

Honoring the Memory of Negro Baseball Leagues Star and Hall of Famer, Leon Day
To Benefit His Widow, Geraldine Day

On March 7, 1995 the nation watched Leon Day receive the news in his hospital bed that Cooperstown's National Baseball Museum had elected him to be the 12th Negro Leagues Baseball Player to join the Hall of Fame. March 13, six days later, Leon Day died.

Benefit on February 15, 1997
The Overlea 6809 Bel Air Road, Baltimore
8:00 PM - 12:00 AM

Special Guests: Former Negro Leagues Stars, Baltimore Orioles, Major Leaguers
Silent and Live Auctions of Negro and Major League Baseball memorabilia
Leon Day commemorative and autographed items

A poster announcing the fundraising dinner organized by Dr. Robert Hieronimus for Leon Day's widow Geraldine Day (courtesy Dr. Robert Hieronimus).

someone special. But the next day, back in Baltimore, the financial pressures continued. Had Leon lived, an appearance schedule would have been arranged that could have brought in $75,000–$100,000, according to sports agent Bob Allen. Geraldine, who faced serious health issues, was left with her pay and some health benefits from Weyerhaeuser, as well as some help from the National and American Leagues that paid her rent and money toward auto insurance, but she was still several thousands of dollars short each year for doctor bills.

Many people stepped forward to help. Dr. Bob organized a fundraiser and auction in February 1997 that was open to the members of the public for tickets priced at $75.

The event was well advertised. A large, integrated crowd turned out. Geraldine was grateful, if a bit embarrassed, for the support. Dressed in a sharp red dress, she told the crowd, "Sometimes a person has to swallow their pride and reach out." Bob Wade, former University of Maryland basketball coach, gave her a check from Mayor Kurt Schmoke. Ken Bancroft, on behalf of St. Agnes Hospital where Leon had learned of his election, gave her a check for $5,000. In other efforts, Molly Dunham, sports editor for the *Baltimore Sun*, asked for people to send checks to her that she would pass on to Geraldine. Hall of Famer Joe Morgan, former second baseman for the Cincinnati Reds and a baseball television commentator, sent a check for $500.[34]

A deeply religious woman, she relied on her faith for strength in tough times. She volunteered at the Central Church of Christ where Leon's funeral had been held. Through it all, she maintained a positive spirit. A fellow worker at Weyerhaeuser, Tim Hill, who had known Geraldine for three years, said of her in 1997, "She's a beautiful lady. She cooks for us sometimes, bringing us fish and corn for lunch. You couldn't ask for a better co-worker. She comes to work even when she's sick."[35]

Geraldine passed away on Christmas Day, 2024, and was interred in the same grave as Leon at Arbutus Memorial Park.

Epilogue

It took Leon Day 25 years to make it to the Hall of Fame, largely because electors knew much less about the Negro Leagues than they knew about the National and American Leagues. A 2020 initiative by Major League Baseball (MLB), a New York City–based organization representing the interests of the National and American League teams, may improve future Hall of Fame electors', as well as the public's, knowledge and appreciation of the Negro Leagues.

On December 16, 2020, MLB commissioner Rob Manfred bestowed, in what he called "long overdue recognition," major league status on Negro Leagues players. All played in one or more of the seven most prominent Negro Leagues between 1920—the year Rube Foster founded the first Negro League, the Negro National League—and 1948—the year after Larry Doby and Jackie Robinson broke the National and American Leagues' color bars. A 16-member committee, the Negro Leagues Statistical Review Committee, consisting of authors, statisticians, executives, and two players under the leadership of John Thorn, official historian of Major League Baseball, has added more than 2,300 players to the permanent MLB database. In Thorn's words, "There's no distinction to be made. They were all big leaguers."[1]

The Hall of Fame and the Negro Leagues Baseball Museum, joint beneficiaries of a 2020 $1 million grant from MLB and MLB Players Association, are hard at work educating the public on the Negro Leagues' impact on baseball and society.

Appendix A: Geraldine Day's Acceptance Speech for Leon Day

FIRST OF ALL, I'd like to give honor to God. Mr. Stack, members of the National Baseball Hall of Fame, on behalf of my late husband Leon Day, I'm honored to accept this plaque. This has been a very emotional year for me and my family. On March the 7th, we received the word that Leon had been inducted into the Hall of Fame. Six days later, his sweet heart gave out, and he was returned to his maker. Leon had very little opportunity to enjoy this great honor. But even though he is not here with us today, I know that he's here in spirit. I only wish that all of you could have known my husband. He was a kind, gentle, and humble man. He was a good family man and a wonderful athlete. He never bragged about his many accomplishments, but he was always quick to praise others. He often talked about how many great athletes there were that played in the Negro Leagues. He never could understand why there was so few that had been elected to the Hall of Fame. Leon was very proud the day he was elected. He was proud to be number twelve, but he was sad that there was only twelve Negro Leagues players in the Hall of Fame. He always said that there are so many of our boys that should be there. For the sake of Leon and all of the Negro Leagues players, I pray that one day it would be made right.

Leon had a vision of this day. Leon told me about his dream. He dreamed that he was inducted into the Hall of Fame. The day that he was inducted, he dreamed that dream that morning. So he called me at home and he says, ah, "Baby, I'm in, I'm in." I say, "You in where?" He says, "I'm in the Hall of Fame." I says, ah, "You, you're in the Hall of Fame?" He says, "Yes. Didn't you hear?" I said, "No." I said, "Leon, do you know what time it is?" He said, "What time is it?" I says, "It's eight o'clock in the morning." I says, "They haven't even voted yet." He said, "Those people up there don't play around like you!" He says, "I'm in, I'm

Appendix A: Geraldine Day's Acceptance Speech for Leon Day

in!" So I noticed that he was real serious about this. So I says, "Leon," I say, "listen," I said, "it's eight o'clock in the morning." I said, "They haven't voted." I said, "Baby, you dreamed that you was in the Hall of Fame." So he got real quiet and he said, "I must've."

So after I went up to the hospital, the TV people, the media, and everybody was up there and after everybody left, I stayed behind. So he said, "Gerry," he says, "let me tell you about this dream I had." He said, "I dreamed that Ed Stack came into my room with the little box saying it was all wrapped up and saying that when he came into my room," he says, "Day, you made it." So he says, he said to Ed, "I made it?" He said, "Yes. You is in, you is in the Hall of Fame." Then Ed passed him the little box. He says, "I was, I was unwrapping the little box," and he says, "I wouldn't open it." So then he says, "Ed says, 'Open it, open it.'" So he says, "I opened the box," and said, "Baby, there was the prettiest ring I have ever seen." He says, "I put my ring on my finger," and he says, "that's when the phone rang." He says, "It was you, and that's when I realized that I wasn't in the Hall of Fame," he said, "but I am now. I know I am." But he was a very happy man that day. He just lit the whole room up, he was saying, "I got to get outta here now and go up to the Hall of Fame and really get my ring." So, I'm so thankful that all of you have helped Leon's dream come true.

I also want to thank all the friends and family that made this trip to be here with me today. I especially want to recognize Leon's family. Will Leon's family please stand. You all meant so much to Leon. And I thank God for you all, and I thank you all for coming to make this day, and to enjoy this day for Leon. And I thank everyone out there that came and made this day possible for Leon. And I just wish all of you just enjoy yourself, and may God bless ya, and thank you, thank you, thank you.[1]

Appendix B:
Questionnaire Completed
by Leon Day in 1951

(See questionnaire on the following page)

Leon Day

A questionnaire completed by Day in 1951 at the request of William T. Weiss, a baseball statistician in San Mateo, California, who sent similar questionnaires to thousands of ballplayers at all levels of the game. Weiss' collection is housed in the San Diego Public Library. Day's responses tell us he was married, aspired to play in the major leagues, considered his 1946 opening day no-hitter against the Philadelphia Stars his most unusual/interesting experience in baseball, participated in track and basketball as well as baseball in high school, and enjoyed fishing and photography. Courtesy of Hunt Auctions. Lot 4, March 25, 2017.

Chapter Notes

Introduction

1. John B. Holway, "Day Crossed a Road Less Traveled to Cooperstown," *Washington Post*, March 19, 1995.
2. Erik Brady, "A Baseball Era Gone By," *USA Today*, June 9, 1987.
3. Dave Anderson, "Leon's Day in the Sun at Last," *New York Times*, March 9, 1995.
4. "818th Amphibious Truck Company," Camp Gordon Johnston WWII Museum, https://www.campgordonjohnston.com/honor/818th-amphibious-truck-company/, accessed July 7, 2024.
5. Ships' manifests and U.S. World War II Enlistment Records, 1938–46, Ancestry, accessed December 15, 2023.
6. Bill Mills, "'Fats' Jenkins Raps Wage Cut for Ballplayers," *New York Age*, April 9, 1938; Doug Davis, "Opinion: We All Lost When MLB Excluded Black Players," *Portland (Maine) Press Herald*, June 29, 2024.
7. Kent Baker, "Ex-Negro Leaguer Is 'Hall' Material," *The Sun*, February 20, 1963; Leslie Heaphy, "Shadowed Diamonds: The Growth and Decline of the Negro Leagues" (PhD diss., University of Toledo, 1995), 239.
8. Larry Lester, "Day, Leon," https://doi.org/10.1093/acref/9780195301731.013.35244, accessed June 25, 2024.
9. A comment by Day's widow Geraldine during her January 28, 2021, interview with Jorge Colón Delgado, official historian of Puerto Rican Professional Baseball, https:www.youtube.com/watch?v=z2NBGegd41A, accessed March 16, 2024; Lester, "Day, Leon."
10. Heaphy, "Shadowed Diamonds," 110–11.
11. Fred Lindsey, "Salute to a Local Legend," *Afro-American*, June 17, 1989.
12. Lew Zeidler, "Just below the Majors," *Brooklyn Eagle*, August 28, 1935.
13. Bill Glauber, "Elite Giants: The Pride of Baseball History," *Baltimore Sun*, April 2, 1990.
14. "Local Baseball Legend Waits for Next Year," *Afro-American*, March 28, 1992.
15. "Former Negro Leagues Star, New Hall of Famer Leon Day Is Dead at 78," *Iola Register* (Iola, KS), March 14, 1995.
16. Heaphy, "Shadowed Diamonds," 110–11; Wayne Coffey, "Players from Negro Leagues Remember Good—and Bad—Old Days," *The Sun*, August 18, 1991.
17. Ron Rapoport, *Let's Play Two: The Legend of Mr. Cub, the Life of Ernie Banks* (New York: Hachette, 2019), 55–56.
18. "Money Was No Concern in Early Days," *News Record* (North Hills, PA), August 14, 1994; James A. Riley, *The Biographical Encyclopedia of the Negro Baseball Leagues* (New York: Carroll & Graf, 1994), 42, 465.
19. "Negro Leaguers Can't Relate to Today's Pay," *Kokomo Tribune* (Kokomo, IN), August 14, 1994.
20. Heaphy, "Shadowed Diamonds," 127.
21. Randy Weller, "Old Timers Honoring McCord," *Nashville Banner*, February 16, 1996.
22. "Money Was No Concern in Early Days"; Jackie Robinson, "What's Wrong with the Negro Leagues," *Ebony*, June

1948; Riley, *Biographical Encyclopedia*, 529.

23. Mark Kram, "It Seemed like It Happened in Another Century," *Baltimore News American*, August 1, 1981.

24. John Holway, "One Day at a Time: Leon Day Waits for Hall of Fame Call," *Baseball Research Journal*, 1983; Riley, *Biographical Encyclopedia*, 264.

25. James A. Riley, *Dandy, Day and the Devil* (Cocoa, FL: TK Publishers, 1987), 71.

26. Riley, *Biographical Encyclopedia*, 223.

Chapter 1

1. Interview with Geraldine Day, October 30, 2023.

2. "Ashburn Tops Hall of Fame Inductees," *Brazosport Facts* (Clute, TX), March 8, 1995.

3. "Ford C. Frick Awards," National Baseball Hall of Fame, https://baseballhall.org/discover-more/awards/887, accessed September 17, 2024.

4. "Leon Day, Pitcher," National Baseball Hall of Fame, https://baseballhall.org/hall-of-famers/day-leon, accessed April 9, 2025; Anderson, "Leon's Day in the Sun at Last"; Holway, "Day Crossed a Road Less Traveled to Cooperstown"; James A. Riley, *Of Monarchs and Black Barons* (Jefferson, NC: McFarland, 2012), 246; Richard Goldstein, "Bob Gibson, Feared Flamethrower for the St. Louis Cardinals, Dies," *New York Times*, October 4, 2002.

5. Brad Snyder, "'You Made It, Man,'" *The Baltimore Sun*, March 5, 1995; Anderson, "Leon's Day in the Sun at Last"; Geraldine Day interview, October 31, 2023.

6. Brad Snyder, "300-Plus Pay Last Respects to Day," *The Sun*, March 18, 1995.

7. Noah Frank, "Sunset in Hagerstown? City, Team Fight for Minor League Survival," wtopnews, December 5, 2019, https://wtop.com/mlb/2019/12/sunset-in-hagerstown-city-team-fight-for-minor-league-survival/; Funeral Program, "In Loving Memory of Leon Day," March 17, 1995. Day's burial plot is Section U, Lot 33, Space 1.

8. Mike Klingaman, "For Leon Day's Widow, 'Baseball Is Mental Therapy,'" *Baltimore Sun*, October 29, 2014.

9. Ibid.

Chapter 2

1. Tim Wendel, "In His Day, Leon Day Was the Best," National Pastime Museum, last updated January 7, 2024, https://www.thenationalpastimemuseum.com/article/his-day-leon-day-was-best/.

2. Cum Posey, "Homestead Grays Stars Dominate 'Dream Team,'" *Pittsburgh Courier*, November 7, 1942; "To Make Plans for 1943 at Meeting," *Pittsburgh Courier*, January 23, 1943.

3. "Gas-Electric Employees Hold Gala Field Day," *Afro-American*, September 21, 1929.

4. Brad Snyder, "For Leon Day, Dream Is No Longer Deferred," *The Sun*, July 31, 1995.

5. Geraldine Day interview, August 31, 2023; Riley, *Dandy, Day and the Devil*, 79.

6. Riley, *Of Monarchs*, 104.

7. Riley, *Dandy, Day and the Devil*, 93; Snyder, "For Leon Day."

8. Riley, *Dandy, Day and the Devil*, 92–93.

9. Lot 4, Hunt Auction, March 25, 2017.

10. Riley, *Biographical Encyclopedia*, 52, 739, 53; Geraldine Day interview, August 31, 2023.

11. Geraldine Day interview, October 31, 2023.

12. Stevie Peters, "Interview with Geraldine Day," Cooperstown Graduate Program, Fall 2022.

13. Anderson, "Leon's Day in the Sun at Last."

Chapter 3

1. "Mount Winans/Mt. Winans," Westport CEDC, https://www.westportcedc.org/neighborhoods-1/mount-winans%2Fmt.-winans, accessed February 27, 2024; "Gives Glad Hand to the Working Girls," *Afro-American*, January 22, 1921.

2. Geraldine Day interview, August 31, 2023; 1920 and 1930 Federal Census, Virginia Birth Certificate 43082. Several accounts cite the Westport Glass Company as Ellis' employer. No reference could be found to the Westport Company. More likely the company's name was the Carr-Lowrey Glass Company, a large firm located in Westport.

3. Riley, *Dandy, Day and the Devil*, 78; Riley, *Biographical Encyclopedia*, 889.

4. Baker, "Ex-Negro Leaguer Is 'Hall' Material."

5. Lot 4, Hunt Auction, March 25, 2017.

6. Riley, *Dandy, Day and the Devil*, 81; "Silver Moons Take Twin Bill from Dem'crats," *Afro-American*, September 3, 1932; "Silver Moons Top Gray Sox," *Afro-American*, May 26, 1934.

7. Bernard McKenna, *The Baltimore Black Sox: A Negro Leagues History, 1913–1936* (Jefferson, NC: McFarland, 2020), 152–55; "Double Plays, Heavy Blows, Feature Two Sox Victories," *Afro-American*, May 3, 1930; "Two and Two," *Afro-American*, July 21, 1928; "The Seamheads Negro Leagues DB: A Brief Introduction," Negro Leagues Database, https://www.seamheads.com/NegroLgs/year.php?;earID=1934&lgID=NN2, accessed March 17, 2004.

8. Orrin C. Evans, "Sports Shorts," *Delaware County Daily Times*, August 1, 1949; Rick Hines, "Leon Day: The Man Cooperstown Forgot," *Sports Collectors Digest*, March 13, 1992.

9. Geraldine Day interview, October 31, 2023; Riley, *Biographical Encyclopedia*, 240; Riley, *Dandy, Day and the Devil*, 79; "Sox Boss Tells Why No More Games Were Played in Baltimore," *Afro-American*, August 25, 1934.

10. Riley, *Biographical Encyclopedia*, 391.

11. "1934 Baltimore Black Sox," Negro Leagues Database, https://seamheads.com/NegroLgs/team.php?yearID=1934&teamID=BBS&tab=pit, accessed April 9, 2025; Riley, *Biographical Encyclopedia*, 370; "Sox Make Late Bow by Losing Pair to Nashville Giants," *Afro-American*, July 14, 1934.

Chapter 4

1. Riley, *Dandy, Day and the Devil*, 80–81.

2. Bob Luke, *The Baltimore Elite Giants* (Baltimore: Johns Hopkins University Press, 2009), 6–7; Riley, *Biographical Encyclopedia*, 508, 399, 875–708, 636–37, 630.

3. Bob Luke, *The Most Famous Woman in Baseball: Effa Manley and the Negro Leagues* (Washington, DC: Potomac Books, 2011), 10–13, 17.

4. Riley, *Biographical Encyclopedia*, 889–90.

5. "Yokely Fans Ten but Sox Lose to All-Stars, 8–2," *Afro-American*, October 13, 1934; "Black Sox Lose," *Afro-American*, October 27, 1934; "Radcliffe, Dixon, and Balto. Lad on Brooklyn Eagles," *Afro-American*, April 6, 1935.

6. John Holway, *Blackball Stars* (Westport, CT: Meckler Publishers, 1988), 347.

7. Riley, *Biographical Encyclopedia*, 648–50; Riley, *Dandy, Day and the Devil*, 82. See Thomas Kern's biographical article on Radcliffe that raises well-researched questions about the true origin of Duty's nickname: "Ted 'Double Duty' Radcliffe," Society for American Baseball Research, https://sabr.org/bioproj/person/ted-double-duty-Radcliffe/, accessed November 5, 2023. One published comment on the issue is that of former Negro Leagues player turned sportswriter Chico Renfro. He stated in 1987, without attribution, that Runyon gave Duty his nickname in June 1932 after watching a doubleheader in

which Radcliffe caught the first game and pitched the second. Chico Renfro, "Sports of the World," *Atlanta Daily World*, June 16, 1987.

8. "Radcliffe, Dixon, and Balto. Lad on Brooklyn Eagles"; Riley, *Biographical Encyclopedia*, 598.

9. "Brooklyn Eagles Add to Lineup," *New York Age*, April 13, 1935.

10. "Belting Eagles Defeat Dodgers in Double Bill," *New York Age*, May 11, 1935; "Eagles Swamp the Dodgers in Double Bill," *Brooklyn Citizen*, May 6, 1935.

11. "1935 Brooklyn Eagles," Negro Leagues Database, https://seamheads.com/NegroLgs/team.php?yearID=1935&teamID=BE&tab=pit, accessed November 5, 2023.

12. "Philly Stars Win Two of Three from Brooklyn Eagles," *Afro-American*, May 18, 1935; "Bolden's Stars Take Three from Eagles," *New York Amsterdam News*, May 18, 1935; "Day Again Ace for Eagles Nine," *Times Union* (Brooklyn), May 13, 1935; "Eagles Swamp the Dodgers in Double Bill."

13. "Mayor to Toss First Ball at Brooklyn-Grays Series," *Chicago Defender*, May 18, 1935; "Grays Win 2, Lose 2, to Brooklyn," *Pittsburgh Courier*, May 25, 1935.

14. "Cuban Stars in Pair Win over Brooklyn Team," *Chicago Defender*, June 8, 1935.

15. Riley, *Biographical Encyclopedia*, 317.

16. "Brooklyn Team Starts West; To Meet Chicago," *Chicago Defender*, June 29, 1935.

17. "Black Yankees' Owner Not in Spiteful Mood," *New York Amsterdam News*, June 15, 1935.

18. "Eagles Play at Home on Sunday," *New York Amsterdam News*, July 6, 1935.

19. "Brooklyn Shows Giants How Easterners Play Baseball," *Chicago Defender*, July 6, 1935.

20. "Crawfords Split 4 Games with Brooklyn Eagles," *Afro-American*, July 20, 1935; "Stars Lose 1, Win 3 from Brooklyn," *Times Union* (Brooklyn), August 22, 1935.

21. "Rookie to Stardom," *Times Union* (Brooklyn), August 9, 1935.

22. Randy Dixon, "Sports Bugle," *Philadelphia Tribune*, July 29, 1937.

23. Lewis E. Dial, "The Sport Dial," *New York Age*, November 9, 1935; "Cum Posey's Pointed Paragraphs," *Pittsburgh Courier*, December 14, 1935; Harold Parrott, "Reds to Meet Eagles," *Brooklyn Daily Eagle*, January 14, 1936; "Brooklyn Eagles and Reds Divide Honors," *Bristol Herald Courier*, March 2, 1936; "Brown Defeats Dihigo," *Pittsburgh Courier*, March 21, 1936; Riley, *Biographical Encyclopedia*, 745.

24. Thomas Barthel, *Baseball's Peerless Semipros: The Brooklyn Bushwicks of Dexter Park* (Haworth, NJ: St. Johann Press, 2009), 275.

25. Ibid., 148, 189.

26. "Gotham Fans to Get Peep at Josh Gibson," *New Journal and Guide*, July 24, 1943.

27. Luke, *The Most Famous Woman*, 22–24.

28. Ibid., 21.

29. Alan Richardson, "A Retrospective Look at the Negro Leagues and Professional Negro Baseball Players" (MA thesis, San Jose State University, 1980), 158; Marriage Application, Effa Manley File, National Baseball Hall of Fame and Museum, Cooperstown, NY.

30. Luke, *The Most Famous Woman*, 7–8.

Chapter 5

1. "Report of N.J. Survey Body Stresses Job Ills," *Afro-American*, January 22, 1940.

2. Ibid.

3. Luke, *The Most Famous Woman*, 17–21.

4. Ibid., 20–27.

5. Riley, *Biographical Encyclopedia*, 75; "Brooklyn Eagles Add to Lineup."

6. "Elites Belt Eagles," *New York Amsterdam News*, May 21, 1936; "Elite Giants Win, Lose with Newark," *Chicago*

Defender, May 23, 1936; William E. Clark, "Cubans Win Three out of Four Games from Newark Eagles over Weekend," *New York Age*, June 13, 1936; Riley, *Biographical Encyclopedia*, 234–35, 74–75, 536; Luke, *Most Famous Woman*, 169.

7. "Cubans Win Three out of Four Games from Newark Eagles over Weekend; Elite Giants Coming," *New York Age*, June 13, 1924; Riley, *Biographical Encyclopedia*, 105, 234; "Great Day," *New Pittsburgh Courier*, August 1, 1936.

8. Riley, *Biographical Encyclopedia*, 271, 209.

9. "Puerto Rico News," *Philadelphia Tribune*, November 12, 1936; W. Rollo Wilson, "Thru the Eyes," *Pittsburgh Courier*, February 27, 1937; Newark Eagles Sail for Winter Baseball Season," *Afro-American*, December 5, 1936; Pas-senger List, S.S. *Coama, Ancestry*, accessed October 11, 2023; "Eagles, Ball Hawks, Sail for Islands," *New Pittsburgh Courier*, December 5, 1936.

10. Riley, *Biographical Encyclopedia*, 170, 753, 22.

11. E.R. Rae, "Newark Eagles Take Three Games from Winston," *New Journal and Guide*, May 8, 1937.

12. E.B. Rea, "From the Press Box," *New Journal and Guide*, May 15, 1937.

13. "Dexter Parkers See Why Eagles Lead Negro Race," *Times Union* (Brooklyn), June 1, 1937; "Farmers Combat Eagles Tonight," *Brooklyn Daily Eagle*, June 22, 1937; "Eagles Suffer 1st Loop Setback by Yankee Nine at Dexter Park," *Brooklyn Eagle*, June 1, 1937.

14. "Eagles Take Double from Black Yanks," *New York Amsterdam News*, August 7, 1937; Warren Corbett, "George Earnshaw," Society for American Baseball Research, https://sabr.org/bioproj/person/george-earnshaw/, accessed November 21, 2023; "Day Fans 16 as Eagles Tie in 11 Innings," *Philadelphia Tribune*, August 12, 1937; "Eagles with Best NL Infield," *New York Age*, August 7, 1937.

15. "Newark Eagles Put out 1937 Averages," *Philadelphia Tribune*, March 10, 1938.

16. Riley, *Dandy, Day and the Devil*, 68.

17. Luke, *The Most Famous Woman*, 33–34.

18. *Ibid.*, 34–35.

Chapter 6

1. "Cuban Sportsways," *New York Amsterdam News*, November 13, 1937; "Cuban Sportsways," *New York Amsterdam News*, November 27, 1937; Midget Alberts, "Cuban Sportsways," *New York Amsterdam News*, January 29, 1938.

2. Hines, "Leon Day."

3. "Newark Eagles Expect Few Changes," *Philadelphia Tribune*, February 17, 1938; "Day Recovering from Ailing Arm," *New Journal and Guide*, March 5, 1938; Passenger List, S.S. *Florida, Ancestry*, accessed October 11, 2023.

4. "Leon Day among Quartet Balking for More Money," *Philadelphia Tribune*, March 24, 1938; Leon Day, "Arm on Bum, Out," *Afro-American*, June 4, 1938; Roch Eric Kubatko, "Maryland Honors Day, Star in Negro Leagues," *The Sun*, May 19, 1992; "Leon Day Asking Highest Salary," *New Pittsburgh Courier*, March 26, 1938.

5. "Eagles Encounter Parkways Sunday," *Brooklyn Eagle*, May 4, 1938; H.R. Webber, "Eagles Spank Craws Twice, Lose Once," *Afro-American*, May 28, 1938; "Newark Pilot Worried over Pitcher Day's Injured Arm," *Pittsburgh Courier*, June 4, 1938; "Homestead in Twin Victory over Eagles," *Philadelphia Tribune*, June 9, 1938; "Injuries Hamper Eagles," *Philadelphia Courier*, June 18, 1938; "Smitty's Sports Spurts," *Pittsburgh Courier*, June 18, 1938; "Grays 'Walk Away' with First Half Honors," *Pittsburgh Courier*, July 16, 1938.

6. Riley, *Dandy, Day and the Devil*, 8, 7; Cum Posey, "Posey's Points," *Pittsburgh Courier*, September 10, 1938.

7. Riley, *Biographical Encyclopedia*, 437.

8. *Ibid.*, 535; "Eagles Trade McDuffie to Yanks for Rookie Hurler," *Philadelphia Tribune*, August 25, 1938.

9. "Satchel Paige 'Not Wanted,'" *Chicago Defender*, December 17, 1938.
10. Riley, *Dandy, Day and the Devil*, 87.
11. "New Hurling 'Find' Slated for Birth [sic] with Newark," *New Pittsburgh Courier*, April 22, 1939.
12. Harry B. Webber, "Baseball's Bosses Meet," *Afro-American*, February 18, 1939; "New Hurling 'Find' Slated for Birth [sic] with Newark."
13. "Maconites Thrill to 2 Games," *Atlanta Daily World*, May 3, 1939; Riley, *Dandy, Day and the Devil*, 87.
14. Riley, *Biographical Encyclopedia*, 872; "Grays and Newark in Crucial Series," *Pittsburgh Courier*, July 8, 1939; "Eagles Divide Doubleheader with the Grays," *Afro-American*, July 15, 1939; "Eagles Break Even with Homestead Grays Retain League Lead," *New York Age*, July 15, 1939.
15. "Elites Divide 2 with Newark," *Afro-American*, July 29, 1939; "Ex-Black Crax Keep Baltimore in League Lead," *Atlanta Daily World*, July 29, 1939; Art Carter, "From the Bench," *Afro-American*, July 29, 1939; "Newark Eagles Divide Pair with Baltimore," *New Journal and Guide*, July 29, 1939.
16. "Leon Day Loses as Eagles Drop Two to Phillies," *Afro-American*, August 19, 1939.
17. "Suttles Socks Home Run But Eagles Lose," *Afro-American*, September 16, 1939; Ralph Boyd, "Elites Whip Eagles to Gain Championship," *Afro-American*, September 16, 1939; Riley, *Biographical Encyclopedia*, 270–71.
18. "Bushwicks End Arc Schedule," *Brooklyn Eagle*, September 20, 1939; "Campanella in Star's Role as Elites Score," *Afro-American*, September 30, 1939.
19. "N.L. Players Dominate Posey's All-American '9,'" *Pittsburgh Courier*, January 6, 1940.
20. Riley, *Dandy, Day and the Devil*, 88.
21. Ibid., 93.
22. Riley, *Biographical Encyclopedia*, 370.
23. Victor M. Calderon, *The Wager Nobody Cared to Win: My Life with ADHD* (Bloomington, IN: Xlibris, 2011), n.p.; Riley, *Biographical Encyclopedia*, 370–71.
24. Thomas E. Van Hyning, *The Santurce Crabbers: Sixty Seasons of Puerto Rican Winter League Baseball* (Jefferson, NC: McFarland, 1999), 9; Daniel, "Satchel Paige May Pitch Newark Opener," *New York Amsterdam News*, May 4, 1940.
25. Riley, *Dandy, Day and the Devil*, 88.
26. "Gang of Rookies Brings Joy to the Hearts of the Manleys as Newark Eagles Head to South for Training," *Philadelphia Tribune*, April 11, 1940; "Newark Eagles to Train in Savannah," *New Pittsburgh Courier*, March 30, 1940.

Chapter 7

1. Riley, *Dandy, Day and the Devil*, 89–90.
2. Pedro Treto Cisneros, *The Mexican League, Comprehensive Player Statistics* (Jefferson, NC: McFarland, 2002), 123, 338.
3. Kubatko, "Maryland Honors Day."
4. John Holway, "Historically Speaking: Ray Dandridge," *Black Sports*, September 1977, 52, as cited in John Virtue, *South of the Color Barrier: How Jorge Pasquel and the Mexican League Pushed Baseball* (Jefferson, NC: McFarland, 2008).
5. William Marshall interview of Ray Dandridge, November 12, 1979.
6. Cum Posey, "Posey's Points," *Pittsburgh Courier*, August 10, 1940; Virtue, *South of the Color Barrier*, 7–22; Kubatko, "Maryland Honors Day."
7. Virtue, *South of the Color Barrier*, 83, 88; Paul Dickson, *Baseball's Greatest Maverick* (New York: Walker, 2012), 122–23.
8. "Leon Day First Outlaw Player to Sign Contract," *Afro-American*, April 5, 1941; "Eagles Seek Return of Outlaw Players; Release Suttles," *Afro-American*,

Notes—Chapter 8

March 15, 1941; "Leon Day Rejoins Newark in South," *New York Age*, April 5, 1941.
   9. "Day Joins Newark Eagles," *Chicago Defender*, April 12, 1941; "Leon Day First Outlaw Player to Sign Contract."
   10. Art Carter, "From the Bench," *Afro-American*, January 11, 1941.
   11. Interview of Irvin by the author, February 10, 2008; Wendell Smith, "Wells to Succeed Hornsby," *Pittsburgh Courier*, May 6, 1944.

Chapter 8

   1. James Overmyer, *Effa Manley and the Newark Eagles* (Metuchen, NJ: Scarecrow, 1993), 15; Barbara J. Kukla, *Swing City: Newark Night Life, 1925–50* (New Brunswick, NJ: Rutgers University Press, 2002), 7–10.
   2. "Gets Apology from Railway," *New York Amsterdam News*, February 15, 1940; William O. Walker, "Letter Box," *Cleveland Call and Post*, June 24, 1950.
   3. Harry B. Webber, "Plan $15,000 Lawsuit," *New York Amsterdam Star-News*, November 12, 1941; "Potato Pickers Win $9,000 Verdict," *Philadelphia Tribune*, May 16, 1941.
   4. Stanley Glenn interview by the author, January 12, 2006.
   5. Effa Manley letter to "Dear Friend," July 19, 1946, Newark Eagles Files, Newark Public Library.
   6. Luke, *The Most Famous Woman*, 76; "Judge William Hastie, 71, of Federal Court, Dies," *New York Times*, April 15, 1976.
   7. "Hastie Ends Jim Crow of 3,000 Workers," *Afro-American*, December 5, 1942.
   8. "Newark Reports Refute Hastie," *New York Amsterdam Star-News*, December 12, 1942.
   9. "New Jersey C.I.O. Hits Army Segregation," *Chicago Defender*, December 18, 1943.
   10. Paul Dickson, *The Rise of the G.I. Army 1940–41: The Forgotten Story of How America Forged a Powerful Army Before Pearl Harbor* (New York: Atlantic Monthly Press, 2020), 144–46.
   11. "Plants Plead Ignorance of F.D.R. Job-Bias Order," *Pittsburgh Courier*, February 21, 1942; "Report Gains in War Employment," *New York Amsterdam Star-News*, March 7, 1942; "Tells 8 Concerns to Lift Racial Bars," *New York Times*, May 27, 1942; "Newark Booms with War Work: Negroes Fail to Get Their Share," *New York Amsterdam Star-News*, November 21, 1942.
   12. "Wm. Jackson Is on Board of Education," *Newark Herald*, July 4, 1942.
   13. "Congressmen Join Fight for Mixed Army Units," *Chicago Defender*, June 2, 1945.
   14. Charlie Cherokee, "National Grape-vine," *Chicago Defender*, April 10, 1948; Dickson, *The Rise of the G.I. Army*, 342–43.
   15. "Executive Order 9981, Desegregating the Military," Charles Young Buffalo Soldiers National Monument, National Park Service, https://www.nps.gov/articles/000/executive-order-9981.htm, accessed April 27, 2024.
   16. Walt Napier, "A Short History of Integration in the U.S. Armed Forces," 447th Fighter Group, July 1, 2021, https://www.477fg.afrc.af.mil/News/Commentaries/Display/Article/2679252/a-short-history-of-integration-in-the-us-armed-forces/; "Negro Soldiers Prove Courage in Mixed Units," *Michigan Chronicle*, May 5, 1945; "Hidden Report Blow to Jim Crow Army," *Afro-American*, October 27, 1945.
   17. "NJ State Constitution," New Jersey State Legislature, https://www.njleg.state.nj.us/constitution, accessed June 16, 2024.
   18. "New Jersey Approves New 'Equal Rights' Constitution," *Afro-American*, November 14, 1947.
   19. "Majority of Schools in N.J. Segregate," *Philadelphia Tribune*, June 15, 1948.
   20. "Newark Board Agrees to End School Jim Crow by Residence," *Afro-American*, March 24, 1962.

21. "On the Desegregation Front," *Louisville Defender*, September 8, 1955.

Chapter 9

1. "Day Joins Newark Eagles," *Chicago Defender*, April 12, 1941.
2. "Cubans Take NNL Lead as Other Teams Split Bills," *Afro-American*, May 17, 1941; "Cubans in Win over Newark," *Chicago Defender*, May 17, 1941; "12,500 Fans Attend Opening at Ruppert Stadium in Newark," *New York Age*, May 17, 1941; Riley, *Biographical Encyclopedia*, 42.
3. Riley, *Biographical Encyclopedia*, 391, 509, 383, 196, 223, 120–21; "Newark Nine Discovers 2nd Satchel Paige," *Chicago Defender*, April 19, 1941.
4. "Newark Takes League Lead: Nip Quakers," *New York Amsterdam Star-News*, May 24, 1941; "Eagles Soar to NNL Lead with Twin Win: Elites Top Bushwicks," *Afro-American*, May 24, 1941; "Newark Eagles Take Two from Star [sic]; Go into First Place," *New York Age*, May 24, 1941.
5. "Newark Eagles Defeat Cubans," *Harrisburg Telegraph*, June 26, 1941.
6. "Eagles Defeat Bushwicks, 5–1," *Afro-American*, June 7, 1941; "Campanella Leads Loop in Batting," *Philadelphia Tribune*, June 12, 1941; "Pitchers Perfect as Elite Giants and Eagles Split," *Philadelphia Tribune*, July 31, 1941; "Newark Eagles Defeat Cubans."
7. Dick Powell, "Day Scores Seven Runs for Newark," *Afro-American*, August 16, 1941.
8. "Homestead Grays and Newark All Set for Benefit Game at Polo Grounds This Saturday," *New York Age*, September 13, 1941.
9. "Newark Splits 4 Games with Black Yankees," *Afro-American*, August 9, 1941.
10. "History 1940–1948," Negro Leagues Database, https://www.seamheads.com/NegroLgs/history.php?tab=years&first=1940&last=1948&lgID=NN2&lgType=All, accessed October 31, 2023.
11. Dan Burley, "Confidentially Yours," *New York Amsterdam Star-News*, March 15, 1941.
12. "Athlete Bio: John Borican," National Track & Field Hall of Fame, https://www.usatf.org/athlete-bios/john-borican, accessed April 9, 2025.
13. "John Borican," NJSports.com, https://www.njsportsheroes.com/johnboricantf.html, accessed October 31, 2023; "Elites, Grays Win Twin Bill at Borican Day," *Afro-American*, September 6, 1941.
14. Art Carter, "From the Bench," *Afro-American*, February 14, 1942; "Here and There," *Pittsburgh Courier*, February 14, 1942; Riley, *Biographical Encyclopedia*, 124.
15. Thomas E. Van Hyning, *Puerto Rico's Winter League: A History of Major League's Launching Pad* (Jefferson, NC: McFarland, 1995), 4, 86–87, 241, 252, 255; Riley, *Biographical Encyclopedia*, 607.
16. "Nation Needs Baseball, Say Congressmen," *Chicago Daily Tribune*, January 9, 1942.
17. "Diamond Stars in Puerto Rico May Be Victims of Axis Blockade," *Afro-American*, March 14, 1942; Diz Dismukes, "Looks at Baseball," *The Call* (Kansas City, Missouri), March 20, 1942; Riley, *Dandy, Day and the Devil*, 72.
18. Lem Graves, Jr., "Eagles Gain 3–0 Decision over Hilldales," *New Journal and Guide*, May 2, 1942.
19. "Grays Bow Twice to Newark Eagles," *Chicago Defender*, April 25, 1942.
20. "Elites Take Lead with Double Win over Newark," *Afro-American*, May 30, 1942; "Eagles, Stars Divide Bill," *Afro-American*, May 23, 1942; Art Carter, "Teams Split Baltimore Holiday Bill," *Afro-American*, June 6, 1942.
21. "Philly Stars, Newark Victors Before 17,000 in Yankee Stadium," *Pittsburgh Courier*, June 6, 1942; "Willie Wells Revamps Newark Eagles Lineup," *Chicago Defender*, June 13, 1942; "Strengthened Newark Eagles Return Home to

Face Yanks," *New York Amsterdam News*, June 20, 1942.

22. "Willie Wells Revamps Newark Eagles Lineup."

23. "Black Yankees Win Doubleheader from the Newark Eagles," *New York Age*, June 27, 1942; "Newark Gets Mad and Beats Grays 2 Games," *Chicago Defender*, July 4, 1942; "9,000 Watch Eagles Trim Grays in 14," *Chicago Defender*, July 4, 1942; "McDuffie Blanks Eagles, 10–0," *Philadelphia Tribune*, July 11, 1942.

24. "McDuffie Blanks Eagles"; Lem Graves, Jr., "Grays Sweep Four Game Series with Eagles," *New Journal and Guide*, July 11, 1942; "First Half Honors Go to Elites," *Afro-American*, July 11, 1942; "'No First-Half Champion,' Says League Secretary," *Pittsburgh Gazette*, July 11, 1942.

25. John G. Palmer, "Great Pitching by Leon Day Ends Bushwicks' 9-Game Winning Streak," *Brooklyn Citizen*, July 13, 1942; "Harris Winner over Eagles as Bushwicks Split," *Brooklyn Eagle*, July 13, 1942.

26. "Elites Drop 3 Straight as Grays Take Twin Bill," *Afro-American*, August 1, 1942; "Eagles Edge Grays in 14 Innings, 6 to 5," *New Journal and Guide*, July 4, 1942; Art Carter, "From the Bench," *Afro-American*, August 8, 1942; Cum Posey, "Posey's Points," *Pittsburgh Courier*, August 8, 1942; "Barons' Pitcher Whiffs 20," *Philadelphia Tribune*, August 28, 1943.

27. "Win and Lose in 2 Games," *Afro-American*, August 29, 1942; "Grays Win NNL Flag; Play K.C.'s," *Afro-American*, September 12, 1942; "1942 Season," Negro Leagues Database, https://www.seamheads.com/NegroLgs/year.php?yearID=1942, accessed November 3, 2023.

28. Riley, *Dandy, Day and the Devil*, 66–68; Riley, *Of Monarchs*, 161; "Protested Game Kicked Out," *Chicago Defender*, October 3, 1942; "Grays Win, 4–1, but Monarchs Protest Use of Day," *Afro-American*, September 26, 1942; "Charge Grays Used 'Ringers' in Fourth World Series Game," *Pittsburgh Courier*, September 26, 1942; "Posey's All-American Team for '42," *Pittsburgh Courier*, November 7, 1942; Riley, *Biographical Encyclopedia*, 91–92, 613, 176, 237.

Chapter 10

1. "Major League Heads Say Negroes Can Play Baseball," *Cleveland Call and Post*, July 25, 1942.

2. Ibid.

3. Ibid.

4. "Alva Bradley, 69, Indian Ex-Owner," *Washington Post*, March 30, 1953; "Indians Turn Thumbs Down on Woods, Parnell, Bremer," *Cleveland Call and Post*, September 12, 1942.

5. Lucius Jones, "Philadelphia Phillies Try Out Baltimore Elites' Roy Campanella After Landis Edict," *Atlanta Daily World*, July 26, 1942.

6. "Major League Heads Say Negroes Can Play Baseball"; "Barney Brown, Spearman, Clarks 'n Shine as Stars Beat Eagles, 20–5," *Philadelphia Tribune*, July 25, 1942.

7. "Indians Turn Thumbs Down on Woods, Parnell, Bremer."

8. Lem Graves, Jr., "From the Press Box," *New Journal and Guide*, August 8, 1942.

9. Edgar T. Rouzeau, "The Sportoscope," *New Journal and Guide*, September 23, 1939.

10. Jay Don Davis, "From the Press Box," *New Journal and Globe*, June 26, 1942.

11. Wendell Smith, "Smitty's Sports-Spurts," *Pittsburgh Courier*, August 15, 1942.

12. "Move to Get Negro Players in National and American League Fails,'" *Washington Post*, December 4, 1942.

13. Wendell Smith, "Frick Says Owners Were Impressed by Publishers," *Pittsburgh Courier*, December 11, 1943.

14. John Fuster, "No Negro Stars Signed Yet: National and Local Effort, W.O. Walker's Plan, Starts," *Cleveland Call and Post*, September 5, 1942.

15. "Notables to Demand Negroes in National and American League," *New York Amsterdam Star-News*, October 31, 1942.
16. Jones, "Philadelphia Phillies Try Out Baltimore Elites' Roy Campanella After Landis Edict."
17. Donn Rogosin, *Invisible Men*, 124 as cited in Virtue, *South of the Color Barrier*, 33.
18. "Veeck Planned to Scrap Phillies for Negro Club," *Philadelphia Tribune*, August 14, 1954.
19. Larry Gerlach, David Jordan, and John Rossi, "A Baseball Myth Exploded: Bill Veeck and the 1943 Sale of the Phillies," *National Pastime* 18 (1998). The *National Pastime* was published by the Society for American Baseball Research.
20. Jules Tygiel, "Phillies," *Baseball Research Journal* (2006); Norm King, "Abe Saperstein," Society for American Baseball Research, https://sabr.org/bioproj/person/abe-saperstein, accessed November 28, 2023.
21. Paul Dickson, *Bill Veeck: Baseball's Greatest Maverick* (New York: Walker, 2012), 357–66.
22. Peter Susskind, "The National and American League Could Use Leon Day," *New Journal and Guide*, June 5, 1943.
23. "Eagles Begin Spring Grind on April 12th," *New York Amsterdam News*, April 3, 1943.
24. "Day Heads Fine Mound Corps as Eagles Launch Training," *New Journal and Guide*, April 17, 1943; "Hurling Staff, Headed by Day, Newark's Best Asset," *Afro-American*, April 17, 1943.
25. "Trenton Packers Franchise History (1942–1944)," Stats Crew, https://www.statscrew.com/minorbaseball/t-tp15025, accessed November 21, 2023; "Leon Day Shows Old Form in Initial Hurling Stint," *Afro-American*, May 8, 1943.
26. "Grays Beat Newark, 5–3, in Extra Inning Battle," *New Journal and Guide*, May 15, 1943.
27. "Stars Lose Opener, 4–2, as Eagles Rally in 11th," *Afro-American*, May 22, 1943; "Leon Day Breaks Jinx as Eagles Win, 9–1," *Afro-American*, May 22, 1943.
28. "Stars Top Blk. Yanks 6–1," *Afro-American*, June 5, 1943; "Grays Whip Newark, 6–0," *Michigan Chronicle*, May 29, 1943; Riley, *Biographical Encyclopedia*, 265.
29. "Homestead Grays Take Two from Newark Eagles," *New Journal and Guide*, July 3, 1943; Ric Roberts, "Grays and Eagles Split 2 Games," *Pittsburgh Courier*, August 14, 1943; "Grays Whip Newark, 6–0"; "Newark Eagles and Homestead Grays Winners in Twin-Bill Game Sunday," *New York Age*, July 31, 1943; Riley, *Biographical Encyclopedia*, 883.
30. "Gibson and Martinez Lead Poll for All-Star Game," *New Journal and Guide*, July 24, 1943.
31. "Interracial Game in D.C. Features Bushwicks vs. Grays," *New Journal and Guide*, July 3, 1943; "Grays Defeat Bushwicks Before 10,000," *Philadelphia Tribune*, July 17, 1943.

Chapter 11

1. "Negro Leaguers in World War II" and "Negro Leaguers in World War II by Team." Lists provided to the Baseball Hall of Fame, Cooperstown, New York, by Larry Lester, Noir Tech Research Inc., Kansas City, Missouri.
2. "Many Leading Ball Players in the Army," *Pittsburgh Courier*, January 1, 1944.
3. Franklin Penn, "League All-Stars Lose 3-Game Series," *Philadelphia Tribune*, September 25, 1943.
4. "Baltimore May Face Gray Team," *The Call* (Kansas City, Missouri), September 24, 1943; "Winter Loop Baseball Plans Told," *California Eagle*, September 16, 1943.
5. Cornelius Ryan, Foreword to *The Longest Day: June 6, 1944* (New York: Simon & Schuster, 1959), https://www.nationalww2museum.org/students-teachers/student-resources/research-starters/research-starters-d-day#:~:

Notes—Chapter 12

text=Whether%20by%20parachute%2C%20glider%2C%20or,2%2C400%20were%20on%20Omaha%20Beach, accessed June 6, 2024.

6. "Research Starters: The Draft and World War II," National WWII Museum, New Orleans, https://www.nationalww2museum.org/students-teachers/student-resources/research-starters/draft-and-wwii#:~:text=On%20September%2016%2C%201940%2C%20the,draft%20in%20United%20States'%20history, accessed December 2, 2023; Leon Day in the U.S. World War II Draft Cards Young Men, 1940–1947, on Ancestry.com, accessed December 2, 2023; "818th Amphibious Truck Company."

7. "Newsmen Score War Department Policy," *Chicago Defender*, December 13, 1941.

8. John Jasper, "Hastie Fought Army Jim Crow to the End," *Afro-American*, March 13, 1943.

9. "Newark to Lose Battery Aces," *Pittsburgh Courier*, September 18, 1943; Art Carter, "From the Bench," *Afro-American*, January 30, 1943; "Leon Day, Newark Pitcher, Inducted at Fort Dix, N.J." *Afro-American*, October 2, 1943.

10. "Medal of Honor Profile: COL Gordon Johnston," https://web.archive.org/web/20091231210810/http://www.gordon.army.mil/ocos/ac/Edition,%20Summer/Summer%202002/johnston.htm, accessed December 2, 2023; Patrick Connolly, "Florida Woman Retraces Father's Past as Captain of the WWII 818th Amphibious Truck Company," *Orlando Sentinel*, November 11, 2022.

11. Everette Coppock, Email to author, February 17, 2024.

12. "Motor Pool," Camp Gordon Johnston WWII Museum, Campgordonjohnston.com/motor-pool/, accessed April 14, 2024.

13. "About the Army DUKW," Rainforestation Nature Park, https://www.rainforest.com.au/army-dukw/, accessed April 24, 2024.

14. "Army Recruiting Caravan to Visit Ironwood, Bessemer," *Ironwood Daily Globe* (Ironwood, Michigan), September 10, 1946; "Army Amphibious DUKW Is Shown," *Ironwood Daily Globe* (Ironwood, Michigan), September 13, 1946.

15. Paul Dickson, *G.I. Jive: A Dictionary of Words at War: 1939–1946* (manuscript in progress), 151.

16. W.P. Lambertson, "The Cloakroom," *Fairview Enterprise*, October 28, 1943.

17. Ollie Stewart, "Ex-Newark Hurler Drives DUKW in English Channel," *Afro-American*, June 15, 1944.

18. Robert Weintraub, *The Victory Season: The End of World War II and the Birth of Baseball's Golden Age* (New York: Little Brown, 2013), 56–60; Robert Weintraub, "Three Reichs, You're Out: The Amazing Story of the U.S. Military's Integrated 'World Series,' in Hitler Youth Stadium in 1945," *Slate*, April 2, 2013, https://slate.com/culture/2013/04/baseball-in-world-war-ii-the-amazing-story-of-the-u-s-militarys-integrated-world-series-in-hitler-youth-stadium-in-1945.html.

19. Edna Green Medford and Michael Frazier, "Keep 'Em Rolling: African American Participation in the Red Ball Express," *Negro History Bulletin*, December 1993, 57–62.

20. Chris Jackson, "The Red Ball Express," *Chicago Defender*, July 22, 1955; "White Press Pays Tribute to Gallant Negro Soldiers," *Cleveland Call and Post*, January 13, 1945; "'Red Ball Express' Wins Eisenhower Citation," *Chicago Defender*, September 10, 1944; Ollie Stewart, "There Was Only One Red Ball Express," *Afro-American*, March 7, 1953.

21. Sean Axmaker, "Ride Lonesome: The Career of Budd Boetticher," Senses of Cinema, February 2006, https://www.sensesofcinema.com/2006/feature-articles/boetticher/.

Chapter 12

1. Weintraub, "Three Reichs, You're Out"; Weintraub, *The Victory Season*,

56–59; Riley, *Biographical Encyclopedia*, 127–28.
2. Author source missing.
3. Weintraub, *The Victory Season*, 59–62; Gary Bedinfield, "The 1945 GI World Series," in *When Baseball Went to War*, ed. Todd Anderson and Bill Nowlin (Chicago: Triumph Books, 2008), 208–11; "TSFET Trumps 3rd Army, 2–1," *Southern France Stars and Stripes*, September 5, 1945; "3rd Army Ties Diamond Series for ETO Title," *London Stars and Stripes*, September 8, 1945; Stephen R. Bullock, "Vital Connections: Baseball and the American Military During World War II" (PhD diss., University of Nebraska, 2001), 126.
4. Ollie Stewart, "Leon Day Gives 4 Hits in Outpitching Pirate," *Afro-American*, October 20, 1945.

Chapter 13

1. "Women Quit When Whites Just Hired, Get More Pay," *New Jersey Afro-American*, August 28, 1943; "Plan Housing in Newark for War Workers," *Newark Herald*, September 13, 1943; "Status of New YW Is Cleared," *Chicago Defender*, December 25, 1943; "Jersey C.I.O. Hits Army Segregation," *Chicago Defender*, December 18, 1943; "Discrimination Exposed in 'It's Midnight over Newark,'" *New York Amsterdam Star-News*, May 7, 1944; "N.J. Hospital Board Upholds Ban Against Negroes on Staff," *New York Amsterdam Star-News*, June 17, 1944.
2. "Newark Is Disturbed," *Afro-American*, November 23, 1940.
3. "N.J. Medics in Bitter Fight to Avoid Jim Crow," *Chicago Defender*, June 1, 1935.
4. "White War Vets Refuse to Use 'Jim Crow' Park," *Pittsburgh Courier*, February 11, 1939; "Color Bar Causes Vets to Reject Park's Invitation," *Chicago Defender*, March 11, 1939.
5. "N.J. Beach Fight Won," *Afro-American*, April 12, 1939.
6. "'Jim Crow Dishes' for Negro Patrons Is Latest Addition at Jersey Resort," *Pittsburgh Courier*, September 10, 1938.
7. "Segregation in Movies Calls for Technique," *Newark Herald*, July 11, 1942.
8. Michael Carter, "Jersey Jives Colored People: An Interview with Governor Charles Edison of N.J.," *Afro-American*, August 21, 1943.

Chapter 14

1. Geraldine Day interview, October 31, 2023.
2. Wayne Coffee, "Players from Negro Leagues Remember Good—and Bad—Times," *The Sun*, August 18, 1991.
3. Riley, *Biographical Encyclopedia*, 537; Effa Manley, letter to Art Carter, May 9, 1946, Moorland-Spingarn Research Center, Howard University, Art Carter Papers, Box 170–16, Folder 9; "Day Hurls; No Hits, No Runs," *Chicago Defender*, May 11, 1946; Hines, "Leon Day."
4. Riley, *Of Monarchs*, 154–55.
5. "Play that Caused Near Riot in Newark Eagles' No Hit Win from Philly," *New York Amsterdam News*, May 11, 1946; Effa Manley, letter to Mr. Ed Gottlieb, May 8, 1946, Newark Eagles Files, Newark Public Library; "8 Players Get 5-Year Suspensions for Mexico Jump," *Baltimore Afro-American*, May 25, 1946; Riley, *Biographical Encyclopedia*, 328, 207; "Police Halt Philadelphia Stars-Newark Eagles Riot," *New York Amsterdam News*, May 11, 1946.
6. National Negro League Bureau, "Around and About with the NNL Baseball Teams," *Afro-American*, May 18, 1946; "Newark Eagles Whip Yankees, 8–2 in Fourth," *New York Amsterdam News*, May 18, 1946.
7. Luke, *The Most Famous Woman*, 125–26.
8. Wendell Smith, "The Sports Beat," *Pittsburgh Courier*, July 13, 1946; "Eagles, Stars, in Tie for NNL Lead; Newark Tops Cubans Twice," *New Journal and Guide*, July 15, 1946; "Cubans Take Over Lead

in National League," *New Journal and Guide*, June 8, 1946; "Newark Twice Blanks Stars to Nab Title," *Philadelphia Tribune*, July 2, 1946; "Eagles Down Cubans, 7–1, 4–2, to Gain First Place," *New York Age*, June 15, 1946.

9. Wendell Smith, "The Sports Beat," *Pittsburgh Courier*, July 13, 1946.

10. "Newark Eagles Defeat Grays, by 8–7 in 15th," *New York Amsterdam News*, August 17, 1946; "Strikeout King," *Afro-American*, August 10, 1946.

11. "Newark Eagles Rout Satchel Paige 7–4," *Cleveland Call and Post*, August 17, 1946; "Strikeout King," *Afro-American*, August 10, 1946; "Day Hurls Newark Victory, Clouts Homer for Winning Run," *New Journal and Guide*, August 17, 1946.

12. "1946 Season," Negro Leagues Database, seamheads.com/NegroLgs/year.php?yearID=1946, accessed August 12, 2024; "Newark Eagles Rout Satchell Paige 7–4."

13. "Kansas City Monarchs, Newark Eagles Ready for World Series," *Alabama Tribune*, September 20, 1946; "Newark Eagles Defeat Grays, by 8–7 in 15th."

14. Lem Graves, Jr., "Press Box," *New Journal Guide*, September 14, 1946.

15. "Newark Eagles Win World Series Crown," *Afro-American*, October 5, 1946.

16. Steve Wulf and David Conrads, *Buck O'Neil, I Was Right on Time* (New York: Simon & Schuster, 1996), 178–79.

17. "Satchel Paige, Monarch's Ace-in-Hole as Negro World Series Opens," *Cleveland Call and Post*, September 1, 1946; Lem Graves, Jr., "Kansas City Edges Newark 2–1 in Series," *New Journal and Guide*, September 21, 1946; "Army Vet Hurls Newark to World Series Title," *Chicago Defender*, October 5, 1946; Riley, *Biographical Encyclopedia*, 589, 481, 723; "Newark Eagles Win World Series Crown," *Afro-American*, October 5, 1946.

18. Effa Manley and Leon Herbert Hardwick, *Negro Baseball Before Integration* (Chicago: Adams Press, 1976), 37; Riley, *Biographical Encyclopedia*, 715; "World Series Moves to Kansas City Sept. 22," *Chicago Defender*, September 21,

1946; "Newark Eagles Win World Series Crown"; "Barney Brown, Austin Join Satchel's Stars," *Philadelphia Tribune*, September 28, 1946.

Chapter 15

1. Luke, *The Most Famous Woman*, 140; "1946 Season: Negro Leagues vs. Major Leagues," Negro Leagues Database, https://www.seamheads.com/NegroLgs/year.php?yearID=1946&lgID=NvM, accessed January 28, 2024.

2. "The Seamheads Negro Leagues DB"; James A. Riley, "Johnny Davis," *Baseball Research Journal* (1982), https://sabr.org/journal/article/johnny-davis/; Timothy M. Gay, *Satch, Dizzy & Rapid Robert: The Wild Saga of Interracial Baseball Before Jackie Robinson* (New York: Simon & Schuster, 2010), 222, 224.

3. Monte Irvin and James A. Riley, *Nice Guys Finish First: The Autobiography of Monte Irvin* (New York: Carroll & Graf, 1996), 68; Monte Irvin interview, March 2, 2005; "First Black Doctor to Practice at City Hospital Was a Trailblazer," Newark Public Library, February 26, 1998, https://knowingnewark.npl.org/first-black-doctor-to-practice-at-city-hospital-was-a-trailblazer/.

4. Melvin B. Johnson, "Discrimination in Jersey Jobs Seen on Increase," *New York Amsterdam News*, February 23, 1946; "YMCA Abolishes Separate Camps," *Newark Herald*, April 20, 1946; "Seeks End of Jim Crow in N.J. National Guard," *Chicago Defender*, April 27, 1946; "First Negro Medic at Newark Hosp. a Woman," *Chicago Defender*, January 26, 1947; "New Jersey Park Revives Former Anti-Negro Policies," *Chicago Defender*, August 24, 1947; "Won After All," *Afro-American*, December 7, 1946.

5. "John Doe Is Up on Charge of Jim Crow," *New York Amsterdam News*, October 11, 1947; "Club Owner to Appeal Verdict in Bigotry Suit," *Chicago Defender*, July 3, 1948; "GOP Leader Files Complaint with DAD," *Afro-American*,

December 2, 1950; Samuel Hoskins, "Far Eastern Ends Club Policy; Service to All," *Afro-American*, December 9, 1950.

Chapter 16

1. "1946 Newark Eagles," Negro Leagues Database, https://www.seamheads.com/NegroLgs/team.php?yearID=1946&teamID=NE&tab=pit, accessed Secember 20, 2023.
2. Interview of Day conducted by William Marshall in Three Points, Ohio, on June 24, 1980, for the Louie B. Nunn Center for Oral History, University of Kentucky Libraries.
3. "Leon Day, Ruffin Jump the Eagles," *New York Amsterdam News*, May 22, 1947.
4. Riley, *Dandy, Day and the Devil*, 94; Cisneros, *The Mexican League*, 123, 338; Sam Lacy, "From A to Z," *Afro-American*, May 4, 1948.
5. Hines, "Leon Day"; Interview of Day conducted by Marshall.
6. "Traipsing over the Country," *Pittsburgh Courier*, June 26, 1947; Riley, *Biographical Encyclopedia*, 531.
7. Interview of Day conducted by Marshall.

Chapter 17

1. The Jackie Robinson Papers, Container 1, Folder 17, Manuscript Reading Room, Library of Congress, Washington, DC.
2. Virtue, *South of the Color Barrier*, 184.
3. Ibid.
4. "Grays Quit League; New Circuit Formed," *Afro-American*, December 11, 1948.
5. Riley, *Dandy, Day and the Devil*, 95; "Memphis Red Sox Set for Houston Exhibition," *Pittsburgh Courier*, April 9, 1949; Riley, *Biographical Encyclopedia*, 299–300.
6. Ted Waters, "Numbers Found Lucrative Industry," *Afro-American*, May 10, 1947; Clarence Brown interview by author, September 2, 2006; Riley, *Biographical Encyclopedia*, 809–10.
7. An exception was the New York Giants, which were founded in 1883 as the Gothams and renamed the Giants in 1885.
8. Riley, *Biographical Encyclopedia*, 681; "Kansas City and Baltimore Play at Lloyd Field Tonight," *Delaware County Daily Times*, May 4, 1949.
9. "Day's Homer Tops Chi for Balto," *Afro-American*, June 18, 1949.
10. "Elites Rally to Beat Philadelphia, 13 to 12," *The Sun*, September 3, 1949; "Elites Take Pair from Birmingham," *Afro-American*, August 13, 1949.
11. "Elites Take Pair from Birmingham"; "Clowns Break Losing Streak Down Giants, 7–1," *New Journal and Guide*, May 14, 1949; "Elite Giants Beat Phila. Stars, 3–2," *Delaware County Times*, May 20, 1949; "Elites, Memphis Split Twin-Bill," *Afro-American*, June 4, 1949; "Elites Set Hot Pace Flag Race," *Afro-American*, June 11, 1949; Riley, *Biographical Encyclopedia*, 65, 404. The *New Pittsburgh Courier*, June 18, 1949, listed Hutchinson's first name as Jim. Riley lists it as Willie (Ace). "Elites Win Both Ends of Twin Bill," *New Pittsburgh Courier*, June 18, 1949.
12. "Negro American League Opens World Series Play, Sept. 16th," *Atlanta Daily World*, September 14, 1949; "Negro World Series to Open Sept. 16," *Black Dispatch*, September 17, 1949; "Baltimore Tops Giants in Title Tilt Here, 8–4," *New Journal and Guide*, September 24, 1949.
13. "Elites Win NAL Championship," *Afro-American*, October 1, 1949.
14. Clinton "Butch" McCord interview with author, May 5, 2006; Riley, *Bio-graphical Encyclopedia*, 529–30; R.S. Simmons, "Baltimore's Elite Giants Win Negro World Series," *Philadelphia Tribune*, September 27, 1949.
15. "We Didn't Do So Badly," *Afro-American*, October 1, 1949; Riley, *Bio-*

graphical Encyclopedia, 600, 241, 426–27, 780, 261.

16. Jules Tygiel, *Baseball's Great Experiment: Jackie Robinson and His Legacy* (Oxford: Oxford University Press, 1983), 157.

17. Clinton "Butch" McCord interview with author, October 18, 2006; "Effa Manley 'Hotter than Horse Radish,'" *Chicago Defender*, September 18, 1948.

18. Art Rust, *Get That Nigger Off the Field* (Los Angeles: Shadow Lawn Press, 1992), 39 as cited in Virtue, *South of the Color Barrier*, 179.

19. Luke, *The Baltimore Elite Giants*, 138–39.

20. "10 States Enact Anti-Bias Laws," *Afro-American*, September 17, 1949; "Caitlin Passes MD Plumbing Exam," *Afro-American*, December 3, 1949; "Discrimination Topples as Building Goes Up," *New Journal and Guide*, January 28, 1950.

21. "Mayor, Former City Solicitor Assail Rampant Prejudice," *Afro-American*, January 10, 1948.

22. Ibid.

23. "Residents of Mixed Areas Like Situation," *Afro-American*, April 3, 1948.

24. Geraldine Day interview, October 31, 2023.

25. Luke, *The Baltimore Elite Giants*, 124.

26. Biddy Wood, "York School's Stand Hailed," *Afro-American*, May 6, 1950.

27. "How to Fight Jim Crow," *Chicago Defender*, March 25, 1950.

28. Lerone Bennett, Jr., and Robert E. Johnson, "Racial Progress Noted in Headlines of '49," *Atlanta Daily World*, January 1, 1950; "Open U. of Md.," *Afro-American*, April 22, 1950; Elwood Watson, "William Levi Dawson [Politician] (1886–1970)," BlackPast, January 23, 2007, https://www.blackpast.org/african-american-history/dawson-william-l-1886-1970/; Albert Barnett, "Author Says 'Negro Problem' Is Now 'White Man's Problem,'" *Chicago Defender*, February 22, 1950.

Chapter 18

1. Van Hyning, *The Santurce Crabbers*, 32.

2. Sam Lacy, "From A to Z," *Afro-American*, July 1, 1950; "Bushwicks Keep Right on Rolling," *Brooklyn Eagle*, June 17, 1950; "Black Hurls Baltimore Win," *Afro-American*, June 24, 1950; "ANL Teams Prep for Tight Loop Race," *Afro-American*, April 15, 1950; Riley, *Biographical Encyclopedia*, 379.

3. Wendell Smith, "25,000 Fans Expected at Memorial Stadium," *Pittsburgh Courier*, May 6, 1950; Riley, *Biographical Encyclopedia*, 139.

4. Kyle McNary statement in the audio book edition of his *Ted "Double Duty" Radcliffe: 36 Years of Pitching & Catching in the Negro Leagues* (n.p.: McNary Publishing, January 1994) as cited in Gary Gillette, "The True Greatness of the ManDak League," Society for American Baseball Research, https://sabr.org/journal/article/the-true-greatness-of-the-mandak-league/, accessed April 9, 2025.

5. Wilmer Fields, *My Life in the Negro Leagues: An Autobiography* (McLean, VA: Miniver Press, 2013), 39, as cited in Gillette, "The True Greatness of the ManDak League"; Riley, *Biographical Encyclopedia*, 281.

6. Barry Swanton and Jay-Dell Mah, *Black Baseball Players in Canada: A Biographical Dictionary, 1881–1960* (Jefferson, NC: McFarland, 2009), 6; Riley, *Biographical Encyclopedia*, 281; "The Ligon Colored All-Stars," Western Canada Baseball, https://attheplate.com/wcbl/ligon.html, accessed June 7, 2024.

7. Barry Swanton, *The ManDak League: Haven for Former Negro League Ballplayers, 1950–1957* (Jefferson, NC: McFarland, 2006).

8. "Brief History of Athabasca," Town of Athabasca, https://web.archive.org/web/20130320090712/http://www.athabasca.ca/content/brief-history, accessed March 18, 2024; "Group that Fled Okla. Hatred Thrives in Canada Province," *Afro-American*, January 7, 1950.

Notes—Chapter 19

9. Dan Burley, "Confidentially Yours," *Philadelphia Tribune*, August 12, 1950; Swanton, *The ManDak League*, 2; Riley, *Biographical Encyclopedia*, 635, 97.
10. Swanton, *The ManDak League*, 8; "Diamond in the Rough," *Winnipeg Free Press*, October 31, 2004.
11. https://en.wikipedia.org/wiki/Osborne_Stadium, accessed April 23, 2025; William O. Little, "Red Sox Upsets Chicago Giants in Recent Canadian Junket," *Atlanta Daily World*, July 15, 1952.
12. Swanton, *The ManDak League*, 16–17.
13. Ted Bowles, "Day's Three Hitter Blanks Minot," *Winnipeg Free Press*, August 15, 1950; Glenn Flynn, "Buffs Stampede in 14th to Sink Minot," *Winnipeg Free Press*, August 23, 1950; "Buffs Win 'Story-Book' Contest," *Winnipeg Free Press*, August 30, 1950; https://en.wikipedia.org/wiki/Osborne_Stadium, accessed April 23, 2025; Bob Moir, "Buffs' Barrage Levels Brandon," *Winnipeg Free Press*, July 13, 1950.
14. Glenn Flynn, "Buffaloes Cop Marathon Opener," *Winnipeg Free Press*, September 7, 1950.
15. Riley, *Biographical Encyclopedia*, 581; Swanton, *The ManDak League*, 144; "Black Baron Hurler Jumps Team to Play in Canadian League," *Atlanta Daily World*, June 22, 1950.
16. Swanton, *The ManDak League*, 20–21, 95; Glenn Flynn, "Cop Clincher 1–0 in 17 Innings," *Winnipeg Free Press*, September 13, 1950.
17. Glenn Flynn, "Record Crowd Sees Buff Victory," *Winnipeg Free Press*, May 21, 1951.
18. Ted Bowles, "Buffs Hammer Minot," *Winnipeg Free Press*, June 28, 1951.
19. Swanton, *The ManDak League*, 23–24, 95.

Chapter 19

1. "Satchel Paige, Scheduled to Report to St. Louis Browns Monday," *Philadelphia Tribune*, July 14, 1951; Dickson, *Bill Veeck*, 187; "Toronto Signs First Negro Players," *Los Angeles Tribune*, August 11, 1951.
2. *The Jacksonville Daily Journal*, July 11, 1951; Riley, *Biographical Encyclopedia*, 825.
3. "St. Louis Browns to Call Up Negro Ball Players," *Arizona Sun*, July 13, 1951; "Wendell Smith's Sports Beat," *The Pittsburgh Courier*, July 21, 1951; Riley, *Biographical Encyclopedia*, 825; "New Maple Leafs Here for Visit, Open Important Series Tonight," *The Ottawa Journal*, July 16, 1951; Swanton, *The ManDak League*, 25.
4. "Six Players En Route to Join Buffs," *Winnipeg Free Press*, July 16, 1951.
5. Swanton, *The ManDak League*, 25.
6. Jim Vipond, "Negroes Augment Fleet St. Fanfare," *Globe and Mail*, July 16, 1951.
7. Riley, *Dandy, Day and the Devil*, 95.
8. "Minor League Notes," *The Call City Ed.* (Kansas City, Missouri), August 10, 1951.
9. "Shore Is Brilliant as Leafs Prevail over Chiefs, 11–5," *Globe and Mail*, July 24, 1951.
10. "Rhaun Delivers Playoff Smashes as Leafs Win Two," *Globe and Mail*, July 16, 1951.
11. https://www.baseball-reference.com/bullpen/Toronto_Maple_Leafs, accessed April 23, 2025; Hugh Fullerton, "Sports Round-Up," *Ironwood Daily Globe* (Ironwood, Michigan), July 16, 1951.
12. Bill Reddy, "Keeping Posted," *Post Standard* (Syracuse, New York), July 31, 1951.
13. "Satchel Paige Loser in Exhibition Tilt," *Philadelphia Tribune*, August 18, 1951.
14. Joseph L. Reichler, ed., *The Baseball Encyclopedia* (New York: Macmillan, 1988), 1655.
15. Kurt Blumenau, "Maple Leaf Stadium (Toronto)," Society for American Baseball Research, https://sabr.org/bioproj/park/maple-leaf-stadium/, accessed January 14, 2024.
16. Ralph Matthews, "Listening Post," *Cleveland Call and Post*, August 5, 1951.

Notes—Chapter 19

17. The Editors of Encyclopedia Britannica, "Fair Employment Practices Committee," *Britannica*, Britannica.com/topic/Fair-Employment-Practices-Committee, accessed March 20, 2024.

18. "FEPC Can Investigate Philly Big League Clubs' Failure to Drop Tan Player Ban," *Afro-American*, April 22, 1950; "Loesher Named FEPC Head in Philadelphia," *Atlanta Daily World*, November 3, 1948; Bill Ladson, "These Players Integrated Each MLB Team," MLB, August 14, 2020, https://www.mlb.com/news/players-who-broke-color-barrier-for-every-team.

19. "High Court Ruling Dooms Segregation on Railroads," *Michigan Chronicle*, November 15, 1952; "Railroad Sued for $200,000," *African-American*, July 8, 1950; "President Truman Still Adamant in Stand for Full Civil Rights," *Afro-American*, February 4, 1950.

20. "Leon Day a Busy Boy," *Winnipeg Free Press*, July 17, 1951; "Orioles Blank Toronto by 2–0," *Post Standard* (Syracuse, New York), August 25, 1951; "Hetki Chalks Up 17th for Toronto," *Daily Record* (Long Branch, New Jersey), September 4, 1951; David E. Skelton, "Pete Burnside," Society for American Baseball Research, https://sabr.org/bioproj/person/pete-burnside/, accessed January 11, 2024; Swanton, *The ManDak League*, 95; Blumenau, "Maple Leaf Stadium." Marion E. Jackson, "Campanella All-Stars Open Tour Friday," *Atlanta Daily World*, October 9, 1952.

21. "Camp's Stars Split in Va," *Pittsburgh Courier*, October 27, 1951; "Campanella Team Wins All-Star Tilt," *Waco-News-Tribune*, October 31, 1951.

22. Norm King, "Zack Taylor," Society for American Baseball Research, https://sabr.org/bioproj/person/zack-taylor/, accessed September 14, 2024.

23. "Miners Find Hill Staff Problem," *Troy Record* (Troy, New York), April 23, 1952.

24. Marion E. Jackson, "Sports of the World," *Atlanta Daily World*, August 20, 1952; "Puzzled by Miners," *Williamsport Sun-Gazette*, June 12, 1952; "Albany's Lead to Half Game," *Williamsport Sun-Gazette*, June 9, 1952; "Albany Widens Eastern Lead with Elmira 7–6," *Evening Times* (Williamsport, Pennsylvania), June 26, 1952; "Elmira Draws Record Crowd," *Evening Times*, August 25, 1952; "Pinch Hitter Comes Through," *Plain Speaker*, July 24, 1952; "Wildness by Foe's Hurlers Helps Albany," *Times Record* (Troy, New York), July 16, 1952; George Lyle, Jr., "Out on the Limb," *Alabama Tribune*, May 23, 1952; "Hamley Stops Miners 10–3, After Bengals Bow in Opener, 5–2," *Daily Gazette and Bulletin*, June 11, 1952.

25. "Wild Pitch Leads to March's Downfall in Duel with Barnes," *Daily Gazette and Bulletin*, July 30, 1952.

26. Marion E. Jackson, "Campanella All-Stars Open Tour Friday; Play Here Monday Night," *Atlanta Daily World*, October 9, 1952; "Campanella All-Stars Win," *Oakland Tribune*, October 30, 1952; "All Barnstormers Quit Except Campanella's," *Cleveland Call and Post*, November 1, 1952.

27. "Comes to Terms," *Lethbridge Herald* (Alberta, Canada), May 10, 1953.

28. "Eskimos Blanked on Five Hits," *Lethbridge Herald* (Alberta, Canada), May 15, 1953.

29. "Tri-City Snaps Eskimo Streak," *Lethbridge Herald* (Alberta, Canada), June 10, 1953.

30. "Eskimos on Rampage," *Lethbridge Herald* (Alberta, Canada), June 30, 1953.

31. "Leon Day to Edmonton," *Winnipeg Free Press*, February 20, 1953; "Salem Skein, Sliced at 7," *Herald and News* (Klamath Falls, Oregon), June 5, 1953; "Pitcher Released," *Daily Chronicle* (Centralia, Washington), August 18, 1953; "1953 Edmonton Eskimos Roster," Stats Crew, https://www.statscrew.com/minorbaseball/roster/t-ee11370/y-1953, accessed January 15, 2024.

32. Interview of Day conducted by Marshall.

33. Swanton, *The ManDak League*, 194, 196.

34. "Kaline-Nine, NAL All-Stars Here Oct. 16," *New Journal and Guide*, October 15, 1955.
35. Riley, *Biographical Encyclopedia*, 96.

Chapter 20

1. Larry Lester, *Black Baseball's National Showcase* (Lincoln: University of Nebraska Press, 2001), 1.
2. Ibid., 3; "More than 150,000 Voted for All-Stars," *Chicago Defender*, August 10, 1935.
3. Ed R. Harris, "East-West Game East?" *Philadelphia Tribune*, July 11, 1935.
4. Lester, *Black Baseball's National Showcase*, 37.
5. "Satchel Paige Was in His Prime by 1933," *Pecan Park Eagle*, https://bill37mccurdy.com/2014/02/01/satchel-paige-was-in-his-prime-by-1933/, accessed February 10, 2024; Lester, *Black Baseball's National Showcase*, 41; Riley, *Biographical Encyclopedia*, 398.
6. Lester, *Black Baseball's National Showcase*, 78; Riley, *Dandy, Day and the Devil*, 82.
7. BR Bullpen, "1937 East-West Game (Negro League)," Baseball Reference, https://www.baseball-reference.com/bullpen/1937_East-West_Game_%28Negro_League%29#:~:text=The%201937%20East-West%20Game%20was%20the%20fifth%20East-West,4%20errors%20while%20the%20East%20made%20just%20one, accessed January 13, 2024; "East Triumphs over West in All-Star Game," *The Call* (Kansas City, Missouri), August 13, 1937; "West Nine Wins Colored Classic," *Times Union* (Brooklyn), August 12, 1935.
8. 8 "40,000 Watch West Defeat East 4–2," *Afro-American*, August 12, 1939.
9. Harry B. Webber, "East Beats West, 10–2," *Afro-American*, September 2, 1939.
10. Lester, *Black Baseball's National Showcase*, 172–206; "Hall of Famers at War—Leon Day," *Baseball in Wartime Blog*, February 19, 2010; "East Shows Batting Power to Top West, 5–1," *New Journal and Guide*, August 22, 1942.
11. Lem Graves, Jr., "From the Press Box," *New Journal and Guide*, August 21, 1943.
12. Lester, *Black Baseball's National Showcase*, 257–79.
13. Ibid., 194, 441.

Chapter 21

1. Lester, "Day, Leon."
2. Peters, "Interview with Geraldine Day."
3. Geraldine Day interview, August 31, 2023.
4. Geraldine Day interview, August 31, 2023; Lester, "Day, Leon"; Holway, *Blackball Stars*, 345.
5. Riley, *Biographical Encyclopedia*, 613; Mike Klingaman, "For Leon Day's Widow, Rich in Memories, Little Else," *Afro-American*, August 10, 1996.
6. Geraldine Day interview, August 31, 2023; Lester, "Day, Leon."
7. Geraldine Day interview, August 31, 2023.
8. Frank Hunt, "Protesters Hit Route 301 Cafes," *Afro-American*, May 5, 1962.
9. Geraldine Day interview, August 31, 2023.
10. "Pigtown Main Street," https://www.pigtownmainstreet.org/, accessed February 22, 2024; Justin Klugh, "Who Is Leon Day?" Society for American Baseball Research, December 17, 2018; Sandra McKee, "Fame and Misfortune," *The Sun*, February 7, 1997.
11. Kenneth Meeks, "Ex-Negro Leagues Baseball Players Sign Autographs," *New York Amsterdam News*, June 6, 1992; author interview with Thomas Kern, August 14, 2024.
12. "Old Black Players Honor Clint Thomas," *Chicago Defender*, June 23, 1979; Frank Saunders, "Frankly Speaking," *Michigan Courier*, June 23, 1979; "Negro Leagues Reunion Begins," *Chicago Defender*, June 21, 1982; "Coopers-

Notes—Chapter 22

town Honors Blacks," *Michigan Chronicle*, September 21, 1985; Riley, *Biographical Encyclopedia*, 773–74.

13. Peters, "Interview with Geraldine Day."

14. "National Baseball Hall of Fame Inductees," Baseball Reference, https://www.baseball-reference.com/awards/hof.shtml, accessed May 28, 2024.

15. "Black Players Honored at Dedication of Hall of Fame in Ashland," *Louisville Defender*, June 24, 1982; "Annual Negro Baseball League's Reunion, November 2–4," *Atlanta Daily World*, October 25, 1983; "Cooperstown Honors Blacks," *Michigan Chronicle*, September 21, 1985; Chico Renfro, "Sports of the World," *Atlanta Daily World*, August 25, 1991; "National Negro Leagues Hall of Fame Idea Proposed at Reunion," *Atlanta Daily World*, June 29, 1980.

16. "Hall to Honor Negro Leaguers," *Chicago Defender*, May 15, 1991.

Chapter 22

1. "Puerto Rican Hall to Induct Leon Day," *Baltimore Sun*, October 15, 1993; Roderick C. Willis, "Edmondson Indians Highlight Leon Day Festival," *Afro-American*, June 21, 2003.

2. Peters, "Interview with Geraldine Day."

3. Snyder, "You Made It, man"; January 22, 2024 email from Cassidy Lent, Director, Library, National Baseball Hall of Fame and Museum; "Late Sox Star Fox Gets New Shot at Hall of Fame," *Chicago Defender*, March 5, 1996; "Veterans Get Shutout at Hall of Fame," *Defender Chicago*, February 24, 1993; David Ogden and Kevin Warneke, *The Call to the Hall: When Baseball's Highest Honor Came to 31 Legends of the Sport* (Jefferson, NC: McFarland, 2018), 66; Wulf and Conrads, *I Was Right on Time*, 214.

4. Ogden and Warneke, *The Call to the Hall*, 66.

5. A comment by Day's widow Geraldine, as told to Jorge Colón Delgado, official historian of Puerto Rican Professional Baseball League, https:www.youtube.com/watch?v=z2NBGegd41A, accessed March 16, 2024.

6. Ogden and Warneke, *The Call to the Hall*, 68.

7. Snyder, "You Made It, Man."

8. Ogden and Warneke, *The Call to the Hall*, 66.

9. "History Meets Vice President," *The Call* (Kansas City, Missouri), April 29, 1994; Sally Badger, "Yule Begins at Crab Feast," *The Sun*, October 4, 1992; Display Ad, *The Sun*, September 24, 1992.

10. "O's Plan Leon Day Day," *Afro-American*, October 19, 1992.

11. Kubatko, "Maryland Honors Day."

12. Riley, *Of Monarchs*, 156, 235–36.

13. John Steadman, "Orioles Fans Could Manage Nicely with Weaver and Hanlon in Hall," *The Sun*, April 14, 1996.

14. Stephen R. Greenes, *Negro Leaguers in the Hall of Fame: The Case for Inducting 24 Overlooked Ball Players* (Jefferson, NC: McFarland, 2020), 20–21.

15. Riley, *Biographical Encyclopedia*, 292, 826–28, 677, 856, 739–40, 723.

16. Sam Lacy, "Leon Day: The Tragedy of Tardiness," *Afro-American*, July 22, 1995.

17. Holway, "Day Crossed a Road Less Traveled to Cooperstown."

18. "1995 Baseball Hall of Fame Induction Ceremony," Clark Sports Center, https://www.clarksportscenter.com/events/1995-baseball-hall-of-fame-induction-ceremony/.

19. Richard Goldstein, "Bob Wolff, Sports Broadcaster for Nearly 80 Years, Dies at 96," *New York Times*, July 17, 2017; "Annual Program: Fifty-Sixth Induction Ceremonies," compliments of Dr. Bob Hieronomous.

20. Lester, *Black Baseball's National Showcase*, 418.

21. R.D. Miller, *A Hall of Fame Salute to Leon Day* [DVD], viewed January 20, 2024.

22. Brad Snyder, "For Induction, Negro Leaguers Left Without Tickets to the Big Show," *The Sun*, July 31, 1995; Ogden and Warneke, *The Call to the Hall*, 69.

23. "Van Pelt Goes to Vikings; Banks Signs," *Washington Post*, July 13, 1984.
24. Lindsey, "Salute to a Local Legend."
25. "Negro League History Exhibit Featured in Exhibition," *The Sun*, April 22, 1990.
26. "Former Negro Leaguers to Be Honored at Old Timers Game," *Chicago Defender*, April 23, 1990.
27. Gabby Richards, "Negro Leagues to Be Honored at All-Star Week," *Washington Post*, May 25, 1993.
28. "Baseball Minutes," *Washington Post*, September 25, 1994.
29. Riley, *Biographical Encyclopedia*, 642.
30. Howie Evans, "Sports and Entertainment Figures Join Celebration of Negro Leagues Oldtimers," *New York Amsterdam News*, November 25, 1995; "2nd Annual Celebration for Negro Baseball League," *New Journal and Guide*, November 8, 1995.
31. "Leon Day's Event Planned at Douglass," *Afro-American*, May 17, 1997.
32. James Smith, "Take Me Out to the Leon Day Park," *The Sun*, August 24, 1997.
33. "Sculpted Legends," *Salina Journal* (Salina, Kansas), July 2, 1997; "Players, Sportswriters Pick All-Star Teams," *Los Angeles Sentinel*, June 10, 1993.
34. McKee, "Fame and Misfortune"; Gregory Kane, "Friends Lend a Hand to Day's Widow," *The Sun*, February 19, 1997; Dan Rodricks, "Baseball Still Owes Day One Thing: A Little Help for His Widow," *The Sun*, August 25, 1995.
35. McKee, "Fame and Misfortune"; Rodricks, "Baseball Still Owes Day One Thing"; Kane, "Friends Lend a Hand."

Epilogue

1. Anthony Castrovince, "MLB Adds Negro Leagues to Official Records," MLB, mlb.com/history/negro-leagues/features/mlb-adds-negro-leagues-to-official-records, accessed October 11, 2024.

Appendix A

1. Transcribed from Miller, *A Hall of Fame Salute to Leon Day*.

Bibliography

There are no other biographies about Leon Day. The works below contain information about the Negro Leagues in general as well as information on Day's performance on the field, the important people in his life, his memories, the times in which he played (1934–57), and his life after baseball (1957–95)—including his long trek to baseball's Hall of Fame. Many have an extensive bibliography for the reader who wants to pursue a particular topic.

- Barthel, Thomas. *Baseball's Peerless Semipros: The Brooklyn Bushwicks of Dexter Park*. Haworth, NJ: St. Johann Press, 2009.

  Many Negro League games featured semipro teams as opponents in exhibition and barnstorming venues. Barthel gives a detailed and sparking account of one of the most famous semipro teams during the early and mid-twentieth century. Babe Ruth, Lou Gehrig, Josh Gibson, Waite Hoyt, Max Patin, Stan Musial, Leon Day, Jackie Robinson, and a host of others whose names will forever stand as milestones to the game put in an appearance, as do a panoply of players and teams whose names have long been forgotten.

- Dickson, Paul. *Bill Veeck: Baseball's Greatest Maverick*. New York: Bloomsbury, 2012.

  An in-depth, extensively researched and smoothly written book about the man considered by many to be the most innovative and daring baseball executive of all time. Among other aspects of his life, Dickson describes Veeck's interest in integrating the National and American Leagues, his integration of the American League by signing Larry Doby, and his plan (never carried out) to buy the 1942 Philadelphia Phillies and restock the team with Negro Leaguers.

- Holway, John B. *Blackball Stars: Negro League Pioneers*. Westport, CT: Meckler Books, 1988.

  Written by the pioneer historian of Negro Leagues baseball, this book contains 25 chapters devoted to in-depth profiles of Negro Leaguers who could have easily starred in the National and American Leagues, including such figures as Rube Foster, Oscar Charleston, Biz Mackey, Norman "Turkey" Stearnes, Mule Suttles, and Leon Day. Nineteen of the 25 are in the Hall of Fame.

Bibliography

- O'Neil, Buck, with Steve Wulf and David Conrads. *I Was Right on Time*. New York: Simon & Schuster, 1996.

    An insider's view of the Negro Leagues told candidly and with humor by one who knew the game intimately as a star player, coach, scout, and ambassador for the Negro Leagues after his retirement. O'Neil's vivid account includes his disappointments as well as his high moments in a society where racial segregation and discrimination impacted where and how the game was played and by whom.

- Riley, James A. *The Biographical Encyclopedia of the Negro Baseball Leagues*. New York: Carroll & Graf, 1994.

    Riley's exhaustive research and interviews with more than 100 players is an invaluable source of information about players' careers and lives. The 926-page book is, in Riley's words, "a blend of anecdotal archives and player profiles; it envelops the statistical skeletons with flesh and blood to reconstruct ballplayers who will be remembered as *real* people." My copy is worn and coming apart at the seams due to constant use over the past 15 years.

- Riley, James A. *Dandy, Day, and the Devil*. Cocoa, FL: TK Publishers, 1987.

    Although Day was often reluctant to talk about himself, he opened up to Riley, whose short paperback, consisting of interviews with Ray Dandridge (Dandy), Day, and Willie Wells (The Devil) is by far the best account of Day's career in his own words. Riley has preserved Day's manner of speaking.

Index

Numbers in *bold italics* indicate pages with illustrations

Aaron, Hank 104
African Americans: civil rights movement and 3, 53, 123; defense industry jobs for 52, 74, 86, 123; in Jim Crow era 50–55, 76, 88, 90, 104, 112; in World War II 1, 5, 8, 54, 56, 74–82, *80*, 90; *see also* discrimination; integration; segregation
Alemán Valdés, Miguel 47
Allen, Bob 156
Allen, Mel 10
Allison, Hughes 86
American League: executives on prospect of Black players in 1, 65–68; games against Negro Leagues teams 19, 69; integration of 3, 10, 66–70, 104, 108–109, 157; lifestyle of players in 4, 6; Mexican summer league players from 47; salary of players in 6; *see also* Major League Baseball; *specific players and teams*
Andrews, William T. 69
Ashburn, Richie 9, 148
Atlanta Black Crackers (Negro Leagues) 41, 42, 113
Atlanta Braves (National League) 151
Awkard, Russell 6, 7, 56

Babcock, Jim 126
Baird, Tom 64, 108
Baker, Kent 4
Baltimore: Arbutus Memorial Park in 12, 156; Day family residences in 17; discrimination in 111–112; Enoch Pratt Free Library in 151; integration efforts in 110–112; numbers games in 105–106
Baltimore Black Sox (Negro Leagues):

Day's career with 1, 8, 14, 20–22, 25; Day's sneaking into stadium of 14, 18–19; Dixon as player/manager for 8, 14, 19–21; exhibition games played by 19; failure due to financial reasons 22, 25; games against white teams 19, 25; recruiting strategies used by 7–8
Baltimore Elite Giants (Negro Leagues): Butts as player for 128; in California Winter League 74; Campanella as player for 41, 66; Day's career with 1, 105–108, 113; Ferrell as pitcher for 11; integration's impact on 105; lifestyle of players with 7; matchups against Day 41, 42, 63; pennant won by 21; Porter as pitcher for 115; Villodas as catcher for 142; Walker as manager of 107; Wilson as owner of 23–24, 74, 107; in World Series 108
Baltimore Orioles (American League) 12, 128, 145, 151–152
Baltimore Silver Moons (semipro team) 19
Bancroft, Ken 156
Bankhead, Sam 15–16, 62, 64, 66
Banks, Ernie 142
Banks, Ray 12
Baraka, Amiri 30
Barber, Red 10
Barnes, Frank "Buster" 122, 126
Barnett, Albert 112
Barthel, Thomas 29
Baseball Writers' Association of America (BBWAA) 9, 67, 146
"Baseball's Unsung Heroes" program 151
Baselice, Lou 125
Bassett, Lloyd "Pepper" 107–108

Index

Bauers, Russ 83
Bavasi, Buzzie 143
BBWAA (Baseball Writers' Association of America) 9, 67, 146
Bearden, Gene 127
Bell, Bill 33, 39, 42
Bell, James "Cool Papa" 46, 132, 139, 140, 146, 154
Benson, Gene 11, 13, 139
Benswanger, William E. 65–68
Bethlehem Gray Sox (semipro team) 19
Birmingham Black Barons (Negro Leagues) 63, 74, 107, 115, 118, 142, 152
Black, Joe 107, 109, 126, 127
Black Americans *see* African Americans
Black Panthers 54
Blackwell, Ewell "The Whip" 82, 83, 85
Blumstein, William 31
Boetticher, Budd 81
Bolden, Ed 63
Bolton, Frances P. 69
Bolton, Ida Mae 5, 11, 17
Bolton, Todd 12, 137
Borge, Victor 122
Borican, John 58
Bostic, Lyman 115, *116*
Boston Braves (National League) 66, 109
Boston Red Sox (American League) 3, 66, 67, 125
Bottomley, Jim 29
Bradley, Alva 65–67
Brady, Eric 1
Bremer, Eugene 66, 67
Brewer, Chet 15, 33
Brickhouse, Jack 143
Briggs, Spike 99
Britton, Johnny *116*
Broeg, Bob 143
Brooklyn Bay Parkways (semipro team) 29
Brooklyn Bushwicks (semipro team) 29, 33, 39, 57, 63, 73
Brooklyn Dodgers (National League): Campanella and 112; Durocher as player/manager for 65; Earnshaw as pitcher for 36; Great Depression and 29; integration of 3, 67, 104; lifestyle of players with 7; MacPhail as president of 65; Nahem as pitcher for 83; New York Cubans against 69; renting of Ebbets Field to Brooklyn Eagles 24; Robinson and 3, 67, 104, 108–109, 112; spring training invitees 11–12
Brooklyn Eagles (Negro Leagues): Day's career with 1, 4–5, 23, 25–29; Dixon as player/manager for 23; exhibition games played by 25; Giles as player/manager for 1, 26; lifestyle of players with 4–5; Lundy as manager of 40; Manley as owner/manager of 23–27, 29; moving of team to Newark 29; scouts in attendance at games 66; Taylor as manager for 12, 24–26
Brown, Al 112
Brown, Clarence 106
Brown, James 56
Brown, Joe L. 143
Brown, Raymond *28*, 58
Brown, Wesley A. 112
Brown, Willard "Home Run" 68, 83–85, *84*
Brown v. Board of Education (1954) 55, 112
Bullock, Ollie 87–88
Burke, Ernest 150
Burley, Dan 58
Burnside, Pete 124
Bush, George H.W. 144
Bustard, John L. 55
Butts, Tommy "Pee Wee" 113, 128
Byrd, Bill 15, 43, 58, 107, 108, 113

Caitlin, John 110
Calderon, Victor M. 43
Cambria, Joe 20
Camden Yards 12, 111, 145, 149–150, 154
Campanella, Roy: All-Star team assembled by 125–127; Baltimore Elite Giants and 41, 66; Brooklyn Dodgers and 112; Mackey as mentor to 41; reunions attended by 140; on Robinson's barnstorming team 98; rumors regarding Veeck and 70; strikeouts against Day 1; tryout with Philadelphia Phillies 66, 67; on Veterans Committee 142, 143
Canada: Athabasca community in 115; Day's baseball career in 1–2, 8, 114–119, *116*, 121–122, 124–125, 127–128, *129*; ManDak League in 2, 114–119,

Index

116, 128; treatment of Black players in 114, 127–128
Cantor, Ernest *116*
Carlisle, Matt 64
Carter, Art 41, 48, 63, 91
Cash, Bill 91, 92
Chandler, A.B. "Happy" 140
Charleston, Oscar 27, 63, 91, 132, 146, 154
Cherry, Hugh 105
Chicago American Giants (Negro Leagues) 27, 58, 74, 107–108, 115, 117, 120, 130
Chicago Cubs (National League) 6, 142
Chicago White Sox (American League) 36, 90, 125, 152
Christopher, Thadist 35
Churchill, Winston 77
Cincinnati Reds (National League) 28–29, 66, 82, 156
CIO (Congress of Industrial Organizations) 52, 68, 86
Citizens' Committee to End Discrimination 69
civil rights movement 3, 53, 123
Clark, J.L. 133
Clarkson, "Bus" 48, 59, 63
Cleveland Buckeyes (Negro Leagues) 66, 67
Cleveland Indians (American League): Bradley as owner of 65–67; Doby and 10, 66, 67, 70, 104, 109, 120; Feller as pitcher for 90, 97; integration of 10, 66, 67, 70, 104; Paige as pitcher for 109, 120; Veeck as owner and president of 10, 47, 66, 120
Coffey, Wayne 5
Cole, Bob 130
Cole, Cecil *96*
Comiskey Park 6, 94, 108, 130, 132, 133
Congress of Industrial Organizations (CIO) 52, 68, 86
Cooke, Jack Kent 121–122
Cortner, Laura 2
Cozart, Haywood "Big Train" 56
Crecy, Warren G.H. 54
Crosley, Powel, Jr. 66
Crowe, George 126
Crutchfield, Jimmy 35, 144
Cuba, winter baseball in 1, 4, 38
Curry, Homer 91, 92

D-Day invasion (1944) 1, 75–78, *79*, 82
D'Alessandro, Thomas, Jr. 110–111
Dalton, A.A. 50
Dalton, Letteria May 50
Dandridge, Ray: Hall of Fame induction 144, 146; in ManDak League 114; in Mexican summer league 45–48, 102; Newark Eagles and 35, 38; reunions attended by 139; salary disputes involving 38, 47; statue at Negro Leagues Baseball Museum 154; suspension for jumping to Mexico 92; winter baseball played by *28*, 34, 45, 46, 58, 59
Davis, B.O. 76
Davis, Buster 117
Davis, Doug 3
Davis, Eric 154
Davis, Jay Don 67–68
Davis, Johnny 93
Davis, Lomax *116*
Davis, Robert "Butch" 108, 120
Dawson, William 112
Day, Ellis, Jr. 17
Day, Ellis, Sr. 17, 19–21
Day, Geraldine: at Camden Yards ceremony 150; death of 156; at dedication of Leon Day Park 154; on demeanor of Leon 16; on discrimination in apparel stores 111; family background 135–136; fundraising event for *155*, 156; grief following Leon's death 12; at Hall of Fame induction ceremony 146, 148, *149*, 159–160; jobs held by 135–137; love for Baltimore Orioles 12; marriage to Leon 136; reunions attended by 140
Day, Hattie Lee 17
Day, Helen Elizabeth 2, 4
Day, Ida Mae *see* Bolton, Ida Mae
Day, Leon: athleticism of 8, 10, 13; autograph signings by 2, 137, *138*; birth and early life 17–19, *18*; death and funeral service for 2, 10–12; demeanor and personality of 8, 14–16, 119; honors and recognition given to 151–154, *153*; injuries and health challenges 9, 11, 34, 38, 39; love for baseball 4, 5, 8, 12, 18–19, 21; marriage to Geraldine Ingram 136; marriage to Helen Johnson 2, 4; National Baseball Hall

187

Index

of Fame induction 2, 9, 146–151, *147–150*, 159–160; *Negro Leagues Baseball Minutes* on 152; Newark Hall of Fame induction 142; *Not in Our League* featuring 152; photographs of *60*, *84*, *116*; post-retirement jobs held by 2, 135–137; Puerto Rican Professional Baseball Hall of Fame induction 142; questionnaire completed by 15, *162*; retirement from baseball 2, 8, 128, *129*; reunions attended by 139–141, 151; statue at Negro Leagues Baseball Museum 154; White House meetings attended by 144; World War II service of 1, 8, 56, 75–79, 90; *see also* Day's baseball career; Negro Leagues
Day, Robert 17
Day, William H. "Piggy" 17
Day's baseball career: Baltimore Black Sox 1, 8, 14, 20–22, 25; Baltimore Elite Giants 1, 105–108, 113; Baltimore Silver Moons 19; Brooklyn Eagles 1, 4–5, 23, 25–29; Campanella's All-Stars team 125–127; in Canada 1–2, 8, 114–119, *116*, 121–122, 124–125, 127–128, *129*; career statistics 13; East-West game appearances 2, 26, 27, 73, 132–134; games against white teams 36, 69, 72, 83–85; Homestead Grays in World Series 63–64; in ManDak League 2, 114–119, *116*, 128; mentors to Day during 25, 26; Mexican summer league 1, 4, 45–46, 102–103; in minor leagues 2, 8, 109, 121–122, 124–127; Newark Eagles 1, 3, 5–6, 8, 10, 17, 29, 33–42, 48, 56–57, 61–65, 71–74, 90–96, 102; OISE All-Star team 83–85, *84*; pitch delivery and strategy 13, 14; tryout with Pittsburgh Pirates 66; World War II as interruption to 1, 8, 56, 75–79, 90; *see also* Negro Leagues; winter baseball season
Dean, Dizzy 69
DeHaven, Gloria 122
Detroit Stars (Negro Leagues) 15
Detroit Tigers (American League) 66, 99, 125, 128
Dewey, Thomas 24
Dickson, Paul 71
Dihigo, Martín 33–34, 146, 154
discrimination: antidiscrimination legislation 87, 100, 101, 110, 122–123; in apparel stores 111; Citizens' Committee to End Discrimination 69; Manley's protest against 31; in military 51–54, 56, 75–76; by railroads 50, 109, 112, 124; in restaurants 100–101; stresses brought on by 2; in workplace 32, 52, 53, 86, 110, 122–123; *see also* segregation
Dismukes, William "Dizzy" 64
Dixon, Paul 20
Dixon, Randy 28
Dixon, Rap 8, 14, 19–21, 23, 24, 27
Doby, Larry: on Campanella's All-Stars team 126; Cleveland Indians and 10, 66, 67, 70, 104, 109, 120; integration of baseball and 10, 66, 67, 70, 104, 157; *Negro Leagues Baseball Minutes* on 152; Newark Eagles and 30, 91, 93, 94; praise following Day's death 10, 11; on Robinson's barnstorming team 98
Dominican Republic, winter baseball in 4
Ducey, John 127
Duckett, Mahlon 11
Ducks (DUKWs) 76–79, *79*
Duncan, Frank 27, *28*
Dunham, Molly 156
Durham, Millard G. 54
Durocher, Leo "The Lip" 65

Earnshaw, George 36
East-West games (Negro Leagues) 2, 26, 27, 68, 73, 130–134, *131*
Easter, Luke 70, 109, 120, 125
Ebbets Field 5, 24, 26, 30
Edison, Charles 88–89
Edmonton (Washington) Eskimos (minor leagues) 2, 127
Eggelston, Maeajah "Mac" 8
Eig, Jonathan 71
Eisenhower, Dwight D. *80*, 81, 84
Elam, Jake 72
Equal Employment Opportunity Commission 123
Evans, Bob 34, 38, 42

Fair Employment Practice Committee (FEPC) 52, 53, 123
Farrell, Jack 20

Index

Felder, William 90
Feller, Bob 90, 97, 98, 139
Ferrell, Leroy "Toots" 11–12, 107, 154
Fields, Wilmer 114, 151, 152
Flowers, Virginia 87
Forbes Field 62, 73
Foster, Rube 132, 146, 152, 154, 157
Foster, Willie 132, 145
Foxx, Jimmie 19
Frazier, Michael 81
Frick, Ford C. 9–10, 70

Gaedel, Eddie 125
Gaines, Jonas "Lefty" 105
Gerlach, Larry 70
Gibson, Bob 10–11, 16
Gibson, Josh: in East-West games 132; Hall of Fame induction 21, 146; Homestead Grays and 15, 21, 62, 66; matchups against Day 15, 27, 62; in Mexican summer league 46; *Negro Leagues Baseball Minutes* on 152; Pittsburgh Crawfords and 15, 27; rumors regarding Veeck and 70; statue at Negro Leagues Baseball Museum 154; tryout with Pittsburgh Pirates 66; winter baseball played by 15, 34, 46, 47
Gibson, Josh, Jr. 144
Giles, George 1, 26, 135
Gilliam, James "Junior" 109, 113
Gipson, Alvin "Bubba," Sr. 63
Glauber, Bill 5
Glendale Farmers (semipro team) 29
Glendening, Parris 11
Glenn, Stanley 15, 51, 151
Goebbels, Joseph 83
Gore, Al 144
Gottlieb, Eddie 92
Graves, Lem, Jr. 67, 94, 133
Great Depression 22, 24, 29
Green, Elijah "Pumpsie" 3, 67
Green, Vernon 75
Greenlee, Gus 23, 35–37, 40, 130
Griffith, Clark 65, 73
Griffith Stadium 6, 33, 41, 61–62, 72–73, 93, 131, 133
Grimm, Charlie 142
Grove, Lefty 19
Guilfoyle, Bill 145
Gumpert, Randy 125
Gunther, Henry 87

Hairstone, J.B. 20
Hargrave, Frank, and Hargrave Commission 32
Harris, Ed 131
Harris, Vic **28**, 39, 132
Harris, Wilmer 6
Harrison, Smokey **116**
Hartzog, Ernie 112
Harvey, Bob 93, 139, 140
Harwell, Ernie 143
Haskin, Aaron 99
Hastie, William H. 51–52
Haverstock, B. **116**
Hayes, Burnalle "Bun" 22
Hayes, Johnny **28**, 43
Hayes, Tom 118
Hector, Jack **116**
Heintzelman, Ken 83–84
Hemond, Roland 149
Hieronimus, Robert ("Dr. Bob") 2, 12, 143–145, 154–156, **155**
Hieronimus, Zohara 144
Hill, Jimmy 56, 57, 72
Hill, Samuel **116**
Hill, Tim 156
Hines, Ed 21
Hines, Rick 38, 91
Hitler, Adolf 75, 83
Hodges, Gil 125
Holden, William 110
Holway, John 10, 13, 25
Homestead Grays (Negro Leagues): Bell as pitcher for 33; in California Winter League 75; Day as World Series pitcher for 63–64; exhibition games played by 61; games against white teams 73; Gibson as player for 15, 21, 62, 66; integration's impact on 105; Leonard as member of 21, 39, 62; matchups against Day 39, 41, 62, 72, 74, 92, 93; pennants won by 21, 36, 58, 63, 73, 74; Posey as player/owner/manager of 21, 24, 40, 63, 71–72; semipro team games against 29; Williams as pitcher for 146; in World Series 63–64
Hooker, Lenial 56, 95, 133
Hopkins, Gordon 150
Householder, E.R. 75–76
Howard, Percy **116**
Hughes, E.S. 81
Hughes, Sammy T. 113

Index

Hulbert, William 9
Hull, Charles J. 17
Hutchinson, Hutch *116*
Hutchinson, Jim 107

Illidge, Eric 5
Indianapolis ABCs (Negro Leagues) 113
Indianapolis Clowns (Negro Leagues) 107
Ingram, Geraldine *see* Day, Geraldine
integration: in Baltimore 110–112; of baseball 3, 10, 66–71, 104–105, 108–109, 122, 157; of beaches in New Jersey 88; civil rights movement and 3; of military 8, 54, 86; in Newark 3, 52, 86, 87, 99; in Toronto 122–123
Irvin, Monford "Monte": on Campanella's All-Stars team 125, 126; on competitiveness of Day 14; on food at Newark's Grand Hotel 30; Hall of Fame induction 146; injuries sustained by 41; on lifestyle of Negro League players 6; in Mexican summer league 48, 49, 104; New York Giants and 109; Newark Eagles and 10, 36, 41, 48, 57, 58, 93–95, 99; praise following Day's death 10, 16; reunions attended by 139; on Robinson's barnstorming team 98; rumors regarding Veeck and 70; on Veterans Committee 142; White House meetings attended by 144; winter baseball played by 49, 58, 59; World War II service of 74
Israel, Clarence "Half-Pint" 74, 151
It's Midnight Over Newark (Hughes) 86

Jackman, Bill "Cannonball" 26
Jackson, Rufus "Sonnyman" 24
Jackson, William R. 53
Jaros, Tony 84
Jethroe, Samuel 66, 109
Jim Crow era 50–55, 76, 88, 90, 104, 112
Johnson, Helen Elizabeth 2, 4
Johnson, Jack 20
Johnson, Jimmy "Slim" 20, 40
Johnson, John H. 31
Johnson, Josh 139
Johnson, Judy 132, 139, 140, 146, 154
Jones, Slim *28*
Jordan, David 70

jumping 4, 37, 45–49, 92, 97, 104, 115, 118

Kaline, Al 128
Kansas City Monarchs (Negro Leagues): Baird as owner of 108; Bell as pitcher for 33; Brown as player for 83; Manley's acquisitions from 26; Paige as pitcher for 63–64, 68, 93, 94, 97, 132; Robinson's tenure with 7; Rogan as member of 145–146; Smith as pitcher for 42, 68, 94, 97, 146; in World Series 63–64, 94–97, *95*
Kennedy, John *116*, 120, 124
Kern, Tom and Emily 139
Kimbro, Henry 107
Kimbrough, Larry 6
King, Larry 144
Klingaman, Mike 136
Ku Klux Klan 99, 112
Kubatko, Roch Eric 46

Lacy, Sam 67, 146
La Guardia, Fiorello H. 26
Lambertson, W.P. 78
Landis, Kenesaw Mountain 59, 65–68, 70
Latin America: food and living conditions in 48; hesitancy of jumping to leagues in 104; Pearson on loneliness of players in 48; thinning of baseball talent pool in 105; treatment of Black players in 114; *see also* winter baseball season; *specific countries*
Lausche, Frank 69
Lawrence, Mary 152
Lemon, Bob 98
Leon Day Park (West Baltimore) 152, 154
Leonard, Walter "Buck": in East-West games 133; Hall of Fame induction 146; Homestead Grays and 21, 39, 62; honors and recognition given to 151; Pittsburgh Crawfords and 27; reunions attended by 139; statue at Negro Leagues Baseball Museum 154; winter baseball played by *28*
Lester, Larry 74, 130
Lett, Harold 101
Lewis, Allen 143
Lewis, Ira 68

190

Index

Lewis, Rufus 28, 94, 96
Ligon, Marvin 114
Lindsay, James H. 87
Lloyd, John "Pop" 146, 154
Lobert, Hans 66
Lockett, Lester 139
Loescher, Frank S. 123–124
Lombardi, Ernie 29
Lopat, Eddie 127
Lopez, Al 142
Louis, Joe 94, 130
Lucchino, Larry 151
Lundy, Dick "King Richard" 40–42, 56
Lyle, George, Jr. 126

Mackey, Biz 41–42, 56–57, 61, 95, 99, 132
MacPhail, Larry S. 65
Major League Baseball (MLB): Chandler as commissioner of 140; Landis as commissioner of 59, 65–68, 70; major league status bestowed upon Negro Leagues players 157; Manfred as commissioner of 157; Negro Leagues Statistical Review Committee 157; Roosevelt's "green light letter" on continuation of 59; threats in response to 1995 players' strike 11; *see also* American League; National Baseball Hall of Fame; National League; *specific players and teams*
Malloy, James 104
Manfred, Rob 157
Manitoba-Dakota (ManDak) Baseball League 2, 114–119, *116*, 128
Manler, Larry 127
Manley, Abraham Lincoln: as Brooklyn Eagles owner/manager 23–27, 29; chief scouting duties of 36–37, 39; efforts to sign Satchel Paige 36–37, 40; as Newark Eagles owner/manager of 29–30, 33–41, 56, 63, 93, 97; player salary disputes with 38–39, 46; trades and acquisitions by 26, 34–36, 40
Manley, Effa: Borican Day organized by 58; on Day's opening day no-hitter 91; on desertion of Negro Leagues by fans 109; on healthy entertainment for African Americans 51; letter to Gottlieb regarding umpires 92; McDuffie's relationship with 40; National Baseball Hall of Fame induction 31; *Negro Leagues Baseball Minutes* on 152; Pearson's relationship with 63, 135; player salary disputes with 46; protest against discrimination led by 31; reunions attended by 140; role with Newark Eagles 30, 31, 34, 35, 38, 102; at World Series game 96
Manning, Max: on Day's Hall of Fame induction 143; love for game of baseball 5; Newark Eagles and 56, 57, 94, 102; on Paige's All-Stars team 98; as pallbearer at Day's funeral 11; World War II service of 5, 74
March, Herb 68
Marr, Dave *149*
Marshall, George 75
Marshall, William 102–103, 128
Mathews, C.H., Jr. 50
Matthews, Ralph 123
Matthis, Verdel 68
Mauriello, Tami 94
Mays, Willie 95, 139
McCarroll, Mae 99, *100*
McCord, Clinton "Butch" 7, 108, 109
McCready, Esther 112
McDaniels, Booker 103
McDonald, Webster 140
McDuffie, Terris 28, *28*, 33–36, 39–40, 62, 92
McHenry, Henry 91
McKeldin, Theodore 111
McNary, Kyle 114
Medford, Edna Green 81
Medlinger, Irvin 124
Memphis Red Sox (Negro Leagues) 107, 117, *131*, 152
Mexico: summer baseball in 1, 4, 45–49, 102–104; treatment of Black players in 47–49, 103; winter baseball in 1, 4, 46, 49
Mfume, Kweisi 11
Mills, Bill 38–39
Milwaukee Braves (National League) 120–121
Miñoso, Orestes "Minnie" 120, 140
MLB *see* Major League Baseball
Morgan, Joe 156
Morse, Wayne 53
Mulzac, Hugh N. 53
Munzel, Edgar 143

Index

Murphy, Howard 68
Murphy, Vincent J. 53
Musial, Stan 98, 142, 146

Nahem, "Subway" Sam 83
Nashville Black Vols (Negro Leagues) 113
Nashville Elite Giants (Negro Leagues) 21, 107
National Association for the Advancement of Colored People (NAACP) 55, 69, 101, 110, 112
National Baseball Hall of Fame (Cooperstown): broadcasters in 9–10; Day's induction into 2, 9, 146–151, *147–150*, 159–160; Hieronimus campaign for Day's election to 12, 143–145; Manley as only female member of 31; public education on Negro Leagues 157; reunion for Negro Leagues players hosted by 141; special committee for Negro Leagues 24; Veterans Committee 9, 142–143, 145–146
National Housing Agency 86
National League: executives on prospect of Black players in 1, 65–68; games against Negro Leagues teams 19, 69; Hulbert as founder of 9; integration of 3, 66–69, 104, 108–109, 157; lifestyle of players in 4, 6; Mexican summer league players from 47; salary of players in 6; *see also* Major League Baseball; *specific players and teams*
National Negro Congress 53
National Negro Newspapers Publishers Association 68
Negro Leagues: criticisms by players 7; East-West games 2, 26, 27, 68, 73, 130–134, *131*; games against white teams 3, 25, 29, 36, 69, 72, 73; Great Depression and 22, 24, 29; Hall of Fame's special committee for 24; as haven for African Americans 51; incompleteness of statistics from 13; integration's impact on 104–105, 109; jumping in 4, 37, 45–49, 92, 97, 104, 118; lifestyle of players in 3–8; major league status bestowed upon players from 157; Mexican summer league players from 1, 4, 45–49, 102–104; raiding of players within 27; recruiting strategies for 7–8; reunions for former players 139–141, 151; Roosevelt's "green light letter" on continuation of 59; salary of players in 3–4, 6, 20–21, 36–37, 46; stadium conditions for 6–7; World War II service of players from 1, 5, 8, 56, 74–79, 90; *see also specific players and teams*
Negro Leagues Baseball Minutes (television program) 152
Negro Leagues Baseball Museum (Kansas City) 152, 154, 157
Negro Leagues Baseball Players Association 6, 137, 144
New York Black Yankees (Negro Leagues): integration's impact on 105; matchups against Day 35–36, 62, 72–73, 92; semipro team games against 29; Semler as owner of 24, 26–27; trades with Newark Eagles 40
New York Cubans (Negro Leagues): Brooklyn Dodgers against 69; Great Depression and 29; integration's impact on 105; lifestyle of players with 6; matchups against Day 5, 33, 56, 57, 61, 72, 92; Pompez as owner of 24; Santiago as pitcher for 142
New York Giants (National League) 6, 10, 24, 29, 109
New York Yankees (American League) 29, 30, 128
Newark: antidiscrimination legislation in 100, 101; Day's induction into Hall of Fame in 142; defense industries in 51, 52, 86; Grand Hotel in 30, 136; housing for Blacks in 86; integration efforts in 3, 52, 86, 87, 99; segregation in 50, 55, 88; workplace discrimination in 32, 52, 53, 86
Newark Bears (minor leagues) 30, 34, 94
Newark Dodgers (Negro Leagues) 25, 30
Newark Eagles (Negro Leagues): Bell as player/manager for 33, 39, 42; Day's career with 1, 3, 5–6, 8, 10, 17, 29, 33–42, 48, 56–57, 61–65, 71–74, 90–96, 102; exhibition games played by 36, 41, 57, 61, 74; games against white teams 29, 36, 72; integration's impact on 105; lifestyle of players with 5, 6; Lundy as manager of 40–42, 56; Mackey as player/manager for 56, 57,

192

Index

61, 95; Manley as owner/manager of 29–30, 33–41, 56, 63, 93, 97; moving of team to Houston 105; pennant won by 93; role of Effa Manley with 30, 31, 34, 35, 38, 102; semipro team games against 29; southern barnstorming tour by 99; Wells as player/manager for 61–62; Winston-Salem as farm team for 33, 35; in World Series 94–97, *95–96*; World War II service of players from 1, 5, 8, 56, 74–79, 90

Newberry, Jimmy 115, *116*, 118, 120
Newcombe, Don 140
Newhouser, Hal 99
Not in Our League (television program) 152
Nunn, Bill 130

O'Crowley, C. 87
Olson, Ole 83
O'Neil, John "Buck" 64, 95–96, 98, 142, 143, 145, 152
Orange Triangles (semipro team) 36
Overseas Invasion Service Expedition (OISE) All-Star team 82–85, *84*

Paige, Janet 34
Paige, Satchel: All-Star team assembled by 97, 98; Chicago American Giants and 120; Cleveland Indians and 109, 120; Day compared to 8, 10, 13, 16, 25, 39, 75, 125–126; death of 151; in East-West games *131*, 132–133; Hall of Fame induction 146; integration of Cleveland Indians 70; Kansas City Monarchs and 63–64, 68, 93, 94, 97, 132; in ManDak League 114; Manley's efforts to sign 36–37, 40; National and American League teams faced by 69; *Negro Leagues Baseball Minutes* on 152; pitching duels with Day 8, 10, 43, 63–64, 93, 133; Pittsburgh Crawfords and 132; reunions attended by 139, 140; rumors regarding Veeck and 70; St. Louis Browns and 120, 122; statue at Negro Leagues Baseball Museum 154; winter baseball played by 34, 43
Parks, Charles 58, 74
Partlow, Roy 42, 64
Pasquel, Jorge 46–48, 102, 104

Patterson, Pat 30, 68, 93
Patton, George S. 54, 79, *80*, 82
Paul, Gabe 143
Pearl Harbor attack (1941) 59, 75
Pearson, Lennie: Baltimore Elite Giants and 108; Day as bartender at tavern owned by 135; on loneliness of players in Latin America 48; Newark Eagles and 30, 48, 57, 63, 93, 94, 96, 99; relationship with Effa Manley 63, 135; winter baseball played by 58
Pecora, Ferdinand 37
Pelosi, Nancy 111
Philadelphia Athletics (American League) 36, 66, 92, 123–124
Philadelphia Phillies (National League) 9, 66–67, 69–72, 83, 92, 123–124
Philadelphia Stars (Negro Leagues): Benson as member of 13, 139; Bolden as owner of 63; Curry as player/manager for 91, 92; integration's impact on 105; lifestyle of players with 6; matchups against Day 13–14, 26–27, 41–42, 62, 72, 90–92, 107, *162*; scouts in attendance at games 66; semipro team games against 29
Pittsburgh Crawfords (Negro Leagues): Charleston and 27, 63; Gibson as player for 15, 27; Greenlee as owner of 23, 35–37; Leonard as member of 27; matchups against Day 27, 39; Paige as pitcher for 132; semipro team games against 29; trades with Newark Eagles 35
Pittsburgh Pirates (National League) 65, 66, 83
Pizarro, Terín 59
Plessy v. Ferguson (1898) 55
Polo Grounds 6, 35, 61, 72, 92, 94, 131
Pompez, Alex 24
Porter, Andy 115, *116*
Posey, Cumberland "Cum" 21, 24, 40, 42, 62–64, 71–72
Povich, Shirley 143
Powell, Richard 7, 111
Pride, Charley 152
Puerto Rico: Professional Baseball Hall of Fame in 43, 142; treatment of Black players in 4, 43, 48; winter baseball in 1, 3–4, 14–15, 27–29, *28*, 34, 43–46, *44*, 58–59, *60*, 113

Index

racial issues *see* African Americans; discrimination; integration; segregation
Radcliffe, Ted "Double Duty" 25, 26, 132
Randolph, A. Philip 53
Randolph, Oliver 55
Rea, E.B. 35
Red Ball Express 79–82, *80*
Red Circlers 82–85, *84*
Reinhold, Matt 111
Renfro, Chico 140
Rice, Bob 66
Richards, Gabby 152
Rickey, Branch 72
Riley, James 14–15, 18–19, 21, 36, 40, 43, 45, 59, 64, 78, 91, 102, 105, 121, 128, 132
Rizzuto, Phil 98
Robeson, Paul 68
Robinson, Eddie 152
Robinson, Frank 149
Robinson, Jackie: barnstorming team formed by 98; Brooklyn Dodgers and 3, 67, 104, 108–109, 112; criticism of Negro Leagues by 7; integration of baseball and 3, 67, 104, 157; on Paige's All-Stars team 98
Rodgers, Sylvester 107
Rogan, "Bullet" Joe 145–146
Rogosin, Donn 10, 69
Romby, Bob 107
Roosevelt, Franklin D. 52–53, 59, 75, 86, 123
Rosen, Max 29
Rossi, John 70
Rouzeau, Edgar T. 67
Royko, Mike 109
Ruffin, Leon 102
Runyon, Damon 25
Ruppert Stadium 30, 39, 41, 56–58, 62, 72, 90, 92–96
Russell, Richard B. 123
Ruth, Babe 15, 30, 136
Ryan, Cornelius 75

SABR (Society for American Baseball Research) 70
Sadler, Bill *28*
St. Louis Browns (American League) 8, 120–122, 125
St. Louis Cardinals (National League) 10, 36, 69, 70, 82, 83
St. Louis Stars (Negro Leagues) 57
Santiago, Carlos Manuel 142
Santiago, José 142
Saperstein, Abe 70
Sarbanes, Paul S. 11
Scales, George 34
Schaefer, William Donald 144–145
Schmidt, Mike 9, 148
Schmoke, Kurt L. 11, 150, 154, 156
Schultz, Dutch 24
scouts 7, 24, 36–37, 39, 66
Scranton (Pennsylvania) Miners (minor leagues) 2, 125–126
Seay, Dick 35
Segar, Charles 143
segregation: in education 32, 53, 55; in hotels 3, 55, 109, 112; in Jim Crow era 50–55, 76, 88, 112; in military 51–54, 56, 75–76; in movie theaters 88; of parks and beaches 87–88; stresses brought on by 2; on trains 50, 109, 112, 124; in workplace 32, 52
Selective Training and Service Act of 1940 75
Semler, James "Soldier Boy" 24, 26–27
Sengstacke, John 68
Service, Calvin 33
Shackelford, John 69
Shelley v. Kraemer (1948) 111
Simmons, Bert 139
Simmons, Michael 139
Simpson, Harry "Suitcase" 126
Sklar, Albert L. 110
Smith, Eugene 68
Smith, Hal 128
Smith, Hilton 42, 46, 68, 94, 97, 98, 146
Smith, John Ford 96
Smith, Taylor *116*
Smith, Wendell 39, 49, 66–68, 93, 113
Snyder, Brad 150
Society for American Baseball Research (SABR) 70
Souell, Herb 96
Sparrow, Roy 130
Stack, Ed 9, 141, 160
Steadman, John 145
Stearnes, Norman "Turkey" 15, 132, 146
Steele, Ed and Linda 154
Stewart, Ollie 78, 84, 85
Stimson, Henry L. 52, 54

194

Index

Stone, Ed 28, *28*, 34, 38, 42, 59, 63, 143, 148, *149*
Strauch, Peter 91, 92
Strong, Nat 24
Strong, Ted 68
Stultz, Tom 139
Suskind, Peter 71
Suttles, Mule 35, 42, 132
Swanton, Barry 114–115
Sway, Dickey *28*

Taylor, Ben 12, 24–26
Taylor, Joe *116*
Taylor, Zack 125
Thomas, Clint 139, 140
Thompson, Charles 74
Thompson, Hank 109, 126
Thorn, John 157
Thorpe, Jim 58
Thrasher, Charles 85
Thurman, Bob 93
Toronto Maple Leafs (minor leagues) 2, 8, 121–122, 124–125
Triandros, Gus 128
Trice, Bob 124
Truman, Harry S. 52–54, 123
Tuskegee Airmen 54
Tygiel, Jules 70–71

Van Hyning, Thomas E. 43, 113
Veeck, Bill 8, 10, 47, 66, 69–71, 120–121, 125
Venezuela, winter baseball in 1, 4, 45, 47
Vernon, Mickey 98, 128
Villodas, Luis 142
Vipond, Jim 121

Wade, Bob 156
Walker, Harry "The Hat" 82–84, 127
Walker, Jesse "Hoss" 107
Walker, Moses Fleetwood 137
Walker, Weldy 137
Walker, William O. 68–69
Washington, Booker T. 54
Washington Elite Giants (Negro Leagues) 33
Washington Senators (American League) 9, 65, 128
Watkins, Skeeter 128
Weiss, George 30

Weiss, William T. *162*
Welch, Agnes 11
Welch, Winfield 120
Wells, Willie: in East-West games 132; Hall of Fame induction 145; injuries sustained by 39; in ManDak League 114–118, *116*; in Mexican summer league 46, 48, 49; Newark Eagles and 35, 39, 41, 61–63, 66–67; tryout with Pittsburgh Pirates 66; winter baseball played by 58, 59
Wells, Willie, Jr. 115, *116*
Wertz, Vic 95
Whatley, David 64
White, Charlie 120–122
White, Hal 127
Williams, Harry 35
Williams, "Smokey" Joe 146
Williams, Ted 99, 142
Willis, Vic 9
Wilmore, Al 107
Wilson, Artie 142
Wilson, Ernest Judson "Boojum" 14, 132
Wilson, Fred 41
Wilson, Thomas T. "Smiling Tom" 23–24, 74–75, 107
winter baseball season: in California 74–75; in Cuba 1, 4, 38; in Dominican Republic 4; in Mexico 1, 4, 46, 49; in Puerto Rico 1, 3–4, 14–15, 27–29, *28*, 34, 43–46, *44*, 58–59, *60*, 113; salary of players in 43, *44*, 46, 59, *60*; in Venezuela 1, 4, 45, 47
Wolff, Bob 9, 148
Woo, Pan Ye 100, 101
Woods, Parnell 66
World War II (1939–1945): African Americans in 1, 5, 8, 54, 56, 74–82, *80*, 90; D-Day invasion during (1944) 1, 75–78, *79*, 82; Day's baseball career interrupted by 1, 8, 56, 75–79, 90; discrimination in military during 51–54, 56; DUKWs (Ducks) used during 76–79, *79*; employment opportunities for Blacks during 51; European theater of operations "World Series" 82–85, *84*; Pearl Harbor attack during (1941) 59, 75; Red Ball Express in operation during 79–82, *80*; Roosevelt's "green light letter" on baseball during 59

195

Index

Wright, John 72
Wyrostek, Johnny 82

Yankee Stadium 6, 30, 61–62, 72, 92, 94, 98, 131–132
Yawkey, Tom 3, 99

Yokely, Lamon 19, 25, 26
Young, W.H. 105

Zedd, Stanley 115–119, *116*, 121
Zeidler, Lew 4–5
Zientara, Benny 82

www.ingramcontent.com/pod-product-compliance
Ingram Content Group UK Ltd.
Pitfield, Milton Keynes, MK11 3LW, UK
UKHW042008140426
5217IPUK00015B/1045